Still I

Scratching the su~~rface and plumb~~ing the
depths of prayer

ISBN-13: **978-1542903868**

ISBN-10: **1542903866**

© Derrick Phillips 2017. All rights reserved.

Cover image © Derrick Phillips 2017.

Scripture Quotations

Scripture quotations used in this book are from the following
versions:
KJV – King James Version
MSG – The Message (Eugene H Peterson) Copyright © 1993,
1994, 1995, 1996, 2000, 2001, 2002. Used by permission of
NavPress Publishing Group
NIV - New International Version. Copyright © by International
Bible Society, used by permission of Hodder & Stoughton Ltd, a
member of the Hodder Headline Group.

Still Digging

Acknowledgements

Prayer is usually a solitary activity, but we can help one another to learn better ways to develop this fundamental of our Christian life. Many people helped me on my journey of prayer, but I am especially grateful to individuals whose input was formative in my life. First was the late E. S. A. (Ted) Hubbard, whose weekly Bible School laid the foundations of my faith. Maurice Smith helped me to weather many storms, and to explore important areas of belief and experience. The late Brother Bernard of the Society of St Francis opened the doorway to a deeper experience of prayer. Rebecca (Becky) Widdows helped me to obtain healing for wounds that hindered my prayer life, and taught me more about this vital part of the believers' armoury. I especially thank my wife, Kathleen, who, despite knowing the truth about me, has stood by me through all my years of struggling, learning, failing and growing.

For help in the preparation of this book, I thank Annie Hepburn and Peter Honour, who pored over the text and made valuable suggestions and corrections.

Thanks to Ian Smale (Ishmael) for sharing his story and for giving permission to quote from it in Chapter 44. Thanks also to Stuart Wesley Keene Hine, Stuart K. Hine Trust (Hope Publishing Company), the copyright holders of that beautiful hymn, *How Great Thou Art*, quoted in Chapter 14.

Still Digging

Contents

Introduction

Still Digging is the title of a poem. I wrote poems before that one, but ***Still Digging*** is the earliest that I have kept. I remember when I wrote it. I was at a Christian summer camp where the recreational programme included a creative writing course. "Write a haiku" said the course leader — but she first had to explain what that meant.

Haiku is a traditional Japanese poetic form, with just 3 lines of 5, 7 and 5 syllables. This is how it works:

> Five, seven, five, stop.
> That is how a haiku ends.
> But the thought goes on.

Just 3 lines, but often thought-provoking because it compresses its message into such a tight space. I have often used the format to catch and preserve ideas and inspirations. The pithiness of its compressed style makes for memorable verses. Reflecting that virtue, this book is compressed into brief chapters, because I want it to be easily accessible. Prayer is for everyone, not just a spiritual elite of gifted reclusives. Some people are called to a special prayer ministry. But every disciple of Christ can pray.

Each chapter of this book starts with a poem, a Bible passage, or some other quotation. Most of the poems are my own. That's because poetry works for me as a method of capturing ideas and preserving them for future meditation. If I were good at drawing I would probably paint or sketch my memorable thoughts. Prayer is a personal matter, and the way each of us prays proceeds from our individual personality. Be yourself.

With that in mind, please use this book to feed your personal prayer life and don't feel obliged to copy anyone's style – including mine. My qualification to write this book is that I have made mistakes – many times. There are well-tried ways of praying, meditating and contemplating. But, while some work for many people, and some work for just a few, the approaches that work best for you will be unique to you. Don't feel that you should engage in prayer styles that don't ring true for you. Pass over any chapters that speak to personality types who don't think in the same way you do. Be true to yourself.

This book can be read consecutively, but it doesn't have to be used that way. Most chapters stand on their own. Dip in and choose ideas that chime with *your* spirit, *your* needs, and *your* personality. Read them once or many times. Develop your own pattern of devotions and *pray as you are*.

Still Digging was composed in unpromising circumstances - the words formed in my head while I was in a temporary bathroom on the Staffordshire showground. The setting may have been incongruous, but it was an apt demonstration of the *anytime – anyhow – anywhere* nature of prayer.

Ongoing prayer through the whole of life is the subject of that haiku and this book.

> *I will therefore that men pray everywhere, lifting up holy hands, without wrath and doubting.*
> 1 Timothy 2:8 KJV

The Journey

Prayer is a journey. Are you willing to start? How far will you go?

The Journey

1. Still Digging

I tried to dig down
to the bottom of God's love...
I am still digging.

The River Wensum runs through the city of Norwich, joins the Yare and flows on until it loses itself in the Norfolk Broads. The Norfolk Broads region is a popular tourist destination, with winding rivers, wide lakes and the huge, open skies that characterise flatlands. But there were no open skies for the woman who lived in St Julian's church, near the west bank of the Wensum back in the 14th century. She spent more than 30 years bricked up in a cell on the side-wall of that church. History remembers that lady as Julian of Norwich, the earliest known female English writer, a contemporary of Geoffrey Chaucer, and a true woman of prayer.

Considering all the time she spent in prayer, Julian was well qualified to say what it's about. She said it is about love. In one of her typically compact statements she said, *"Prayer oneth the soul to God"* ('oneth' is an Old English word, meaning 'makes as one'). What more could we want from prayer but to be united with the God we love – the One who loves us more than words can say?

Love? Some men may feel that it's a feminine word. Rubbish! Men and women, mothers and fathers, boys and girls, and all the unique personalities in either sex, want to be loved. Look through the pop-charts, the movie lists, and the novel publications and see how much love matters to all of us. Fathers love their children as much as mothers, though they may express their love differently.

There are emotional forms of expression that come more easily to women than men *in general*. But none of us are 'in general'. We are unique individuals. Whatever our personality, we have hopes, we have desires, and we need to be wanted and valued. Love is the word that brings together the normal needs and desires that we had from the day we started asking for things in the only language we knew – the hearty cry of a new-born baby.

Prayer is a way of asking for things, that's true; but that is a very limited view of the subject. Asking for things certainly comes into the model prayer that Jesus taught his disciples – the so-called *Lord's Prayer*. But there's much more there than our requests for 'daily bread'. It includes requests for other people's needs, praying for forgiveness, recognition of our responsibility to forgive, and yearning for God's kingdom to come. But, overall, prayer – including the *Lord's Prayer* – is about love.

Still Digging is a haiku – one of the briefest and simplest of poetic forms which, by its very simplicity, can convey depths of meaning. Prayer is like that. It's so easy that a child can do it, but so profound that people spend lifetimes probing its depths. The haiku that opens this chapter is not merely a poetical form. It's a statement about a spiritual journey and, particularly, my journey of prayer. The objective is about God's love. I started this journey when I was at school and I am now retired – but I'm still probing its mysteries. It is a journey that constantly brings new discoveries. It's an adventure that continues through the whole of life. I have prayed through good times and bad, through defeats and triumphs, through joys and sorrows, and I don't intend to give up praying – ever.

The Christian life starts with a prayer, when we commit ourselves to the Saviour who died for our sins. But, many Christians admit to struggling with prayer. Why is that? And how can we progress into holy habits that will stand us in good stead for the whole of our lives?

God calls *all* of us to share our faith, but *a few of us* are given a definite call to evangelism. We should *all* look out for and support one another, but *some* are specifically called to be pastors. In the same way, prayer is an essential part of life for *every* Christian, but *some* are called, in greater or lesser degree, to a special ministry of prayer. Where are you on this spectrum?

Some people are free to dedicate themselves full-time to lives of prayer, through monasticism, or by consecrating their lives of singleness or widowhood. For most of us, however, life doesn't provide the freedom to devote ourselves to prayer to that extent. But that does not disqualify us from the calling. For most Christians, prayer life is squeezed into what's left over after the demands of work and family. For a minority, prayer is a major occupation filling much of their day. But all who pray are on the same journey.

If your current circumstances put you in the time-limited majority, start the journey anyway, and follow the path as far as you can. Later life may provide new opportunities to go deeper, and you will have a head start. Scratch the surface now. Plumb the depths as much as you can, when you can.

Not that I have already obtained all this, or have already arrived at my goal, but I press on to take hold of that for which Christ Jesus took hold of me. Brothers and sisters, I do not consider myself yet to have taken hold of it. But one thing I do: Forgetting what is behind and straining toward what is ahead, I press on toward the goal to win the prize for which God has called me heavenward in Christ Jesus.
Philippians 3:12-14 NIV

2. Prayer starts here

> Prayer takes all forms.
> But it doesn't even start
> Until we turn up.

"I would like to pray more, but..."

Have you ever said that? Or have you heard someone else say it? No doubt they have busy lives. The modern world is very demanding; but is it so much more demanding of our time than the lives lived by impoverished labourers in times gone by? Mill workers, farmers, kitchen maids, miners and many more had to get up in the dark, and spend long days doing strenuous work, before collapsing into bed exhausted. The world was demanding for past generations too. They didn't all pray regularly, but many did.

The time we devote to prayer is a matter of choice. If we mean it when we declare an intention to pray, it is up to us to do something about it. There are many ways to pray. A life of prayer can be challenging and exciting. But nothing happens until we turn up at the place of prayer.

However, many of us may face real problems about fitting in a regular time for prayer. Our bodies cannot do without sleep; at least, not for long - and certainly not on a regular basis. If the demands of work, probably exacerbated by commuting, forces us to start our working days early, then it may be impractical to designate time for morning devotions. The start of the day has much to recommend it as an ideal time for prayer. But, if that doesn't work for you, try something else.

I was at a weekend Christian youth conference that included a session when a panel of pastors and youth leaders was answering questions from the audience. Someone raised the subject of prayer times and, after the panel members had spoken, Tony, a young man in the audience, chipped in. He faced the problem of an early start to his working day, but his solution was to pray as he cycled to work. The shocked panel members reacted in a way that reminded me of scenes I had seen in war films. They turned towards Tony in a way that recalled scenes of battleship guns turning to attack the enemy. On his bike! Surely, the panel protested, prayer deserved more concentrated attention than that? I felt for Tony. His solution fell short of the panellists' ideals, but he had taken the trouble to find a resolution and deserved encouragement rather than criticism.

If we can't find an ideal time but we want to pray, then we can choose a less-than-ideal time. Slip into a church at lunchtime. Go for a walk. Close your eyes on the train or bus (people will presume you are sleeping). By whatever means, make a start, somehow and somewhere. Once your prayer habit is established, you may find a better time and place. Life always changes. But nothing will happen about prayer until you make a start.

But there's no value in getting legalistic about this. Don't pray because you must. Pray because you want to. Who do you think has the most to gain by your regular prayer life? God will not become bigger, more powerful, more anything, because you pray. He is God; he never changes. Your prayers may benefit many people, including some you may never meet or know about. But the person who has most to gain by your prayers – is you.

3. Yellow Card

There wasn't time to pray this morning –
Will that earn another yellow card?
Will I receive a second warning?
Or will my whole day now turn out hard?

I have heard people say that their day falls apart if they don't manage to fit in a prayer time before they leave home. It hurts me to hear such sentiments. Should prayer (or lack of it) be the cause for a guilt trip? It is a valuable ideal to start the day with God. But let's remember what kind of god we are talking about. Our Father is not vengeful. He is not a tyrannical schoolmaster looking for an excuse to beat us. He wants the best for us.

Of course, prayer *is* the best for us; but for *our* sake, not God's. If we don't pray he is still God – unchanged in power or mercy – our omission does not diminish him. If we don't pray, we are the losers. But the loss is not a penalty handed out like a football referee's yellow card. God is not keeping the score.

Prayer is not an 'ought to', to be followed in fearful
obedience under a cloud of guilt. It is a 'want to' spurred on
by God's invitation to go his way, and experience his love

An effective way of hindering people's prayers, is to make them feel guilty about their 'performance'.

In fairness to the people who talk of the vital part prayer plays in their day, they may not actually be racked with unnecessary guilt. They may just be acknowledging the value prayer times bring to their day. But, on a day when we wake up late and have to rush out of the house, there is always a solution. Just as we may be able to pick up a sandwich to make up for a missed breakfast, we can slip in a break to enjoy God's presence later in our day. Look out for an open church where you can pause for some quiet moments. Stroll around the block and engage in a prayer walk. Hover over a writing pad or computer tablet and make doodle-notes recalling the people or things you want to pray about. Close your eyes as you sit on the train or bus. Pray when you take the dog for a walk. God is always available – wherever you are.

If you often find yourself in the situation where the morning is so rushed that prayer gets missed, why not review your expectations? Are you going to bed so late that you can't wake up at your planned time? You can deny yourself food for several days (see chapter 15) but you can't deprive yourself of much sleep before it simply overcomes you. Are you trying to model your prayer life on a style more suited to a different kind of personality? Don't beat yourself up. Don't go down under a weight of guilt. Take stock of who you are and what demands you have in your life; then construct a pattern of prayer that suits you.

You have chosen to set out on this journey of prayer. But make sure that it is *your* journey.

> Guilt be gone
> I am who I am
> I'll meet with my God
> Any way that I *can*

4. Maths and Prayer

$C = x + ny^2$
I can't do the rest
– as if I cared!
I can't do maths and I can't do prayer
'cause I can't work it out
and my mind's out there –
trying to solve it,
burdened with care
and I can't find the answers
so the problem's still there.

But, not doing maths
never makes me despair;
I'm at home with *that* weakness
So why should I care
that I can't be an expert
on the subject of prayer?

Lord, cause me to rest
in the now and the here;
to believe that you're present
and there's no need to fear.

I used to have a hang-up about mathematics. Numeracy never gave me a problem during my long business career but, if I saw an equation, it scared me. Some people have similar feelings if they are asked to write an essay, sing, draw a picture or whatever it was that never quite worked for them in their schooldays. But most of us outgrow these problems and build careers based on skills and abilities that come easily to us. We adapt.

Some people worry about their lack of progress in prayer. What's so worrying about it? If a child can do it, surely any of us can. Nevertheless, many people seem to find it difficult – a stumbling block. Even the disciples who were closest to Jesus had difficulties in this area, because they made a point of asking him, "*Teach us to pray*".

Perhaps some guidance might help. Step-by-step, through the chapters of this book, we are going to look at some of the barriers that hinder our prayer life, and various ways we can pray in keeping with our individual personalities and gifts. That last point is important. The root of the problem for many people is that they have a concept of prayer based on the way other people seem to do it; but the 'other people' are also other personality types – people who think and act differently.

But, first, let's be relaxed about it. God is not waiting to catch us out like an impatient schoolmaster. God wants us to succeed in every part of our life. He wants us to live righteously. He wants us to pray – and he'll help us to do it.

5. Holy Habits

Holy habits help
To keep us on the pure path
Of discipleship.

Habit has had a bad press. The word has often been reserved to describe addictions or other, less harmful, but also undesirable, behaviours. But we also have good habits – life skills, like walking, cycling, or driving that we acquired with difficulty and through frequent errors until they became competent skills. We learned to do those things so well that, as adults, we do them automatically, without needing to work them out move by move.

Job had a holy habit. Each day, whatever else was happening, he made a ritual sacrifice to God (Job 1:5). And Job had such a widely-recognised reputation for righteousness that even Satan spoke about his goodness. Worship in modern western society doesn't involve killing animals (I expect you're glad about that!). But there is another thing we talk of killing – and it doesn't cause suffering to any living creature; we speak of 'killing time'. Time is what we need to sacrifice as our primary commitment to forming holy habits.

Where does your time go? After accounting for work, household and parental commitments, sleep, church activities and recreation, what time do you have left? Do you spend any of that time praying and reading the Bible? If so, are you specifically setting time aside for it? Or are you grudgingly squeezing it into 'what's left over' time? Either way, it is *you* who will gain or lose by your decision. This is not a matter of 'must do' or 'ought to' but 'what do you really want?' Don't do it to obey the rules. Do it to maintain your spiritual health.

Holy habits set up our minds to deal with the challenges, the choices, and the temptations that we encounter during our lives.

Have a routine, but don't be so bound by it that you can't cope with changes. What works at home may not work so well on holiday or away on business – in a hotel – at a campsite – in a dormitory – or on an overnight flight.

Take stock of your time. Decide what matters to you. If you feel that prayer is important, *do it* – and make a habit of it.

6. The path

It was a short prayer
an honest prayer
a prayer that changed my life;
But nothing in that moment
showed me where the path ran.
In fact, I didn't notice the path;
I was just vaguely conscious
of a bright, glorious light
way off in an unimaginable future.
But, there was a path;
It led me up into the hills
and down into unforeseen valleys,
so I could rarely see
much of the route ahead.
Sometimes it's been a hard climb,
Sometimes it's revealed glorious views,
But, always, that mysterious light
has glowed in the distance.
I will never turn back.

We tend to think of prayer as an activity, or even a duty, that we engage in at particular times. But it is a journey that lasts for a lifetime. That first real prayer, when we acknowledged God's claim on our lives, was the first step on the path that Jesus called 'the narrow way'. When we took that first step, he was with us. And he continues to accompany us at each part of the journey. Our conversation and walk with Jesus is now the core meaning of our life. The focus of our desire is Jesus. The aim of our life is to be like him. This process is called 'sanctification' and a key tool in the process is prayer. However, this is a tool that holds us as much as we hold it. In a sense, we don't pray – we are prayed.

Lose those thoughts about having a '*time* of prayer', as if must end when we stand up and walk away. It doesn't end. It continues at a different level. We walk in God's sight. He may speak to us at *any* time, grabbing our attention through the events of the day, through the things that we read, through the daily news or through our conversations with friends, colleagues, or companions. Communion with God is a total engagement.

We can, of course, turn off the path, allowing ourselves to be distracted by temptations and bad choices. But the path is still there, calling us back. And our Lord is always ready to resume the journey with us.

How far will you follow the path?

A time for prayer

We live in time. How will you use it?

7. Don't stop praying

When you rise from your knees
        Don't stop praying.
When you walk through the trees
        Don't stop praying.
When you get in your car
        Don't stop praying.
Wherever you are
        Don't stop praying.
When life is a laugh
        Don't stop praying.
When it starts to get rough
        Don't stop praying.
If it's good or it's bad
        Don't stop praying.
If it's happy or sad
        Don't stop praying.
Anytime, anywhere
        Don't stop praying.
Make your whole life a prayer –
        Don't stop praying.

Down among the pots and pans in the community kitchen, or out among the cabbages in the kitchen garden, a man was praying. His lips didn't move and he didn't stop working. Brother Lawrence had discovered a valuable aspect of prayer.

As a young Christian, I developed a habit of signing off correspondence with a text under my signature. The text was 1 Thessalonians 5:17 – "*Pray without ceasing*" (KJV). I'm not sure what that meant to me all those years ago, but it became central to my life in later years.

After a while, I decided that appending a text to my signature was a pretentious habit, so I stopped doing it. But the concept of continual prayer stayed with me. Regular, daily prayer times are invaluable, but, if that's all the praying we do, we will miss out badly. Even if we spent hours on our knees in prayer each day, that would be a small portion of our time. Why not share the *whole* day with God?

In the story of Brother Lawrence, *The Practice of the Presence of God*, he made no distinction between his set times of prayer and his manual work. At all times, and whatever he was doing, he sought to remain in God's presence, continuing an unbroken conversation of prayer and praise. He thought about God at his workbench. He kept his mind on God as he laboured in the garden. He continued his unspoken communion with the Lord as he worked in the kitchen. The late Ruth Bell Graham, wife of the evangelist, Billy Graham, had a notice above her kitchen sink saying "*Divine service will be conducted here three times daily*". The point is the same: Every action can be a prayer if our heart is open to God.

"That's ridiculous! My job is full-on. I couldn't possibly pray while I'm working!"

But do you manage to pick up your coffee cup without stopping work?

Do you manage to laugh at your colleagues' jokes without stopping work?

I'm not suggesting that you concentrate on prayer while you're working. Just keep a line open to heaven.

If the sum total of our praying is the set time we have in the morning or evening, we may be guilty of putting

God into a box. That's what the Israelites did when Samuel was a child and Eli's sons were serving as priests (1 Samuel chapter 4). They ignored God most of the time but carried the Ark of the Covenant into battle on the presumption that God would give them victory because of that box. We cannot – we dare not – shut the lid on God and live the greater part of our lives without involving him.

However far advanced we may be in the manner and structure of our prayer times, necessity forces us to leave the secret place and live in the world. We wash, we eat, we meet people, we work (whether in the home or out in the workplace). Amongst all this, God is still with us and we need to keep up the conversation.

8. First calling

*Now return the man's wife, for **he is a prophet**, and **he will pray for you** and you will live. But if you do not return her, you may be sure that you and all who belong to you will die.*
Genesis 20:7

The first person who the Bible called a prophet was Abraham, and the first activity that the prophet was called to was prayer. Note that – speaking out God's word wasn't the prophet's priority. Praying came first. However prominent our calling in the church, prayer comes first. When should we pray? First! Before any spiritual work. Biblical precedent always places prayer before activity. In the infant church in Jerusalem, the apostles found it necessary to appoint men to take care of practical matters so that they (the apostles) could focus on spiritual priorities (see Acts chapter 6). The tasks were practical, but the appointments were made amidst much prayer (and what incredible men they chose for the task).

What is your calling? Whatever it may be, it starts with prayer. Any work in the service of God needs to be rooted in prayer, surrounded with prayer, and directed by prayer. Without prayer, the work is merely a human endeavour. And, remember the message in the first chapter of this book: prayer is fundamentally about love.

If I speak with human eloquence and angelic ecstasy but don't love, I'm nothing but the creaking of a rusty gate. If I speak God's Word with power, revealing all his mysteries and making everything plain as day, and if I have faith that says to a mountain, 'Jump', and it jumps, but I don't love, I'm

nothing. If I give everything I own to the poor and even go to the stake to be burned as a martyr, but I don't love, I've gotten nowhere. So, no matter what I say, what I believe, and what I do, I'm bankrupt without love.
1 Corinthians 13:1-3 MSG

9. Banking on prayer

When all else fails
    People will pray;
In an emergency
    prayer support
        comes easily
            but why?
Is prayer the bank of last resort –
    to use in desperation
        with glum anticipation
            of a high interest charge
                on repayment?
Why not make prayer
    our savings bank –
        always available
            when it's needed?
Why not
    store prayers in the bank that won't fail?
Let's concentrate our forces
    on spiritual resources
        that will help us get through
            in the hard times?
We could make prayer
    our main account –
        pay in continually,
            draw out any time;
Trusty standby –
    No charge –
        Sign up for free banking for life.
Make it a daily habit
    to make a fresh investment–
It's a much surer place
    to store treasure.

On 11th September 2001, as I was driving south on the M5 motorway, I turned on the car radio to listen to the news. There was only one item. Reports were just coming in about the attacks on the Twin Towers of the New York World Trade Center and all other programmes were cancelled as the horrifying story unfolded. When I got home, I watched the television reports with my wife, until it struck me that this was an occasion for corporate prayer. I phoned one of the leaders of our church:

"We need to get people together for prayer."

"Why? What's happened?"

"Turn on the television and you'll see."

By that evening, the word got around and a significant proportion of the members of our church assembled together to pray.

It is easy to get people to pray in an emergency. At another time, when one of my family members was facing a serious medical emergency, we found that all kinds of people were keen to support us in prayer – even friends who had never previously given any indication of faith.

When all else fails, people *will* pray. That's good. But let's not wait for emergencies. If prayer is an established habit in our lives, it will serve us well in good times and bad.

> *But store up for yourselves treasures in heaven, where moths and vermin do not destroy, and where thieves do not break in and steal. For where your treasure is, there your heart will be also.*
> Matthew 6:20-21 NIV

10. Bye bye QT

Are you there, Lord?

… just checking…

We don't make so much of our talks these days

But I can't go far without sensing your footfall alongside.

"Quiet Times" seem too formal for real friendship

But, when things get intense in the world around me

I like the way you sense my panic

And respond.

Now that I've known you for so many years

I no longer feel the need to prove our relationship,

But don't think that I take you for granted;

You're as close as breathing

And just as vital.

The journey may not always be easy. Sometimes we may find it hard to pray. Sometimes we may feel that we are getting nowhere. A sense of failure blights our prayer times and we wonder where we are going wrong. Such times may be the result of external pressures, like work, illness, family issues or even weather. We are, after all, made of flesh. At other times, the disconnection may result from guilt – and, if we are conscious of sin, we have a solution ready at hand:

> *If we confess our sins, he is faithful and just and will forgive us our sins and purify us from all unrighteousness.*
> 1 John 1:9 NIV

But the reason we sometimes face difficult times may not have anything to do with sin. In that case, confession may fail to completely resolve the problem. Those times when prayer seems hard may well be necessary trials to refine and strengthen us or to force us into re-learning things we thought we knew. In my case, I entered a time like that following a period when I had settled into a very comfortable pattern of prayer. I felt 'successful' – usually a dangerous attitude. Then a friend made a chance comment that she meant as a compliment, praising me for getting up early in the morning to pray. How did she know about my prayer habits? I realised that I must have been loose-tongued, perhaps boasting about my spirituality. It made me question my motives, recognise my pride, and feel ashamed. God used that seemingly trivial event to break up my comfortable habits and set me on course for the next stage of my journey.

For several years, I continued to struggle with prayer, not able to maintain my former habit of 'Quiet Times'. Eventually, recognising the falseness of my previous approach, I restarted my journey based on a simple understanding that God loved me, not for my proficiency or even my diligence, but because he is love.

When my prayer times were effectively taken away from me, I was forced to reconsider the question about what constitutes a time of prayer. How frequent and how long should my prayer times be? And the answer I found was – all day and probably all night. But how can that work? What about work? What about family? What about eating and sleeping? What about the many activities and responsibilities that occupy our time? As the poem hints, we spend a lot of time breathing, but we rarely do it consciously. That's how it is with many things that happen in our lives. The parts that we are conscious of may seem to be the most important, but the unconscious parts are what keep us alive. I eat several times a day, but my digestive system works continually. Let's we live our lives as a continuing prayer, with intermittent times of conscious praying to refresh and re-supply our spiritual resources. The question about how long those times should be seems less relevant when we are living in God's presence all day long.

Most of what God is doing in me is happening by the operation of the Holy Spirit and entirely through God's grace. That also is prayer. The brief times that I spend in conscious prayer are just a small part of my interaction with the Lord. But, because contact is continuous, I can move into conscious prayer at any time. He doesn't depend on my planning or effort. He just wants my submission.

With that understanding I was gradually able to rebuild my prayer times, no longer presuming that I knew how to do it. I was ready to learn - ready to be taught – ready to continue the journey.

We can benefit from lessons about prayer. We can learn helpful techniques that enable us to progress in our prayer life. But we should never suppose that we have 'got   it'.

A place for prayer

What place does prayer have in your life?

11. Abraham haggled

Abraham haggled
   Jacob wrestled
      Moses contended
Aaron gave a blessing
Gideon bargained
   Jephthah vowed
      Hannah wept
Samson called for vengeance
David confessed
   Jabez called
      Job cursed
Nehemiah quietly messaged
Ezra sat appalled
   Jeremiah lamented
      Jonah sulked
Elijah threw in the towel
Paul exulted
   Anna gave thanks
      Mary Submitted
Stephen urged forgiveness
Standing
   Walking
      Prostrate
         Kneeling
            Fighting
               Sitting
                  Working
                  Dancing
Each one,
   Uniquely,
      was praying.

References: - Genesis 18:20-33 – Genesis 32:24-30 – Exodus: 32:31-34 – Numbers 6:24-26 – Judges 6:36-40 – Judges 11:30,31 – 1 Samuel 1:10,11 – Judges 16:28 – Psalm 51 – 1 Chronicles 4:10 – Job 3:1 – Nehemiah 2:4,5 – Ezra 9:4 – Lamentations – Jonah 4:1-3 – 1 Kings 19:3,4 – Romans 11:33-36 – Luke 2:36-38 – Luke 1:38 – Acts 7:60

Abraham really did haggle. He argued with God. He bargained the price down, bid by bid: 50, 45, 40, 30, 20, 10 - and the value was calculated in human lives.

Hannah really wept. She cried her heart out. Her prayers were so affected by her emotions that Eli, the priest on duty in the Tabernacle at the time, accused her of being drunk.

Elijah did throw in the towel. He'd had enough. He had obeyed God's commands, exercised incredible faith, and won a famous victory. So, he was exhausted – burnt out – and he wanted to give up.

Each of them prayed with sincerity and fervour. They weren't 'saying prayers', they were praying from the heart. They prayed with emotion. They told God exactly how they felt.

We don't need to hide our feelings when we approach God. If you think about it, the idea of hiding them sounds ridiculous; could we suppose that he doesn't know the truth? But do we know the truth about *ourselves*? Or are we deceiving even ourselves about the way we feel? To do that is to invite mental problems. Let's be honest. If circumstances are making you angry, recognise the fact and tell God how you feel. I mean, really tell him. Nothing you can pray in your grief, anger or sorrow could make him stop loving you, because *he is love*. Healing begins when the sickness is diagnosed.

12. Standing, sitting...

Standing
　Walking
　　Prostrate
　　　Kneeling
　　　　Fighting
　　　　Sitting
　　　　　Working

　　　　　Dancing

Yes, you did read those same words in the previous chapter. Sorry about that, but I want to make some different points.

There is no 'one size fits all' in matters of prayer. The experience of the saints of the Bible, and in modern times, is that the right position, attitude, and style of prayer is the one that fits the occasion. Faced with a momentary opportunity, Nehemiah could not have run off to pray in his bedroom; he stood where he was (beside the throne) and prayed under his breath before answering the king. Each hero of faith mentioned in the poem (see chapter 11) prayed in a way that fitted the situation they found themselves in. One position that appears surprisingly rarely in Bible stories is kneeling. Some of the people mentioned in the poem may have been in a kneeling position, but the Bible doesn't mention it. Nor does the Bible ever suggest praying with 'hands together and eyes closed'. So much for teachers' instructions!

We can pray anywhere, and we should. According to the venerable Bede, St Cuthbert liked to pray whilst immersed in the sea up to his shoulders (hardly the regulation position for monastic prayer!) Wherever we see a need we can pray for it – right where we are. If someone asks me to pray for them I do – straight away. If the occasion is right and they agree, I pray with them there and then. Otherwise, I pray silently, but still immediately or, probably, as I walk away. It ensures that I don't forget and break my promise. Of course, if God reminds me, I pray for them again when I am back in my normal place of prayer. But, when prayer is needed, no place is unsuitable.

Prayer is not restricted to the narrow confines of 2 or 3 approved methods or positions. Whatever we are doing, wherever we are – at work, on a journey, lying on the beach, sitting on a 'plane – anywhere will do.

13. Kneeling

Kneeling, I submit
It's not a place for boasting;
A place for prayer.

We can pray anywhere and in all manner of positions. But there is a case to be made for kneeling – particularly in the secret place where we hold our daily prayer times. Kneeling is an attitude that few of us use in day-to-day situations other than prayer. Some gardening involves kneeling and so do some aspects of childcare. But most everyday activities at work, at home or at play are done standing, sitting or walking. That makes kneeling a special position that our minds can easily associate with prayer. How often, when someone kneels to do a task, have you heard another person joke "say one for me while you're there!" The association is in our culture. Kneeling is conducive to prayer.

Kneeling is conducive to awareness. It's easy to doze off while sitting down, but not so easy to sleep on your knees. There is no rule that says we must kneel to pray but, in our daily devotions, it can help.

I hasten to say that this can't work for everyone. If you have arthritis, or any similar condition that affects your joints, kneeling may be out of the question. Advancing age may stop you doing what you could easily do when you were younger. Nor does kneeling work in certain types of accommodation or situations (it's not practical on public transport!). As with many aspects of prayer, when we can't have the ideal, the less-than-ideal is better than not praying at all.

If kneeling is OK for your place, situation, age, and health, it's a good idea to make provision for it. Get yourself a cushion or pillow to ease the burden on your knees (discomfort doesn't improve prayer). A purpose-made prayer stool can make it even easier to sustain regular, prolonged prayer times. You may be able to buy one, but here's a design for one you could make yourself (or get someone to make for you).

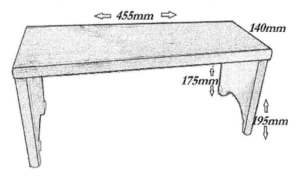

Folding Prayer Stool

This wooden folding stool can be stowed away when not in use, or even packed in luggage to take on holiday or on retreat. The uprights are cut on the slant, so that the front is 20mm shorter than the back. This makes the stool lean forward slightly. The top edge of the legs is cut at a slight angle so that they splay outward a little, thereby increasing stability. Cutting an arc out of the bottom of each side piece turns them into 4 legs, making the stool more stable. The top is joined to the uprights by means of strong door hinges that allow the stool to be folded flat. In a kneeling position the user sits on the horizontal plank with legs underneath it. It is a surprisingly comfortable position that can be maintained for long periods.

This is my preferred design, but there are many types of prayer stool, and the best one for you depends on what space you have available to keep it in, and your personal preferences. You can buy prayer stools online, or even find a design diagram to help you make your own.

Even with such a device, some people may find it impossible to kneel. But that's OK. Kneeling is not obligatory. Unnecessary discomfort does not improve prayer. Whatever position you find appropriate to you – keep praying.

14. Country air

When through the woods and forest glades I
wander,
And hear the birds sing sweetly in the trees;
When I look down from lofty mountain
grandeur,
And hear the brook, and feel the gentle breeze –
Then sings my soul, my Saviour God to thee
How great thou art...
*(Stuart Wesley Keene Hine. Stuart K. Hine Trust – Hope
Publishing Company)*

Walking can be prayerful. Walking in the countryside
can be especially uplifting (you don't need to be a
creationist to appreciate creation). Words are not
needed. It's enough to drink in the beauty and lift your
heart to God in silence. By sparing the words, we allow
the experience to permeate *all* our senses – the sound
of the wind, the patterns of clouds, the rustle of leaves,
the scent of the grass, the songs of the birds. Even rain
can be enjoyable if we suspend our over-civilised
prejudices.

But silence is not mandatory. It's OK to praise the One
who created this beauty. You can sing aloud (though
you may want to check that nobody else is in sight!) or
hum quietly. Savour God's presence and enjoy each
moment, taking time to linger and notice each intimate
detail of the scene around you. These occasions are not
distinct from our regular, daily prayer times. They flow
together as part of the broad stream of a life of prayer.

The rhythm of walking can itself be conducive to
prayer, fuelling meditation. Though it is good to enjoy
the moment and the actuality of the environment, it can

clear the mind to receive inspiration – ideas – even a calling to some special work or service.

But the essence of a country walk with God is praise – with prayer, in song, in the spring of our step, or with silence.

15. Walking with God

Alone, but out in the world.
Quiet, but enveloped in sounds of nature.
Inwardly absorbed, but noticing everything.
Enjoying the rhythm
of walking with God

The expression 'prayer walk' is often taken to mean a stroll around an area, probably with a group of like-minded friends, to intercede for that town, village, parish, or estate. That's not what this chapter is about. A prayer walk (or it may be a jog or a *gentle* cycle ride) is an opportunity to spend time with God in meditation and prayer. Such activities may be particularly attractive to personalities who feel more comfortable with a prayer style based on physical activity. However, anyone who is physically capable of it will find occasions when a prayer walk is the ideal way to get away and enjoy God's company.

The rhythm of walking can be conducive to a sense of inner peace and communion with God. Many people find that rhythm so calming that it can relieve deep feelings of distress. It can be a marvellous way of freeing the mind to discover answers to deep problems. But you don't need to have problems to gain benefits from walking with God.

The poem that heads chapter 76 was composed line-by-line during a prayer walk around the grass banks that mark the historic walls of the Saxon town of Wareham in Dorset. It was one example of the many occasions when walking with God has brought me deep satisfaction and spiritual uplift. Those special times, which create precious memories, may be serendipitous

– but we *can* make prior preparations for a good prayer walk.

Your walks may take you through familiar local scenes, or they may be in unfamiliar territory during a holiday or business trip. But you can usually predict certain things that you are likely to see. Mountains, trees, rivers, meadow-flowers, rocks, sandy beaches, or the urban sights of city and park all contain images that may remind you of Bible stories or texts. So, why not pre-arm yourself with texts to meditate on as you see those sights?

- Notice how trees thrive next to a stream and recall Psalm 1:1-2.
- Look up to the sky and recall how Psalm 19 speaks of the heavens declaring God's glory.
- Remember Psalm 23 as you walk across green pastures or beside still waters.
- If you're near a beach, remember Jesus' parable about the house built on rock and the house built on sand (Matthew7:24-27)
- Notice the wild flowers and think about what Jesus said concerning the "lilies of the field" (Matthew 6:28; Luke 12:27)
- As you read the Bible, make a note of verses that you could use for meditation during your prayer walks

By linking your prayer walks with your Bible readings you will create a more three-dimensional understanding of spiritual truths, strengthen your faith, and increase your enjoyment of it. But, don't do it the same way every time. Vary your experience. There's no need to spiritualise everything you see. Appreciate your environment *as it is*. All of God's creation is holy.

16. Sacred Spaces

Is anything sacred?
Can there be holiness in
>dust,

>>wood

>>>or stones?
What is the difference
>between

>>sacred spaces

>>>and unholy idols?
Do we venerate material things?
Do we idolise places?
No!
>But we sense

>>when a place

>>>has been prayed in.

As a 9-year-old child, knowing little of Christian doctrine or church practices, I recall wandering through a wood in Kent and coming across an area where bench seats were set out in a semicircle facing a low cliff. Maybe it had once been part of a quarry. But, by that time, it was dedicated for use by Boy Scout campers for Sunday worship. Nobody was there when I found the place, but something in me sensed a spiritual dimension to the place. It had been prayed in.

I spent much of my life within Christian traditions that prefer simplicity, and I have sometimes felt repelled by what I considered to be over-elaborate church buildings and shrines. For me, the more gold I can see, the less holiness I sense – but this is a personal prejudice. I have visited places that were meant to be sacred, but which I felt were just expensive. However, I am also aware that some of those places became significant because humble and devout worshippers embellished them with their gifts.   We do not all agree on what is beautiful or what is sacred.

The Jews considered their Temple to be the most sacred place on earth. But God's prophets warned them repeatedly that the sacredness of the Temple meant nothing if their lives were not lived in holiness and obedience. See what Jeremiah said:

> *Will you steal and murder, commit adultery and perjury, burn incense to Baal and follow other gods you have not known, and then come and stand before me in this house, which bears my Name, and say, "We are safe"—safe to do all these detestable things?*
> Jeremiah 7:9-10 NIV

Nevertheless, most of us sense that some places hold an atmosphere that causes us to lower our voices and move with reverence. Some places attract us to God and inspire us to pray. On my travels, I have often been attracted to a wayside chapel, a quiet garden or a beauty spot and have stopped a while to sit in silence and lift my heart to God.   Town or country, simple or elaborate, natural or constructed, I am convinced that any place that has been regularly prayed in over many years picks up some atmosphere of holiness from all that devotion.

Use them.

17. A special place

A place I know,
A place prepared,
A place I love to be,
A place where I feel comfortable,
A place for God and me.
A special place,
A secret place,
A place where I am free.
A place of quiet,
A place of prayer,
A place where I am me.

You can pray anywhere. But, for regular prayer, it is helpful to prepare. Setting aside a special place makes the habit easier to maintain. It's not necessary to be elaborate. It *is* necessary to be yourself. If you are naturally gifted artistically, you may wish to lay out your secret place with special care as an expression of who you are. But the key issue is to identify a place where you will feel comfortable and ready for prayer.

In Mark 1:35 we read that Jesus got up early, while it was still dark, and went to a solitary place to pray. Then, in the next verse, we are told that the disciples went there to tell him that crowds of people were looking for him. That implies that the disciples knew where he would be. He chose a special place for prayer and, no doubt whenever he was in that village, he returned to that spot. We know from the Gospels that the Garden of Gethsemane was one of his favourite places for prayer.

Jesus often chose outdoor spaces. Some people may prefer to do the same thing when weather and other circumstances allow. But, for the purposes of this chapter, I will assume that most people will set up their special place in their home.

Circumstances vary. Some people have roomy homes where it is easy to set aside a whole room as a place for prayer. Most people, however, need to choose a corner, or a small space at the side of a room, which may only be private for part of the day. In that case, some ingenuity may be required. But it helps to have a familiar space that you can return to regularly for prayer.

Make sure that all the things you need are in easy reach in your special place. Keep a Bible there, plus a notebook or journal (or both), a cushion, a firm but comfortable chair and a prayer stool (see chapter 13). This is not so much a secret place as a convenient place. It's not a shrine. Its purpose is not to display your piety but to make it easy for you to spend time in prayer.

I have pointed out elsewhere that prayer is an individual matter and our style of praying will reflect our personality. Undoubtedly, the more introverted personalities will be more attracted to the 'secret place' than the highly active, outgoing extroverts. But we all spend *some* time alone – and it is good that some of that alone-time is spent with our God. Doing that becomes easier if we make provisions that enable the practice to be comfortable and welcoming.

Our special place becomes a sanctuary. It sets the scene for listening to God. It helps us to find ourselves and calm our spirits. By setting aside that special place we improve our chances of establishing a holy habit that will stand us in good stead for a lifetime.

What's it all about?

Do I *have* to pray? Will it make any difference?

What's it all about?

18. Not about duty

Not about duty
Not about ticking boxes
It's all about God.

I'm here, praying – but why? Is it just because I was here yesterday? I've made it a habit, but have I kept my sense of focus? Prayer is not self-sufficient. It doesn't exist for its own sake. It is centrally, solely, and completely about God. If we miss a time of prayer, it's God we're missing. If we remember to pray, but forget why we are praying, we may be engaging in a pointless exercise.

After all I've said about guilt I don't want to be discouraging. But it is possible to slip into a routine that treats prayer as a duty – a task that must be done. Come to pray because you need to – you want to – spend time with your Father God. It is a love affair.

Take that thought and let it lift the burden from your shoulders. God isn't standing by with a clipboard to check that you are keeping up with your commitment. He is watching with a heart of love, waiting to listen to you and make you welcome. Come happily. Come hopefully. Come quietly. Come noisily, if that suits your nature. Come anyway. Don't be in a rush to speak. Maybe you won't speak at all. Just be there. Stand, sit, kneel, walk, draw, paint, sculpt or dance in his presence for however long you can – and don't score yourself on the time you spend there. Whether it's a long time or a short time, don't worry – that's not the issue. The point is that you have been with God.

So don't get ahead of the Master and jump to conclusions with your judgments before all the evidence is in. When he comes, he will bring out in the open and place in evidence all kinds of things we never even dreamed of—inner motives and purposes and prayers. Only then will any one of us get to hear the "Well done!" of God.

1 Corinthians 4:5 MSG

19. Prayer changes things

Prayer changes things;
So, to really see a change,
Do it every day.

Prayer changes things;
So, if you don't want to change,
You're best not to pray.

Prayer changes things;
Just rest in the secret place
And savour God's grace.

Prayer changes things;
But it's not the words that count;
It's listening to God.

Prayer changes things
And the best of it is this:
Prayer changes me.

Point number one in everyone's assumptions about prayer is that there is some possibility that it will make a difference. The young child's prayer asks for results. The person who cries out a prayer of distress in an emergency hopes fervently for a positive answer. The presupposition is that, however weak our faith or slight our hope, prayer changes things.

It does. And sometimes in dramatic ways. However, as we all know, we do not always receive the answers we hope for when we pray. But, if we keep on praying, prayer changes us. I think that's its primary function.

This is not an artful way of sidestepping the issue of unanswered prayers. Nor is it an answer to honest doubts and questions about the world's sufferings. Prayer *is* about changing the world, but in particular ways. In the prayer that most of us learnt in childhood, Jesus taught us to ask for God's kingdom to come and his will to be done on earth... That means *God's* will, not yours or mine. And the process of changing us as we continually pray is the process of conforming us to his will.

The more God's Spirit changes us, the more meaningfully we will pray for the world to change. We will be praying the Kingdom into being.

Ultimately, the Kingdom of God will be fully realised by the return of the Lord, Jesus Christ. But that is the capstone of the building. He laid the foundation during his first coming. What we are dealing with is the ongoing work of building – and a crucial part of that work is prayer. That means praying for change and praying for the needs we see around us. As we pray, God may well move *us* to become agents for change.

My business career went through many changes over the years. Sometimes success followed success and I rose to high positions. On several occasions, following company takeovers, I lost my job or felt unable to continue in the new circumstances. On one occasion, after losing a job, I was offered a new opportunity and wasn't sure whether to accept it. My previous job provided a car. The new opportunity was a casual contract and required me to work in a country village that was impossible to reach by public transport. With no current income and no car, how could I accept the job? My wife said, "*If we get a car, don't expect to get an automatic.*" I decided to pray the matter over with a friend from church.

I called him on the phone:

"Hi Chris, can I come round for a chat and a pray?"

"No problem. Come over straight away."

I spent an hour with my friend, explaining what was happening, and praying for clear guidance whether to take the job or not. Then I walked home. I had scarcely got through the door when the phone rang. It was another member of our church who I had not yet come to know properly. Within minutes of my leaving the house where I had been praying, this man had called Chris to say he wanted to give away his wife's car – and did Chris know anyone who needed one?

By the way, the car was an automatic – and I accepted the job.

On another occasion, on a Saturday morning, my wife said, "I think you should go to Alan P's house this evening and take your guitar"

Alan lived in a village near Dartford in Kent and we lived in another village on the other side of the town. We had known him for several years, and we knew that he opened his home to a group of young people on Saturday evenings; but we had never been to any of those meetings.

When I knocked on Alan's door, his wife took me into the lounge, where the teenagers had already assembled. Alan was stretched out on a couch with his leg propped up, encased in a plaster cast.

He said, "I'm glad you came. Did headquarters send you?"

I led the meeting at his house that evening. His prayers were answered and I was the means.

We have had several occasions in life when we were in financial difficulties and money was provided, sometimes openly by people we knew and sometimes anonymously in letters dropped through our letterbox. Incredibly, the sums provided were often an exact match to the amount we needed at that time. As a balancing element, there have been a few occasions when we felt that we should give to certain people – and the amount we donated turned out to be exactly what they needed.

On such occasions, it may be possible to argue that what happened was just a coincidence. But my credulity about random coincidence is stretched when these coincidences happen again and again. Some people describe these experiences as "God-incidents". I agree. Prayer changes things.

Has everything I ever prayed for been answered in the way it happened in these stories?

No.

Why don't I always receive the answers I expect?

I don't know.

But I know that these, and other examples in my life, were genuine answers to prayer. And I know that, on other occasions when I didn't get what I wanted, something changed in me.

As we pray for God to act we should expect him to enlist us in the action. Whenever we appeal to God we may hear him appealing to us. The decision to develop a prayer life is a commitment to allow God to change us.

Prayer changes people.

20. Lord, I can't find you

> Lord, I can't find you by anxiously seeking
> Lord, I can't reach you by effort of mind
> But, when I attend to your voice gently speaking
> I discover your presence inside.

Where is God? When writing to the church in Colossae, Paul spoke of "Christ in you" (Colossians 1:27 KJV) but, when he preached in Athens, he said of God that "in him we live, and move, and have our being". Is God in here or out there?

Try this experiment: fill a sink or a bucket with water, pick up an empty cup and plunge it under the water. Is the cup in the water or is the water in the cup?

Both are true. God's presence to us is true in the same manner. He is out there and in here.

One psalmist said:

> *Where can I go from your Spirit? Where can I flee from your presence? If I go up to the heavens, you are there; if I make my bed in the depths, you are there. If I rise on the wings of the dawn, if I settle on the far side of the sea, even there your hand will guide me, your right hand will hold me fast.*
> Psalm 139:7-10 NIV

While another said:

> *Awake, Lord! Why do you sleep? Rouse yourself! Do not reject us forever. Why do you hide your face and forget our misery and oppression?*
> Psalm 44:23-24 NIV

Sometimes God seems to be everywhere we look – unavoidable, inescapable, available, dependable. At other times, it seems that God is nowhere to be found

– unavailable, unreachable, impossible, hidden. Is God playing games with us? Is he setting up hurdles for us to jump over? Does he not care?

It's OK to ask questions like that. God will not punish us for it.

It's OK to have doubts (when faith is tested by doubt it becomes stronger).

It's OK to express griefs and fears. Jesus did. When he cried out "*My God, my God, why have you abandoned me?*" (Matthew 27:45-□46 MSG) his words reflected a passage from Psalm 22, but he wasn't just quoting scripture. He was grief stricken and in darkness. In every way possible he took on all the pain and anguish that humanity endures

> *Think of yourselves the way Christ Jesus thought of himself. He had equal status with God but didn't think so much of himself that he had to cling to the advantages of that status no matter what. Not at all. When the time came, he set aside the privileges of deity and took on the status of a slave, became human! Having become human, he stayed human. It was an incredibly humbling process. He didn't claim special privileges. Instead, he lived a selfless, obedient life and then died a selfless, obedient death—and the worst kind of death at that—a crucifixion.*

Philippians 2:5-8 MSG

When God seems distant, don't look for him in the distance. Come back to your centre. You will find the Lord in your heart. Are you suffering? He suffered. Are you anxious? That's how he felt in Gethsemane (Luke 22:41-4). Do you feel rejected and abandoned? He was there too. Consider your humanity and discover his humanity – and his divinity too. Discover his presence inside.

21. If you do not forgive

"But if you do not forgive others their sins, your Father will not forgive your sins"
Matthew 6:15 NIV

Is God unjust? Is he making a hard bargain about our forgiveness? Think about it –

Where is my forgiveness?

Where is my enemy's forgiveness?

Doesn't God hold both answers? And isn't his forgiveness extended to all – including the person who has hurt me?

So, if I don't forgive, where is that *un*forgiveness held? God is not unforgiving so, if God isn't holding onto it, the only other place it can be is in my mind and my heart; and the person who best knows the truth about our feelings is me. By holding onto that unforgiveness I am imprisoning myself.

These words of Jesus amount to sound advice. God is always holding out the offer of forgiveness. It's up to each one of us to accept that offer. But forgiveness changes our situation in this life only if we accept it, and forgive *ourselves*. So long as we harbour sin in our hearts, including the sin of unforgiveness, we will not truly feel the benefits of God's mercy. We will continue to bear the burden and hinder our spiritual journey.

When I am wronged, I may choose to take revenge. But revenge often takes forms that are not only sinful, but criminal. By working out my anger in this way I would be making things worse *for me*. It simply doesn't work. This is not just pious theorising. I have struggled with the need to forgive when I really didn't feel like it. The world of corporate management features a lot of betrayal and backstabbing, and the personal damage from that can be painful. But God's way is still the way of forgiveness. Arguments, threats, and betrayals can even arise within the church, as I have personally experienced.

It is not easy to let go of our pain when somebody wrongs us. Although, for most people most of the time, the damage may be small, it is still hard to let go of our desire to get even. "Surely", we ask ourselves, "shouldn't that person see what they have done and *ask* for forgiveness?" But that is to entrap ourselves in a web that may hold us in a prison of our mind and our making, while the other person feels nothing. Forgiveness starts with me and it affects me.

For some people, the hurt may be extreme. The wrong done may be severe and life changing. We can all recall situations that made world news and turned large numbers of people into innocent victims. And most of us have been impressed by examples where the victims chose the way of forgiveness. Those who chose that path chose the way of life and freedom. They gave up their so-called 'right' to retribution. But, in doing so, they released themselves from the prison of unforgiveness.

If we want to pray effectively, we need to free ourselves to *receive* and to *give* forgiveness.

22. Praying to make a difference

"Dear Lord...
If I give myself to prayer,
    will it show?
If I meditate in secret,
    who will know?
If I shut myself away
    to spend time with you each day
Will my faith grow?
    Will my joy show?
        Will my face glow?
If I point my prayers at mountains,
    will they move?
Can my prayers touch distant countries
    with your love?
If I breathe a heartfelt sigh
    t'wards your mercy seat on high
Will the skies ring?
    Will new life spring?
        Will it change things?
LORD, I want to make a difference
    when I pray
To bring your Spirit's power
    into play
Though I don't know how to do it
I'm resolved to battle through it
I will *seek* you
    I will *sense* you
        I will *trust* you."

The ministry of prayer is not one by which we can earn plaudits. It is carried out in secret. Only I know how much time I spend in prayer or how my prayer times are conducted. I may never know the results of my prayers. I can't even know if any prayer that I pray will make much difference to me. It's all based on faith.

Prayer is not a formalised devotional exercise, going through the motions to maintain a habit. Real prayer is motivated by a desire for change. We want to make a difference.

- We want to get closer to God – why? Because we feel that we're not close enough now.
- We pray for someone to be healed – why? Because they are not well now.
- We plead for peace in the world – why? Because the world is not yet at peace.

Even our praises express yearnings for God's Kingdom to come to its just and rightful completion. We pray because we mean it – don't we?

So, what do we do when we don't yet see the changes we yearn for?

We trust.

We love.

We keep praying.

23. War in heaven
(Daniel 10:1-21)

There was war in heaven
and a man was on his knees.
Powers that controlled kingdoms
battled unseen,
while the man continued in prayer.
Fasting continued for days
as the conflict raged invisibly –
and all Daniel knew
was that God had called him to pray.
Seven days passed,
till, at last, the answer came through.
Conquest in heavenly places.
Victory achieved through prayer.

What really happens when we pray? Daniel's story suggests that it may be much more far reaching than we could imagine. Daniel had been reflecting on Jeremiah's prophecy that Israel's captivity in Babylon would last for 70 years, and he started to pray about it. His prayers were unexceptional at first. He prayed much as he normally did, making his requests, and waiting in faith for God's answer. But, all the time he was praying, furious action was taking place in the heavens. Angels were battling with the spiritual powers whose unseen influence lay behind the powerful nations of that time.

This Old Testament story links with what Paul tells us: For our struggle is not against flesh and blood, but against the rulers, against the authorities, against the powers of this dark world and against the spiritual forces of evil in the heavenly realms. (Ephesians 6:12 NIV).
Rulers?

Authorities?

Powers?

Paul is telling us that governments are not just human affairs; they are subject to unseen spiritual forces. The person who occupies a position of power may have the best plans and intentions, but the place of power can be like the cab of a runaway train. Some of the Psalms refer to God as "Lord of Hosts", which The Message Bible paraphrases as "God-of-Angel-Armies". But there are two armies in this spiritual battlefield. Think about it.

The ministry of prayer is not a soft option.

When we pray for nations and governments, we need to keep these mysterious spiritual powers in mind. Governments change, and some changes may be violent, dramatic, and terrifying. Even democratic systems sometimes produce unexpected outcomes that may worry or offend us. If those changes go against our hopes and aspirations, we will not further God's plans by going into a sulk and turning our back on politics. When we are worried about the outcome of an election it is time to pray more. Pray for those who have come into power. Pray for those who have lost power. Whether the government is the one you voted for, or an alternative, they may be a focus for those spirit forces that Paul warned us about.

Prayer is a serious business.

We don't need to understand these matters intellectually. We are *unlikely* to understand them fully in this life. But we need to recognise the reality of spiritual powers – powers of good and powers of evil. We need to appreciate that prayer reaches beyond the physical world. And we need to be alert and aware.

We are touching heavenly things.

What's it all about?

24. Suffering

I don't blame God
for my suffering, but –
I let him use it.

For 13 years, I ran a website to help sufferers from a chronic pain condition that I had experienced myself. I corresponded with people from many parts of the world and from all kinds of backgrounds, but the one thing they had in common was that they experienced extreme pain. Through correspondence with these patients I discovered that suffering drives people to their extremes. Some become gentle, sympathetic, wanting to help people who suffer like them. Some become spiteful, bitter, wanting to take revenge on a world that they see as cruel.

Suffering is a huge philosophical and theological subject, with big 'why' questions beyond the scope of this book. However, our response to our own suffering is certainly a matter for prayer.

Like most people, I have experienced difficulties and disappointments in my life. The most difficult experiences have tended to drive me back to the Old Testament story of Job. He knew suffering in ways beyond what most of us will ever face; and his response was *"The Lord gave and the Lord has taken away; may the name of the Lord be praise*d." Job 1:21 NIV.

We can't know what pain or suffering we may have to face in our lives, but our response to suffering is in our control. *Consider it pure joy, my brothers and sisters, whenever you face trials of many kinds, because you know that the testing of your faith produces perseverance.* (James 1:2-3 NIV). We can allow suffering to become a noxious weed in our lives, sapping away our energy, our hope, and our faith. Or we can determine that, no matter what happens, God will be glorified in our lives.

Does God have a purpose in our suffering? We can't know unless we have specific revelation about it, as Paul did regarding his *"thorn in the flesh"* (2 Corinthians 1:7 KJV). But we can choose to turn our suffering to good purpose. We can use it to practice perseverance. We can use it to strengthen our faith. We can use it to learn humility (an essential for advancement in prayer). None of us wants to suffer but, when suffering comes our way, our response is our choice.

Though the theory is not scientifically tested, I have come to believe that our capacity to sympathise, to forgive, to care, to love, may be proportionate to the amount we have been hurt, abused, cheated and betrayed or the amount of pain we have suffered. Jesus went through all these trials and demonstrated perfect love.

Some have supposed that suffering is inevitable for those who commit themselves seriously to a life of prayer. The phrase 'the dark night of the soul' has often been misapplied to this presumption. The 'dark night' is a separate, spiritual experience, which will be covered in chapter 68. But be sure that it is not about the random trials and pressures that come into most people's lives, nor about the more extreme physical, financial, and mental trials that some of us face. But the original book, *The Dark Night of the Soul,* includes the following passage which, despite its archaic wording, makes a useful point about the potential value of suffering:

> *"...in suffering [the soul] acquires strength from God, and in actions and enjoyment [the soul] exercises her weaknesses and imperfections"*
>
> (quoted from the 1905 translation by Gabriela Cunninghame Grahame).

God's reply, when Paul's prayed to be relieved of his sufferings makes a similar point:

> *And he said unto me, "My grace is sufficient for thee: for my strength is made perfect in weakness". Most gladly therefore will I rather glory in my infirmities, that the power of Christ may rest upon me.*
>
> 2 Corinthians 12:9 KJV

Suffering is not primarily a spiritual matter, but we can turn it to spiritual advantage.

Teach us to pray

Some people seem to have it all together.
What's their secret?

25. Prayer is not just for specialists

Some are called to mission fields
But all are called to witness
Some are called to heal the sick
But all are called to care
Some are called to lead worship
But all are called to praise
Some are called to constant prayer
But all are called to pray.

There is a difference between the way a specialist works and the ways the rest of us perform similar tasks. We have no problem in understanding that concept in most occupations or, indeed, in most areas of Christian service. But the spread of abilities is not so well understood or appreciated in the subject of prayer. There was a much clearer understanding in medieval times, when monasticism was at its height. Some parts of today's church have a greater understanding of the monastic calling. But all of us have more to learn.

Some people have a special calling to the life of prayer. This may be expressed by joining a religious order or society. It may involve setting up a *House of Prayer* or a retreat centre (you will find links to both resource types on the internet). Or it may take the form of personal, individual commitment to ongoing prayer. In all such instances, we may expect prayer to include more advanced or exploratory forms than may be experienced by the average believer. That doesn't stop the rest of us from exploring different forms of prayer such as we might learn at a retreat; but it doesn't oblige us all to become specialists.

Prayer is not just for specialists. We are all called to pray and we will each benefit from advancing in prayer as far as we are able. But we don't need to go further – let's stick to our calling and ability. Some chapters of this book speak about forms of prayer that are practiced by specialists. Any of us may rightly aspire to such heights; but let's take it one step at a time, and progress *as far as God calls us* to go – and *only that far*. Be who you are. Live as you are meant to.

For all that – let us pray.

26. A method for prayer – or not

A – C – T – S
Got it!
Acronym learnt –
Now I know how to pray.
Really?
Let's see:

A – Adoration
Well, you need to butter up a king.
C – Confession
Well, you should do some grovelling.
T – Thanksgiving
Well, you may gain points by thanking Him
S – Supplication
Hah! Now it's time to ask for things.

Tried that!
But why doesn't it feel right?

Prayer is not about
Talking to God
As I imagine Him to be,
Or
Addressing God
As I would like Her to be.

Prayer is about
Experiencing God
As God is.

Why am I mocking a well-proven and popular aid to prayer? Because we make a mockery of the fundamental principles of prayer when we approach it with wrong attitudes. Prayer is not to be undertaken as a legal duty, a tiresome obligation, a public display of piety, a way of scoring points or an attempt to bribe God.

The ACTS formula has proved helpful to generations of praying people and, though some of the words now seem archaic, it can still be useful. But it can also be a snare. Any method can be a snare – including techniques you may find in this book! Though techniques may help us better understand the process of prayer, prayer is *not* a mechanical process – is it?

The problem is not that the ACTS acrostic is a bad description of prayer. It is a helpful analysis and the next few chapters will examine each element in detail. But the formula can be used mechanistically, like a clockwork engine turning: **A**doration (*click*) **C**onfession (*click*) **T**hanksgiving (*click*) and so on. I fell into that trap at one stage in my life and, when it dawned on me that my prayers had become a hollow ritual, it cast a shadow over my devotions for several years.

Any method, technique, hint, or guidance has the potential to be turned into a law or an obligation, but true prayer flows from grace and love. It is grace that allows us to approach God at all (we would never qualify if it depended on our goodness or ability). In some senses, God is frightening because of his power. But his grace has given us privileged access. And his love draws us to him.

Our love also draws us towards him. We come in the assurance that we are welcome. We don't have to bribe him. We don't need to flatter him. We don't need to grovel. We start with the consciousness that *he is*.

He is...

It's not that he is this or that attribute. Just that he is. Pause in the simple awareness of his being. Wait in the stillness of that certainty. Don't be in a hurry to fill the space with words. Use methods and techniques if you find them helpful; but use them without becoming a slave to them. The object is not to put together a well-structured prayer (as if we could impress God with our word skills). No – the object is to meet with our Lord, the Maker of everything.

Be still and know that I am God.
Psalm 46:10 KJV

27. Adoration

Adoration is
A right sense of proportion –
I bow to the truth.

God does not demand flattery. The purpose of worship is not to get into his 'good books' so we can draw favours from him. We don't need to appease him. When we worship, we are recognising the truth about God and us. He is the monarch; we are his subjects. But that doesn't mean we need to grovel, like supplicants before a tyrannical despot.

The Lord's Prayer starts with an amazingly simple example of worship – "Hallowed be Thy Name" (your name is holy). It isn't extravagant. It isn't effusive. It is a simple acknowledgement of the truth about God. On the other hand, the truth that we acknowledge is beyond our understanding. What does 'holy' mean in this context? We are not suggesting that God could be unholy. We are expressing a mystery. We, who are unfit and undeserving are somehow being allowed to come into the presence, and even to address, One who is perfect and all-sufficient. The best thing to say at that point is:

Nothing.

> *Do not be quick with your mouth, do not be hasty in your heart to utter anything before God. God is in heaven and you are on earth, so let your words be few.*
> Ecclesiastes 5:2 NIV

The Bible does, of course, provide many examples of more fulsome worship. Look, for instance, at the following New Testament verses:

To God only wise, be glory through Jesus Christ for ever. Amen.
Romans 16:27 KJV

Now to him who is able to do immeasurably more than all we ask or imagine, according to his power that is at work within us, to him be glory in the church and in Christ Jesus throughout all generations, for ever and ever! Amen.
Ephesians 3:20-21 NIV

To the only wise God our Saviour, be glory and majesty, dominion and power, both now and ever. Amen.
Jude 1:25 KJV

You are worthy, our Lord and God, to receive glory and honour and power, for you created all things, and by your will they were created and have their being.
Revelation 4:11 NIV

"Worthy is the Lamb, who was slain, to receive power and wealth and wisdom and strength and honour and glory and praise!" Then I heard every creature in heaven and on earth and under the earth and on the sea, and all that is in them, saying: "To him who sits on the throne and to the Lamb be praise and honour and glory and power, for ever and ever!"
Revelation 5:12-13 NIV

Amen! Praise and glory and wisdom and thanks and honour and power and strength be to our God for ever and ever. Amen!
Revelation 7:12 NIV

And, of course, the Psalms provide lots of wonderful examples of worship.

We may do well to include some of these verses in our prayers.

But, always remember-

God is spirit, and his worshipers must worship in the Spirit and in truth."
John 4:24 NIV

No flattery

No insincerity

Not too many words

Simply:

Honest, humble, awed recognition of our incomprehensible God.

Teach us to pray

28. Confession

My dear children, I write this to you so that you will not sin. But if anybody does sin, we have an advocate with the Father—Jesus Christ, the Righteous One.
1 John 2:1 NIV

I have hidden your word in my heart that I might not sin against you.
Psalm 119:11 NIV

Why should we dig out something to confess if we can't recall doing anything wrong? Viewed against the above texts, it's a reasonable question. John said "*if* anybody does sin". His assumption is that we don't sin all the time, but we may do sometimes. Added to that, the psalmist trusts in God's word to protect him from sin. And the salvation deal is that we have power to resist sin. James says:

"Submit yourselves, then, to God. Resist the devil, and he will flee from you".
James 4:7 NIV

This is not to imply that we have suddenly become perfect, but rather that confession should be done truthfully, not grovelingly confessing when we have no awareness of sin to confess. When we sin, we must confess, repent and receive forgiveness. When we don't sin, we praise our victorious God. Sin can be conquered, not at all by our own efforts, but by God's grace and the power of the Holy Spirit. Let's not go through life under a cloud of unnecessary guilt.

Those who have received Christ as Saviour have received forgiveness. But, of course, we do fall into sin and, when we do, confession is necessary. The situation is well illustrated in the story of Jesus washing the disciples' feet:

> *He came to Simon Peter, who said to him, "Lord, are you going to wash my feet?"*
> *Jesus replied, "You do not realize now what I am doing, but later you will understand."*
> *"No," said Peter, "you shall never wash my feet." Jesus answered, "Unless I wash you, you have no part with me."*
> *"Then, Lord," Simon Peter replied, "not just my feet but my hands and my head as well!"*
> *Jesus answered, "Those who have had a bath need only to wash their feet; their whole body is clean. And you are clean, though not every one of you."*
> John 13:6-10 NIV

First century roads were not generally paved; they consisted of stamped-down dirt. No matter how clean a person may have been when starting a journey, his feet would get dusty along the way so, on entering a house, foot washing was necessary. Those who have been cleansed from sin through salvation inevitably pick up the grime of the world as they journey through life. Sin requires confession.

When we do confess, we find forgiveness and cleansing:

> *If we confess our sins, he is faithful and just and will forgive us our sins and purify us from all unrighteousness.*
> 1 John 1:9 NIV

The time to confess is when we become conscious that we have done something wrong. Confession isn't just saying "*I did it*", but "*I did it and I don't want to do it again*" (that means repentance). We shouldn't diminish what we have done, nor should we spice it up by exaggerating its seriousness. All sin is serious, because it cost the life of our Lord.

The purpose of confession is to find peace through forgiveness. Sometimes we may feel low and carry a sense of self-doubt, or even guilt. This may not have anything to do with sin; we have physical bodies and human emotions. We get tired. We experience emotional highs and lows. These are normal variations in the human condition and do not necessarily imply that anything is wrong with us spiritually. Feelings of guilt may arise from the taunts of 'the Accuser' (the literal meaning of 'Satan') but his purpose is to demotivate us. He certainly doesn't want us to receive forgiveness and cleansing. On the other hand, when the Holy Spirit convicts us of sin, he makes us aware of the specific fault. His purpose is to lead us to confession and forgiveness.

Let's re-run that explanation, because this is important. If you have a vague feeling of guilt, but don't know what you might have done to provoke that feeling, adopt an initially neutral attitude. Treat yourself the same as criminal law treats those who are accused – innocent until proved guilty. Then pray for the guidance of the Holy Spirit, whose role includes convicting us of sin. If you then become aware of unconfessed sin, confess it immediately and receive forgiveness through God's grace. If the Holy Spirit doesn't convict you, resist the accusation; it comes from the *"father of lies"* (John 8:44 NIV). Confess only the truth.

A good way to recognise the ups and downs of our emotional life is to keep a journal (see chapter 48). Over time, we can look back in our journal notes and spot patterns that may help us understand what affects our feelings. By understanding ourselves, we may be able to make lifestyle changes that remove the causes of unnecessary guilt or sadness.

Confession brings God's forgiveness, but it also helps us to recognise patterns and identify risks we can avoid. "*Make level paths for your feet*" (Hebrews 12:13 NIV). If particular newspapers or magazines, specific places, certain computer games, TV channels or activities tend to lead us into sin, we need to avoid them. We don't need to be self-righteous about it. We don't need to judge other people (things that lead us into temptation may be no problem to them). We simply need to protect ourselves from avoidable temptations. If we keep back from the edge of the cliff we are less liable to fall over it.

Confession is not just a part of our prayer life; it is a tool for our sanctification.

> "*I am the LORD, who brought you up out of Egypt to be your God; therefore be holy, because I am holy.*"
> Leviticus 11:45 NIV

29. Thanksgiving

If I am thankful
my spirit is uplifted,
so I benefit.

Thankfulness is good,
not just for the one we thank,
but to make us smile.

It is difficult to say 'Thank you' in sincerity without having a smile on your face. Thankfulness is happy. It shows appreciation to the person we received from, and it causes us to remember whatever gift or benefit we received. But it can also transform a disaster. When we suffer a setback or disappointment it is easy to let it get on top of us. But thanksgiving can change the outcome. When something happens that might cause some people to swear, try thanking God for it; it will bring back your smile and lift your hopes.

Thanksgiving is much more than a dutiful obligation. We thank God because we recognise that everything we have depends on him. We came into the world owning nothing, dependent on the love of our parents. And where does love come from? We receive our salvation as an unmerited gift. We live in faith and hope of God's grace and mercy that will lead us to undeserved, eternal blessings. For all this we are moved to thank our heavenly Father. And, in expressing our thanks, we are further blessed.

Thanksgiving features strongly in the prayers of the Bible, and here are some examples:

> *I'll make a list of God's gracious dealings, all the things God has done that need praising, All the generous bounties of*

God, his great goodness to the family of Israel— Compassion lavished, love extravagant.
Isaiah 63:7 MSG

But thanks be to God! He gives us the victory through our Lord Jesus Christ.
1 Corinthians 15:57 NIV

But thanks be to God, who always leads us as captives in Christ's triumphal procession and uses us to spread the aroma of the knowledge of him everywhere.
2 Corinthians 2:14 NIV

Thanks be to God for his indescribable gift!
2 Corinthians 9:15 NIV

Merlin Carothers' book, *'Prison to Praise'* was first published in 1970 and quickly became popular. I didn't read it for myself at that time, but some enthusiastic readers told me about its most distinctive message – to praise God in *everything*. I remember the first time I put that lesson to the test when I was in my garage, trying to fix a problem on my motorbike. The job seemed to be going well until, suddenly, a vital and expensive shaft sheared off and fell to the floor. I stared at it for a moment; then I calmly said "Thank you Lord" and meant it. Any temptation to rage or swear simply dissolved into nothing as my frustration turned to joy. I no longer recall what practical steps I took to sort out that motorbike problem all those years ago, but the thanksgiving lesson stayed with me and has helped me through many crises.

Thanksgiving is a powerful force for transformation. When we thank God, not just *in* every circumstance, but *for* every circumstance – even the ones that seem like disasters – we rob them of their power to get us down. We turn disaster into triumph and bring God into the centre. And we release the power of joy into our lives.

Thanking God for the good things we receive is right, and it's easy. Thanking him *for* the trials, the disappointments and the disasters is hard – very hard, but it's therapeutic. In thanksgiving, we can turn losses into gains. In thanksgiving, we can find release and healing.

This probably seems crazy, so I'll say it again. Thank God for *everything* – the bad as well as the good – and experience renewed strength, faith, peace, and joy. Don't be 'under the circumstances'. Use thanksgiving to rise above them.

> *God gives, God takes. God's name be ever blessed.*
> *Job 1:21 MSG*
> *Although the fig tree shall not blossom, neither shall fruit be*
> *in the vines; the labour of the olive shall fail, and the fields*
> *shall yield no meat; the flock shall be cut off from the fold, and*
> *there shall be no herd in the stalls: Yet I will rejoice in the*
> *Lord, I will joy in the God of my salvation.*
> Habakkuk 3:17-18 KJV

Teach us to pray

30. Supplication

Who do I really care for?
What fills up most of my time?
What have I shed a tear for?
What things weigh most on my mind?
What do my duties require?
Who is relying on me?
What do I deeply desire?
Where do I most like to be?
What is my church's mission?
Who is my worst enemy?
What is my driving vision?
Who do I want to set free?
What have I heard on the news?
What am I doing today?
What do I want to improve?
Has someone asked me to pray?
The answers to these questions
Direct my supplications.

Supplication is the form of prayer that most people in the world think *is* prayer, as if that were all there is to it. God is often seen as a convenient super-being whose primary function is to meet our needs. I'm sure that's not how you see things. But, despite common misunderstandings of the matter, we *can* ask and *should* ask God for things. As James said: "*You desire but do not have ... You do not have because you do not ask God.*" (James 4:2 NIV). We know that the Lord's Prayer includes the words "*give us...*" so, it is right to make requests of God.

There is no virtue in piously saying that we must put other people first in our prayers. Let's be truthful with ourselves and with God and talk with him about the things that we are most worried about, or the things that are most on our minds. If the items that are uppermost in our minds are the desire for material objects it may be that we have our priorities wrong – but not necessarily. When George Müller prayed for bread to supply the needs of the children in his orphan homes, not appealing to men but focussing on God alone as the provider, God supplied that material need repeatedly.

If we do get our priorities wrong, God will teach us. Ask first, see how he answers, and learn from the experience.

Praying for God to act can be an expression of love for our fellow human beings. Think of your prayers as a circle of love, widening as God gives you the capacity to bring more people – and more difficult people – into that circle. Love is part of the fruit of the Spirit (Galatians 5:22,23) and fruit grows. By speaking to our Lord on behalf of others we provide genuine support; and sometimes God will answer those prayers by showing us ways we can take practical action to help the people we pray for. This kind of prayer involves listening at least as much as speaking (see Chapter 50).

As for me, far be it from me that I should sin against the Lord by failing to pray for you.
1 Samuel 1:23 NIV

I urge, then, first of all, that petitions, prayers, intercession and thanksgiving be made for all people— for kings and all those in authority, that we may live peaceful and quiet lives in all godliness and holiness. This is good, and pleases God our Saviour.
1 Timothy 2:1-3 NIV

31. Properly equipped

This is no afternoon athletic contest that we'll walk away from and forget about in a couple of hours. This is for keeps, a life-or-death fight to the finish against the Devil and all his angels. Be prepared. You're up against far more than you can handle on your own. Take all the help you can get, every weapon God has issued, so that when it's all over but the shouting you'll still be on your feet.

Truth, righteousness, peace, faith, and salvation are more than words. Learn how to apply them. You'll need them throughout your life. God's Word is an indispensable weapon.

In the same way, prayer is essential in this ongoing warfare. Pray hard and long. Pray for your brothers and sisters. Keep your eyes open. Keep each other's spirits up so that no one falls behind or drops out.

Ephesians 6:12-18 MSG

I had two dreams in one night. They didn't save the nation like Pharaoh's dreams, nor did I need a Joseph or a Daniel to interpret them. But they provided useful illustrations for this chapter.

In the first, I found myself in a large and beautiful park, facing an escaped tiger. A short way up the hill was a log cabin, so I rushed there for safety, shepherding a bunch of people ahead of me (including several children who hadn't spotted the danger). The cabin was enclosed on three sides, but nothing more than a chest-high bar fence protected the front. The gate closure was flimsy so, when the tiger tried to attack the gate, it seemed unlikely that we would be able to keep him out. I had to admire this magnificent animal, which was in perfect condition – smooth, clean fur, bright eyes, and sharp teeth. Perhaps I was seeing too much of those teeth! It occurred to me that there might be some sharp tools, hanging on the back wall of the cabin, which we could use as weapons. But I couldn't get through the crush of people to reach that wall. And I dared not take my attention off the tiger. As the gate was about to give way, I woke up, tense with excitement and fear – and I recalled the warning given in one the letters of Peter:

> *"Be alert and of sober mind. Your enemy the devil prowls around like a roaring lion looking for someone to devour."*
> 1 Peter 5:8 NIV

tiger?

In the second dream, I was mopping the floor of a shopping mall. I was working enthusiastically, but voluntarily. However, the floor was filthy, with dark footprints and scuff marks, and my efforts weren't making much impression. My mop was too small and the mop head was breaking up under the strain. Eventually, the mop fell apart uselessly, and I had to give up. Then I saw some paid workers cleaning with little enthusiasm, but much better mops. They were making a better job than I had made. But the floor would have been cleaned much more effectively if the job had been done with enthusiasm *and* good equipment!

When I woke from the second dream I quickly recognised that the images contained a message. And I realised that *both* dreams were about being properly equipped. Some of us are called to serve in up-front roles, leading and protecting the flock. Those are the tasks that get noticed and, maybe, commended ('nice sermon, vicar'). Some of us are called to serve in hidden roles, doing the kind of work that only becomes apparent when it is neglected – and it rarely gets commended. Whether we are actively engaged in defending or building the Kingdom of God, or steadily labouring in maintenance roles, we need to have the right tools – or weapons. And we need to know how to use them. This applies equally to those whose ministry is prayer.

The verses at the start of this chapter are quoted from *The Message Bible*, which is a paraphrase. From the more literal versions, many of us know this passage's subject as '*The Armour of God*':

- **The belt of Truth.** This is not just the truth of our Faith, but the truth about ourselves. We need to avoid deceptions that might leave us exposed to attack or embarrassment.
- **The breastplate of Righteousness**. By seeking personal holiness, we can protect ourselves from Satan's accusations.
- **The gospel of peace.** Never forget the Good News by which we have access to God's grace. Keep listening to God and allowing his peace to guide (see Chapter 50).
- **The shield of Faith.** This is not about exceptional faith, but simply trusting the Lord to forgive us, to accept us, and to protect us,
- **The helmet of Salvation.** Our minds may come under attack, creating unnecessary fear or self-doubt. But we are protected by the knowledge that we are saved by God's grace. OK, so I don't deserve it – but my salvation doesn't depend on my deserving.
- **The sword of the Spirit** (the word of God). Know the Bible, but also know how to use it in

> your defence (as Jesus did in the Temptation story – see Matthew 4:1-11)

Prayer is not part of the armour. Rather, it is the arena in which we fight the battle. This is a serious challenge, which we need to face head-on. We dare not retreat (there is no armour for the back). Sometimes our prayer battle may be exciting, with an obvious target (like my tiger!). Much of the time, the task may seem tedious (like my floor cleaning!) but the work is essential.

This matters whether you pray whilst walking the streets, while dancing to music, drawing or doodling your prayerful thoughts, or down-on-your-knees in the traditional prayer position. Whatever way you pray, equip yourself with the best tools – and be sure that you know how to use them.

32. Burning bush
(based on Moses' story in Exodus 3)

Roots in sand – a tenuous hold on soil and life;
branches exposed to the parching desert sun.
survival always in the balance;
the barest spark could destroy me.
But this fire does not consume.
It warms;
    it illuminates;
       it energises;
changing this dried-up thorn bush
into a blazing image of God.
He is –
therefore, I am –
    Alight
      Alive
         Aglow with a fire called love.
And now he can send me;
    still just a small desert plant,
      but a bearer of God's love;
Still essentially me
    But on fire.

This poem is an example of a kind of meditation called *'lectio divina'*. Don't be put off by the Latin name; it is simply a way of reading a passage from the Bible and pausing to allow the passage to inspire you. It is not about Bible study of the kind that examines a passage in detail, trying to work out what it means. The idea is to quietly wait on the Holy Spirit to draw your attention to some part of the story – often a word or short phrase that you hardly noticed was there – and be inspired by it. Learn more about this approach in Chapter 45.

On this reading, it was the bush itself that caught my attention. It wasn't the kind of lush, green shrub that you might want in your garden. It was a parched thorn bush of a kind that somehow manages to survive in the desert – dried up, prickly and unattractive. It represented the man who stood before it: Moses, a man whose desert exile made him feel so useless that God could scarcely persuade him to take on his life's mission.

But God was telling Moses that, although he was worn out, tired and discouraged, God could make use of him. In fact, he could make him into one of the greatest leaders of all time (Moses couldn't have known that, but he needed to recognise that God could use him).

The thorn bush could represent Moses. And it could represent you or me. One of the wonders of grace is that God chooses the weak and the ordinary to take on vital tasks for the Kingdom. There's a place for us.

****

You may often have been told that prayer is about listening to God, rather than just talking to him. Well, *lectio divina* is one way of listening.

I turned this inspiration into a poem, but you don't have to do that. Poetry works for me; but your way might be to simply jot down a brief note. If you are artistically inclined, you may like to produce a drawing or painting to preserve the inspiration. Even non-artists might find doodling a sketch helps the memory. Use whatever method suits your personality. But don't lose touch with your inspirations.

33. Take off your shoes

Take off your shoes
And feel the rough, dirty earth -
That is holy ground

Returning to the 'burning bush' story, have you ever wondered why shoes could be a barrier to holiness? I keep my shoes reasonably clean, though I wouldn't put them on the dining table! But, in a desert, surely we need footwear to protect our feet from dirt, thorns, and venomous creatures? What's the objection to shoes?

This question came to me during another session of '*lectio divina*' meditation on the passage from Exodus quoted earlier (Chapter 32); and the startling thought popped into my mind that, by baring his feet, Moses became closer to the earth. He was put in touch with the world from which he had been retreating. Remember that, in his former life in Egypt, he lived in a palace. It was not the kind of environment where he could have learned the ways of ordinary people.

There are stories about famous saints being seen to float inches above the ground while they were praying. I'm not saying whether those tales were true or not, but, either way, they illustrate the conception that holiness involves separation from the earth. God's instruction to Moses required *closer* contact with earth. Sometimes God turns our ideas upside down.

Prayer takes us into a secret place of communion with God. But God also wants us to face the needs of the world while we are in that place. Spending time with God fits us for spending time with our fellow men and women – and serving them effectively. That is holy ground.

Teach us to pray

34. Let it all out

Cast your cares on the Lord and he will sustain you; he will never let the righteous be shaken.
Psalm 55:22 NIV

"Cast your cares"
That means *throw* them,
    which doesn't sound very holy,
        or gentle,
            or respectful.
This is God we're talking to,
    isn't it?
Won't he be angry if we
    throw things at him?
Shouldn't we hold it in
    out of respect?
Who told us
    we could let it all out?

Psychology tells us that it is unhealthy to bottle up strong emotions. But, therapy may be expensive; so, what can we do when we are raging inside? The text quoted above tells us we can pour out our troubles to God. If that sounds a bit weak, check how the great men of the Bible made use of this privilege: listen, for instance, to Jeremiah:

And I said to GOD: "GOD, listen to me! Just listen to what my enemies are saying.
Should I get paid evil for good? That's what they're doing. They've made plans to kill me! Remember all the times I stood up for them before you, speaking up for them, trying to soften your anger?

But enough! Let their children starve! Let them be massacred in battle! Let their wives be childless and widowed, their friends die and their proud young men be killed.

Let cries of panic sound from their homes as you surprise them with war parties! They're all set to lynch me. The noose is practically around my neck!

But you know all this, GOD. You know they're determined to kill me. Don't whitewash their crimes, don't overlook a single sin! Round the bunch of them up before you. Strike while the iron of your anger is hot!"

Jeremiah 18:19-23 MSG

The prophet was certainly not holding back his anger in that prayer! And the Bible gives many other examples of strongly worded prayers that 'let it all out' to the Lord. The Psalms provide many instances, especially in the ones known as 'imprecatory psalms' (Psalms 5, 10, 17, 35, 58, 59, 69, 70, 79, 83, 109, 129, 137 and 140). Repeatedly, we read heart-wrenching language used – *in prayers*!

If you pour out your heart to God, you are not going to damage him. But, if you pour out your anger, hurt and anguish to another human being you may well shock, hurt and damage them. Prayer is a marvellous resource for 'letting it all out' so that we can find expression for our emotions but nobody else is hurt.

The prophet, Habakkuk, let his feelings out in his prayer:

GOD, how long do I have to cry out for help before you listen? How many times do I have to yell, "Help! Murder! Police!" before you come to the rescue?

Why do you force me to look at evil, stare trouble in the face day after day? Anarchy and violence break out, quarrels and fights all over the place.

Law and order fall to pieces. Justice is a joke. The wicked have the righteous hamstrung and stand justice on its head.
Habakkuk 1:2-4 MSG

Even Jesus found it necessary to express his anguish to the Father in prayer:

Then he said, "This sorrow is crushing my life out. Stay here and keep vigil with me."
Going a little ahead, he fell on his face, praying, "My Father, if there is any way, get me out of this. But please, not what I want. You, what do you want?"
Matthew 26:38-39 MSG

He took Peter, James, and John with him. He plunged into a sinkhole of dreadful agony.
He told them, "I feel bad enough right now to die. Stay here and keep vigil with me."
Going a little ahead, he fell to the ground and prayed for a way out:
"Papa, Father, you can — can't you? — get me out of this. Take this cup away from me. But please, not what I want-- what do you want?"
Mark 14:33-36 MSG

He prayed on all the harder. Sweat, wrung from him like drops of blood, poured off his face.
Luke 22:44 MSG

Somehow, I feel that the words of that Gethsemane prayer, as recorded in the Gospels (especially in the older translations) can't have told the whole story. A man who was under such pressure that he literally sweated blood must have expressed very strong emotions in his prayer – but, perhaps, no words could express such depths of feeling. We can be sure, however, that Jesus knew that his Father always responds with compassion when any child of God calls out to him with passion.

Let's not torture ourselves by holding in our deepest feelings. Let's be truthful with God and with ourselves. If our normal place of prayer is not secret enough for us to 'let it all out', this may be the time to drive out to some secluded spot where only God will hear our rage.

35. Be still

To be really still
means letting go of tension,
muscle by muscle

The advice to 'be still' may be familiar, but how can we do it? It is often said that modern life runs at a hectic pace. But, even when we stop for a while, many of us don't know how to be still. We sit down, but we don't relax. Even in prayer, our muscles remain tensed and our minds continue to race. Well, here's a way to discover relaxation.

Sit in an upright chair, making sure that you are fully supported by the seat and the back of the chair. Close your eyes and breathe in and out normally whilst noticing each breath. Tense the toes of each foot in turn, then relax them, noticing *how* relaxation compares with tension. Tense each ankle and relax it – again taking notice of the difference. Continue to work each muscle in turn, tightening it, then releasing the tension, working gradually up your body to your neck and head.

Now you know what it feels like to be tense, you have discovered what relaxation feels like.

Having found that, stay relaxed and enjoy the moment. Notice your breathing and feel each breath – inward and outward. Listen to your heartbeat. Notice how your clothes touch your body. Recognise the feeling of the seat under you. Sense the quietness. Remain in the moment.

If tensions return, tense the muscles again, one at a time – then release them again.

Do that each time you return to the secret place until stillness becomes a habit.

And, while you are in that place, listen for the still, small voice of God (see Chapter 50). He speaks of love – though he may not say it in words. He speaks of peace – and that doesn't need words. He speaks of acceptance, of hope, of quietness…

BUT, this doesn't work for everyone. For some people, a still body means a busy mind. I'm not talking about distractions in prayer; everyone faces distractions, so we'll talk about that later (chapters 51-57). No, this is a matter of personality and what works for *you* – draw, paint, walk, run, dance – do whatever brings you to the place of calmness. If you are the kind of person whose mind only relaxes when your body is moving, don't be discouraged by your inability to engage with God in ways that others recommend. Stilling exercises work brilliantly for many people and have become a staple of prayer retreats and prayer manuals. But be who *you* are and do what works for *you*. If you find stillness in relaxation, do it. If you need to move, do that. It's your *mind* that you are seeking to calm.

Getting to know me

Sometimes the most difficult person to understand is myself.

36. Getting to know me
(Identity Crisis)

WHO is the person inside this flesh –
choreographing the stage movements of the man
I call me?

WHERE is that soul-centre –
The real me
The true I
The one who bursts out occasionally
when the player fluffs his lines
and the audience boos?

THE player I see in the mirror;
The one they think is me;
The controlled one,
The stage-managed one –
 is a front;
I know he's connected to me;
under my control,
acting to my directions;
playing the parts I worked out in the scripts.
BUT, he isn't really me:
The string puller,
The manipulator,
The puppeteer in black clothes, hidden in the
darkness.

I'M in there somewhere – up – down
out there in the wings;
but I can't see myself.
WILL someone switch the light on PLEASE?

I wrote that poem at a crisis point in my life. But there
have been many crisis points. It may seem hard to get
to know God, but may be even harder to know

ourselves. From childhood, we learn to hide our feelings, to put on a good face and make ourselves acceptable. A key part of our sanctification is getting to know ourselves.

Learning about ourselves us not just a subject for prayer; it is a primary function of prayer. When we go into the secret place with God we want no secrets between us and him. We need the truth. This is not a matter of selfish introspection but simple honesty. We are offering ourselves to him. So, we must offer our true selves. It follows, therefore, that self-examination and self-discovery are not *separate* parts of our spiritual journey. They are part of our prayer life.

Knowing ourselves helps prevent us from fighting against our personality. There's no point in forcing ourselves to act like introverts if extroversion is our true nature. On the other hand, when we understand our natural preferences, we have scope to strengthen and broaden ourselves by deliberately choosing to push our boundaries.

At the time when I wrote the above poem, I realised that, for most of my life, I had been trying *not* to be like my father – but that was to deny the truth about myself. In learning to value my late father I learned to value myself.

There are several tried and tested methods of classifying personalities. Understanding what type of person we are helps direct our prayers more effectively. Not that we are merely personality *types*. No, each of us is a unique individual. But identifying our personality in broad terms is a helpful step to a more thorough self-knowledge.

The details of personality classification are beyond the scope of this book, but an Internet search will quickly lead you to specialised books, courses, seminars or retreats on each method. Examples are the Enneagram (which focuses on 9 personality types), Myers-Briggs (which identifies traits of introversion, extroversion etc.) and Colour Code Personality types (which examines personality under 4 primary driving motivations each of which is represented as a colour). If you're serious about prayer it is worth the effort to read up about these systems or even go on a course. Identifying your personality type may not solve all your hang-ups and problems, but it may contribute to a better understanding of the factors that drive your emotions, preferences, and reactions.

No parent can be perfect, however hard they try. Meanwhile, children often misunderstand even well-intentioned actions and events. Children are excellent recorders of events, but poor interpreters. So many of us grow up bearing mental scars that affect our development and our peace of mind. On the other hand, there may be events from our childhood or youth that, as adults, we remember with shame. As our prayer life develops, we may need to confront those issues and face up to the truth about ourselves.

- We may need to seek forgiveness.
- We may need to forgive ourselves.
- We may need to forgive other people.
- We may need to ask someone to pray with us or provide counselling.
- We may need healing.

For many of us, the biggest problem is not getting to know God, so much as getting to know ourselves. It requires honesty. It requires humility. Both are vital elements of the life of prayer.

37. Our Father

This, then, is how you should pray:
Our Father in heaven…
Matthew 6:9 NIV

A group of sceptical academics gathered together to discuss the New Testament. They were regarded as experts in their field but the list of conference delegates notably excluded scholars who held positive views about the gospel records. They called their conference "The Jesus Seminar" and planned to screen the Gospels for what they called "the authentic voice of Jesus". Their negative conclusions were not surprising, considering their known attitudes. They approached the subject as sceptics and came to sceptical conclusions. But it is instructive to see which of Jesus' sayings were so convincing that even these sceptics couldn't deny their authenticity. Paramount among those phrases were the words 'Our Father'. Despite their scepticism, they were forced to admit that this phrase was original, distinctive, and unique and could only have come from the mouth of Jesus.

'Father' was an original way of addressing God. The Jews did not traditionally use this form of address in prayer. Neither the patriarchs nor the prophets spoke of God in this way. Jesus was, of course, uniquely positioned to see his relationship with God as that of Son to Father; but he taught the disciples to use the same expression. – "*you* should pray: *our* Father".

What does the word 'father' mean to you? Most people look back with some pleasure on their relationship with their earthly father. But, for some unfortunate individuals, the word has unhappy connotations. Are you one of those people? If you have less-than-satisfactory memories of the man who was your father, those memories may cloud your vision of the fatherhood of God. It is not enough for someone to tell you that God is much better than that. Intellectually you know that already. If your concept of fatherhood is damaged, even in a small way, ask a responsible and spiritual person to pray with you. If you have deep problems in this area, seek counselling.

My father was a good man who loved and cared for his family. But my concept of fatherhood was still deficient because of false impressions I formed in childhood. I correctly recognised what was happening, but my immature mind could not properly understand it. My siblings happened to be sickly in childhood, whereas I was healthy. My parents' response to their greater needs was appropriate. But my childish mind interpreted it as a rejection, to which I responded by becoming remote and independent. Thank God for the healing I received in later years, which taught me to become *appropriately* dependent on God.

God is my Father – and it is a special delight to me to address him as 'Father'. I sense his love and care and feel his protection. Coming to him as a valued son I am confident that he hears me and wants the best for me. And I am delighted to be dependent on him.

Prayer is an act of dependence and submission. By saying 'Father' we acknowledge that we are children. As children, we are ready to learn, to be led and to grow.

> *Whoever becomes simple and elemental again, like this child, will rank high in God's kingdom.*
> Matthew 18:4 MSG

38. As I am

As I am, Lord,
that's the way you welcome me.
As I am, Lord,
that is all that I can be.
As I am, Lord,
to myself I must be true.
If I must change, Lord,
I entrust that work to you.

It's obvious. I can't come to God as someone else. I am who I am.

But, Christians often interpret this 'just as I am' concept in relation to a sense of guilt or sinfulness. We know that, based on the grace by which we are saved, we are justified and have access to the presence of God. Most people who write about the life of prayer are on the introvert personality spectrum. So am I. But I recognise that my ways of praying may not be appropriate to people with different personalities. It could be said that introverts have taken over the prayer room. Most books about prayer, and most retreats and seminars on the subject, emphasise methods and habits that come most easily to introverts. Introverts like to recharge their mental/spiritual batteries in solitude. Extroverts prefer to recharge in the company of other people or whilst engaged in physical activity.

The church needs all manner of gifts, personalities, and skills. The church also needs every event, every venture, and every ministry to be bathed, supported, and surrounded by prayer. No one should be excluded *or feel excluded*. Though your prayer language may not be like my prayer language, I'm sure that we both want to maintain contact with our heavenly Father – who loves us both. Humans communicate by nature. We are born to talk. Most children develop language quite naturally between their first and second birthday – and the urge to talk comes *from them*; they don't need a lot of persuasion. In fact, they invent language, coming up with words and word forms they could not have learned from their parents. Even children with hearing or sight problems show a natural desire and a willingness to learn ways to communicate. That's how it is with prayer. With our different personalities, we don't all relate to the same kinds of prayer. But we are born again to pray.

St Teresa of Avila and St John of the Cross were both reformers in the same spiritual tradition. They were close friends. Both were notable for their knowledge and experience of the life of prayer. Each of them suffered persecution for their reforming stand. They both wrote books that have become classics about prayer. But it is instructive to see how their different personalities were reflected in their experience of prayer. Teresa often speaks of 'raptures' and visions and her life story indicates that she had many ecstatic experiences. John was the author of the well-known (though perhaps not so well read) *The Dark Night of the Soul*. Their personality differences illustrate how personality affects our prayers. So, what kind of praying is most suited to you?

In this book, you can find descriptions of many kinds of prayer. They will not all suit you. Some that are ideal for you will seem strange, inappropriate, or incomprehensible to a person with a different personality from yours. Some kinds of prayer that leave you cold will be someone else's ideal. Know yourself.

Experiment to find what works best for you. Be who you are. Try praying as part of an activity, such as dancing, running, walking, cycling (but be safe!). Incorporate your exercise into your prayer life – not as a separate event, but as part of the whole. You are allowed to be individual. I tried dancing as a form of worship and enjoyed it somewhat; but I am not a natural dancer, so it does not fully express who I am. Creativity can be a wonderful expression of prayer, so I tried drawing and painting; but that didn't work for me either. But poetry suited me fine, so it became a frequent aspect of my conversations with God. I love walking, and find that prayer comes easily to me during my solitary walks. But my deepest prayer times happen in my 'secret place'. That's not because it is intrinsically better, but because it suits my personality.

Many people find their expression through art, but that doesn't exclude those whose artistic abilities are limited. In her book, *Praying in Color*, Sybil MacBeth describes visual ways of praying with doodles, shapes, and mind-maps that anyone can do with a few markers or pencils, regardless of their artistic skill (or lack of it). God wants to relate with us *as we are*.

If you are a strong extrovert, you may find strength in sharing some of your prayer time with friends. Link up with a couple of trusted friends to pray together as a prayer-triplet or TiE Group ("Three is Enough"). Explore the possibilities of music and song, visual art, or sculpture. Try action-based prayer styles that feel right for you. Take prayer walks (see chapter 15). Find a style that you can readily and habitually maintain.

However, it is good to stretch ourselves by giving *some* time to different styles – styles more suited to a different personality than yours. Our personalities may be fixed for a lifetime *for the most part*, but healthy development involves broadening ourselves so we understand how life is for other people. Don't force yourself into a mould that you can't fit, but don't be too narrow.

Some personality types find it relatively easy to develop habits involving long, solitary prayer times. If that's you, do it – but don't congratulate yourself too much; you are doing what comes (relatively) easily for your personality. Those whose personality is less suited to this type of prayer are less likely to be called to it; but everyone must live with themselves some of the time. So, for the sake of your spiritual health, be sure to spend some of that alone-time cultivating your relationship with God in prayer.

> *"... pray in the Spirit on all occasions with* **all kinds of prayers** *and requests."*
> Ephesians 6:18 NIV

Prayer is for all, but not all types of prayer are for everyone.

Come just as you are.

Pray just as you are.

39. Nothing is hidden

When I come to the secret place,
Just me and my God,
Alone,
I know that nothing is hidden.
I know that no one can see me.
I know I can't be just acting.
I am what I am –
Sincere.

When people talk about nothing being hidden from God, they are usually talking in sombre terms with an implied threat of future punishment. But God's close knowledge of us can be a comfort. If we are inclined to self-doubt, we may accuse ourselves of insincerity even when we are acting rightly in public ("am I too proud? too loud? too self-centred?") It's easy to hide things from the people we meet – even in church ("yes, I'm fine" "Isn't Jesus wonderful?") But, when it's just us and God, we know we are not just putting it on. Nobody knows what we're doing but God and us. So, when we are in the 'secret place', we're probably there for genuine reasons.

The place of prayer is a place we can be truly ourselves. We don't need to dress in our best clothes. We don't need to put on a false smile. We don't even need to speak. We can just come silently into God's presence and soak up his love. Alternatively, we can rage at him, if that's how we feel at the time. God knows our innermost thoughts and our deepest fears so, since we can't hide them from him, we may as well talk to him about them.

On the other hand, if we have acted wrongly, adopted bad attitudes, or grieved the Spirit in any way, the place of prayer is the place where we can put matters right.

40. I didn't see that coming

Nearly there!
  Just a few more steps and…
        Oh!
                I didn't see that coming.
There's another peak ahead;
  Further to climb;
        so steep,
                so rocky.
It felt so good to be reaching the top,
  but now?

When climbing a mountain, you will often see a summit ahead of you that seems encouragingly close. But, as you reach the top of the ridge, you discover that there's a still higher summit ahead. Unless you are familiar with the mountain you may find that discouraging. But there's a solution – get familiar with the mountain! If you do that you will find future climbs easier. You will recognise the false summits and know what glorious views those way-points can offer. No longer discouraging, they become intermediate targets, assuring you of your progress on the journey.

As we progress in our spiritual lives we often reach false summits. Learning from others, we identify goals we would like to achieve and feel spurred on to reach new heights. Then we discover that the journey is longer and harder than we expected. Or we conquer some difficulty or resolve some longstanding problem, only to discover new issues to deal with.

One summer I was climbing Cairn Gorm, a mountain in the Scottish Highlands. The weather was fine when I started but, as I climbed higher, clouds descended and it began to snow heavily. Everything was grey (it would have been white but for the gloom). There was snow on the ground, snow falling around me and thick cloud surrounding everything. Visibility was almost zero.

Then a voice from the gloom said,

"Well done, you've made it!"

Surprised, I replied -

"Are you telling me this is the top?"

We don't always know when we reach a significant point of progress. Often our greatest advances happen as we press through difficult circumstances, feeling the burden of the journey, and not realising how strong we are or how far we've come. That's when a word of encouragement can transform us in a moment.

Pause in your moments of victory. Celebrate each blessing and each gain. Use each small advance to gather strength for the next part of the journey. Listen for God's "Well done!" – and thank him.

41. Why does prayer live now?

Why does prayer live now
When once it didn't flow?
What have I learned now
That then I did not know?
It's not divine pressure;
He is patient, and waits
Till I grasp the treasure-
A gift of his grace.
So the prayer that failed,
When I made it a rule,
Has now been revealed
As a beautiful jewel.
Now, when I go in
To spend time with my God
It's not to impress him -
I just come to be loved.

I welcome this rest
But it isn't the end;
I've mounted a crest,
But there's new peaks ahead.
There's further to go
On this journey of prayer.
So much I don't know –
Even stages I fear.
It's not God who holds back;
He's waiting for me
There's so much that I lack –
I won't fully be free
Until I move forward
And fully embrace
The calling of God
To the holiest place.

I'm not the only person who has struggled with prayer; and I'm still in the lower classes of this school. But the wonder is that much has changed. How did that happen? It is an ongoing discipleship – an apprenticeship that I must learn in stages by observing the Master.

Progress in our prayer life is a barometer to our overall progress in discipleship, growth, and sanctification. But progress doesn't happen steadily and continuously, like filling a bath from an open tap. Rather, it is like the progress of the incoming tide. Waves roll in, one after another, sometimes reaching further up the beach, sometimes not quite reaching the point that was dampened by the previous wave. Sometimes it's hard to tell whether the tide is coming in or going out. But, if we wait long enough, it becomes clear. Each wave that flows in, also flows out again. Watching the tide is an exercise in patience.

But there is progress.

I wrote the poem that opens this chapter at a time when everything seemed easy. Prayer times were blessed and life felt good. But I was also recalling times when prayer had been much harder for me. In a sense, I was taking stock of what I had been learning over many years. Experience teaches us that life ebbs and flows. Happiness is never guaranteed, but sorrow doesn't last forever. Joy is part of the fruit of the Spirit. It is not like happiness. It doesn't depend on the happenings of the moment, but flows from our inner relationship with God. Joy is what tells us not to fear the downward slope when we are at the top, and not to worry about the upward journey when we are at the bottom.

Give thanks in all circumstances; for this is God's will for you in Christ Jesus.
1 Thessalonians 5:18 NIV

Prayer patterns

What activities count as prayer?

Prayer patterns

42. Unjust judge

Then Jesus told his disciples a parable to show them that they should always pray and not give up. He said: "In a certain town there was a judge who neither feared God nor cared what people thought. And there was a widow in that town who kept coming to him with the plea, 'Grant me justice against my adversary.' "For some time he refused. But finally he said to himself, 'Even though I don't fear God or care what people think, yet because this widow keeps bothering me, I will see that she gets justice, so that she won't eventually come and attack me!'" And the Lord said, "Listen to what the unjust judge says. And will not God bring about justice for his chosen ones, who cry out to him day and night? Will he keep putting them off? I tell you, he will see that they get justice, and quickly. However, when the Son of Man comes, will he find faith on the earth?"
Luke 18:1-8 NIV

Surely nobody supposes that, when Jesus told this story, he was saying that God is unjust? Neither, surely, was Jesus saying that God needs a lot of persuading to answer prayer? However, anyone who prays regularly knows that prayer doesn't work like a slot machine. We don't feed prayers into the machine and expect a chocolate answer to pop out of a slot. The message of this parable is that God wants us to be persistent.

Why does persistence matter? What is going on between our first request and the time when God answers? Many preachers have pointed out that "No" *is* an answer. But, if the answer is "No", that must mean that we should stop praying. How long should we continue to pray before accepting that God is refusing our request?

This parable suggests that we should *not* give up (verse 1). To understand what that means, we must remember that prayer is a two-way conversation. Paul told the Corinthian church a story about one of his prayer experiences that explains this (2 Corinthians 12:7-10). He had a physical problem which he asked God to take away. Paul never fully explains the nature of his infirmity, though many people have tried to identify the condition (often to prove some point of doctrine). It doesn't matter what it was. What does matter is that God told Paul that he would not be relieved of the problem. In other words, God *did* answer with a "No". So, the time when we should stop praying is when we *know* that God has told us so. This might be by a revelatory experience, as it was with Paul – or as with Moses when the Lord refused his plea to be allowed into the Promised Land (Deuteronomy 3:23-26). More commonly, we stop asking because the realisation dawns on us that we have been praying for the wrong things.

Daniel spent three weeks fasting and praying for a revelation and seemed to get no response (see Daniel chapter 10 – and chapter 23 of this book). When the answer came, the angel who delivered the message revealed that there had been a 21-day battle between the angelic forces, who were bringing the message, and some demonic powers, who were trying to resist the revelation. We don't normally think about what might be happening in unseen realms when we pray; but this passage suggests that there may be far more going on than we could imagine. Daniel's persistence was vital.

But sometimes we just *know* that it's time to give up. This may be because circumstances have changed and the things we were praying for are no longer relevant. Or, it may be that we have stopped desiring the things that previously seemed so important. Remember the message from Chapter 19:

> Prayer changes things
> And the best of it is this:
> Prayer changes me.

43. If you ask for a fish

Don't bargain with God. Be direct. Ask for what you need. This is not a cat-and-mouse, hide-and-seek game we're in. If your little boy asks for a serving of fish, do you scare him with a live snake on his plate? If your little girl asks for an egg, do you trick her with a spider? As bad as you are, you wouldn't think of such a thing —you're at least decent to your own children. And don't you think the Father who conceived you in love will give the Holy Spirit when you ask him?
Luke 11:10-13 MSG

In some parts of the world there are cultures that prize snakes as an edible delicacy. What do such people make of this parable? In Britain, few people ever see a snake in the wild (and, in Ireland, never) but most of us have an inbuilt fear of them. Hebrew culture had a view of snakes that is different from both these examples. Snakes were viewed as disgusting; they were unclean animals, marked out by the Law as creatures to be avoided, because any contact with them would make you ritually defiled so that you could not enter the temple (Leviticus 11:41-44). Remember also that, in the story of the Garden of Eden, the tempter took the form of a snake. That shows how controversial this parable was when Jesus first told it. But God will not give you anything evil or unclean; on the contrary, he will give you the Holy Spirit.

To understand that last comment (also the last clause of the above text) we need to look at the story that follows it, in chapter 11 of Luke's gospel. Listening to Jesus that day, there were people who wanted to accuse him of casting out evil spirits by the power of the devil (*'Beelzebul'*). The power Jesus used, and the power God grants us in answer to prayer is the pure power of the

Holy Spirit. When praying for healing, or any miraculous intervention from the Lord, you need not be afraid of the power you are invoking. Ask in faith, with a pure heart, and God's answer will always be pure and holy.

Snakes & Ladders used to be a popular board game, especially for children (though, in this age of digital toys and games, it may be less familiar). In this game, each player takes turns in throwing a dice and then moves forward on the board by as many squares as are shown on the dice. If they land on a square that shows the foot of a ladder, they can move up the board to the top of that ladder. If they land on a square that shows the head of a snake, they must move down the board to the foot of the snake. Landing on a snake puts you at a serious disadvantage. Jesus wasn't referring to Snakes & Ladders when he told his parable, but he certainly wanted to reassure us that prayer will never put us at a disadvantage in the game of life.

44. Written prayers

God, of your goodness give me yourself for you
are sufficient for me.
I cannot properly ask anything less, to be worthy
of you.
If I were to ask less, I should always be in want.
In you alone do I have all.
(Julian of Norwich 1342-1413 – public domain)

In normal circumstances, I pray first thing in the
morning. But circumstances are not always normal. Try
having a concentrated time of prayer on an overnight
flight; it's not easy! And, for any of us, at times in our
life, health problems, tragedies, work demands or
sudden emergencies may disrupt our plans and
intentions. At such times, written prayers can provide
valuable support.

Experiences at school, and in a church where I was a
choirboy, taught me to be sceptical about formal
prayers. I sensed insincerity in what I heard and it made
me cautious, sometimes even derisory, about written
prayers. Extempore praying was the norm in the
nonconformist churches where my faith was nurtured,
and I felt that prayer ought to come from the heart in
the words of the moment. But, for many Christians,
written prayers have always been a staple of spiritual
life. A huge range of prayers has been written and
published over centuries. The Bible provides a valuable
library of beautiful prayers; and there are long-
established resources such as the Anglican Book of
Common Prayer and its equivalents in other traditions.

My attitude towards written prayers was already
changing, when I heard a talk that convinced me of

their usefulness. The talk was a testimony given by Ian Smale (popularly known as Ishmael, the musician and children's worker). When critical illness suddenly put him in hospital, he discovered the value of the familiar. With his mental capacity severely limited by his cancer and the treatment he was receiving, he found that friends who prayed at his bedside using written prayers brought him greater comfort than those who prayed extempore. Deeply embedded memories, formed over many years, made it easier for him to relate to those familiar words and phrases, whereas the unfamiliar wording of extempore prayers, sincere though they were, demanded more brain power than his condition could spare.

My prayer times do not usually include written prayers but, when the pressure is on – perhaps because I am in a noisy environment or in circumstances that create confusion or mental strain – the familiar phrases help me to focus on God.

If you come from a tradition that majors on written prayers, don't allow yourself to be bound by them. God likes to hear your authentic voice. If you come from a tradition that looks down on pre-written prayers, stop being sniffy and start making your own selection of prayers that inspire you. They may prove to be just what you need when things get tough.

The prayer that heads this chapter is one of my favourites. I have assembled a collection of prayers – some Biblical, some that I came across in books, a few that were recommended by friends, a couple from longstanding traditions, and some that I wrote myself –

and I keep them on my computer tablet and my smartphone so I can access them easily.

Whatever the circumstances, I want to be armed at all times, in all circumstances, and always ready to engage with the Lord.

45. I read and I wait

I read and I wait
I read and I notice
I read and I pray
I read and I absorb
I read and I thank
I read and I remember
I read and I am changed

This poem describes a pattern of prayer that uses the Bible. It has a traditional, technical name – '*Lectio Divina*' – which translates as 'godly reading', but let's just call it 'praying with the Bible'. Bible reading can slip into the realm of intellectual study, which is valuable in the right place. But that's not what we're talking about here. This is as much about reading as listening. It is a form of meditation. The object is not to understand the passage rationally, or to seek lessons to teach other people. It is to live within a passage of scripture and listen to God's voice – the voice of inspiration speaking to you or me right now.

Choose a passage – it may be some verses that come into your reading plan for the day, or it may be a reading that pops into your mind. Read it through slowly. Wait prayerfully, then read it again. Notice some part that seems significant for you. It may be a word, a phrase, or a whole verse; or it may be a scene in which you can imagine yourself as a participant. If, for instance, you read the story of Joseph in prison, you might imagine yourself as the jailer or the butler. Sense their situation, their emotions, their joys, or their fears. How does that feel?

Give it time. As you read, some word or phrase may spark a memory – a very personal memory – and that remembrance will teach you something important about yourself. You may find yourself responding emotionally, sensing the scene as if you were there. You may be provoked to thankfulness. You may recognise a personal need for grace and healing. The words of scripture come alive in the moment and become a focus for prayer.

As you read, don't focus too much on the literal meaning. Don't try to understand the passage intellectually. Just allow it to speak to you.

When something in the passage seems to stand out from the text, dwell on that thought. Make it the focus for a period of quiet meditation. Notice your feelings. Repeat the phrase or word that stood out to you, and wait a while longer.

Now – this may be the time to respond. Don't rush it. Allow the prayer to arise from the depths of your being. Speak to God, but not necessarily in words; and if you do use words, don't use too many. Continue to make this a listening exercise in which God can speak to you, rather than you to him.

Then, as you reach the end of your prayer time, thank God for his revelation and bear the thoughts with you as you move out into whatever you need to do next.

46. My song is a prayer

When I worship God
I ride on clouds of wonder.
My song is a prayer.

It is a normal tendency of the human mind to put things into categories. Categories help us to understand the world. But our categories can trick us into seeing things that belong together as if they were separate. In the context of the spiritual life, this can cause us to miss valuable truths. For instance, prayer goes into one pigeon hole and music goes into a different slot.

When we worship in song, whether we use centuries-old psalms, Victorian hymns, or modern songs, we are praying. If we're not entering prayerfully into the mood of the song, we may be missing the point that the composers intended. Worship songs are addressed to God and we need to sing them with a consciousness of his presence. I love the King James rendering of this well-known Psalm:

> *But thou art holy, O thou that inhabitest the praises of Israel.*
> Psalm 22:3 KJV

The idea that God can inhabit our praises is strong motivation for putting heart and soul into our worship. That doesn't necessarily mean that we jump about, wave our hands in the air, or dance about. If we have a hand-waving, jumping personality, that's fine. If we have a head-bowing, hands clasped personality, that's also fine. But let's *feel* what we sing.

My experience is that, while God is riding the waves of our worship, so am I. The heartfelt expression of songs of praise lifts my spirit and draws me closer to the Lord.

It's true that some Christian songs fail to live up to our ideal. There have been good songs and bad ones in every age. But the good ones stand out and survive over time for our continuing edification.

Music is universal and broad. It is enjoyed by extroverts and introverts, by those who like to be demonstrative and display their excitement, and by those who feel a sense of reverence and prefer to reflect calmly on the words they are singing. We are not allowed to judge one another. We are encouraged to be authentic, which means being ourselves. Whatever our personality, we can pray our songs.

We generally use Christian songs in corporate worship, but not do much in private prayer. But there's no reason why we can't bring them into our personal devotions (depending, perhaps, on where we pray). Maybe you can't sing aloud at home, but you may be able to sing on a prayer walk (especially if your walk takes you to remote places). Or you may like to listen to recorded music that resonates with your spirit.

Don't let your prayer life be restricted to one kind of prayer. And don't forget to pray what you sing in corporate worship. Sing with God-consciousness.

47. Creativity

Creativity
is in the nature of God -
Inspiration,
  Intention,
      Conception,
          Thought,
              Action,
                  Word.
God,
The Creator –
  Mother,
      Father,
          Maker of all,
  is reflected in what we do
  when we create.

If you thought that prayer was just about sitting/standing/kneeling, or whatever, so as to engage with God in words, or even in silence, think again. Prayer is much broader than that. It certainly involves personal engagement with God, but that may include all kinds of activities that people usually classify under the 'hobbies' heading. Your favourite hobby can be turned into prayer.

If that sounds strange, think about all the artwork that has been created over the centuries to glorify God. Think of the stained-glass windows, the illustrated manuscripts, the paintings, the sculptures, the poems, the plays. These creative activities reflect the creativity of God. Creative work can be a process of meditation – of prayer.

Images have had a mixed status in Christianity over the centuries. There have been times when so-called religious art has been used inappropriately, verging on idolatry, fraud, or for merely commercial purposes. It's an issue of intention and sincerity. Many people find it helpful to bring their creative art into prayer – or their prayer into creative art. These activities can be thoroughly engaging, taking the mind off the mundane issues that commonly hinder our prayers. And, for many people, such engagement suits their personality better than more conventional prayer formats.

I have said several times in this book that I don't have a talent for visual art. However, I keep one of my pictures on my bedroom wall, because it has had great significance in my life. One evening, during a weekend prayer retreat, I felt a strong urge to pick up a packet of marker pens and start drawing. Totally absorbed, I covered a large sheet of paper, using bold strokes, to create an abstract picture that proved hugely significant for me.

The image was not formed in my mind, so much as on the paper and, though I didn't initially know what it represented, I immediately recognised that it was important. Gradually, over several years, the meaning of each part of that picture became clear as God led me on a path of mental healing and self-discovery. Little by little I recognised what each image represented. The picture identified issues in my childhood and family life that had affected my personality and damaged my self-esteem. Because the issues became clear *gradually,* I could deal with them progressively at a pace that I could cope with – and I received healing. That little burst of uncharacteristic creativity was a prayer, it instigated prayer, and it answered my prayers. No wonder I value that picture.

If you have creative ability, whatever form that may take, offer your talent to God and take time to hone and develop your skill. "Do it heartily, as to the Lord" (Colossians 3:23 KJV). Let it be an expression of your true self and a vehicle for your engagement with God.

Prayer is not, and never has been, a narrow process to be carried on according to strict, inflexible conventions.

...whatever you do, do it all for the glory of God.
1 Corinthians 10:31 NIV

48. Count your blessings

Count your many blessings
Name them one by one
And it will surprise you
What the Lord has done.
(Edwin Othello Excell, Johnson Oatman Jr. – Public
Domain)

I use four notebooks. That may seem excessive, but it
suits my needs. I have a spiral notebook that I use for
my daily journal. I have a similar-sized, bound notebook
that I use to record items that have spiritual importance
for me. A shorthand notebook sits beside my bed, so I
can note down thoughts as they come to mind. And I
keep a smaller one that I take with me when I'm
travelling.

The daily journal is important. I scarcely miss a day,
although I may not write much. Many days pass with
little to report that could ever interest anybody but me.
But that's the point; it *is* for me. That's where I count
my blessings. It is a valuable discipline to sit down at
the end of the day and think through what happened
and how I felt about it. Ignatian teaching encourages an
exercise called the Examen, which involves asking *"what
am I most grateful for about today?"* and writing down the
answer. Then ask *"what am I least grateful for about today?"*
and writing that down too. I don't follow that routine
rigidly every day, but its thinking lies behind what I
record in my main journal.

Sometimes I feel less enthusiastic about writing up my
daily notes. Maybe the day has seemed uneventful.
Maybe I'm just feeling a bit low. At such times, the task
may seem like a chore; but that demonstrates the value
of the exercise. The discipline of this daily routine

forces me to notice my moods, my health, and my spiritual condition. It is a health-check on my body, mind, and spirit, and helps me to live in wholeness and peace.

Every so often, my journal provides valuable answers to my worries and concerns. For example, one December I was berating myself for feeling out-of-sorts for several days in a row. Suddenly, it occurred to me to check back on my journals for previous years. It immediately became apparent that, year-by-year, I had been writing much the same complaint around that time of the year. My problem was not spiritual weakness or failure, but lack of vitamin D! That was a great relief and enabled me to find practical solutions for my winter blues. And it helped my prayers.

Amongst the mundane that occupies much of my life (no doubt that is most people's experience) there is also a developing pattern of encouraging information. I can track my own progress on the path of discipleship. And I can see how God has blessed me repeatedly.

My spiritual journal doesn't get used every day. Sometimes I may not open it for weeks. Sometimes I use it for several days in succession. But I always know that I can go to it to find gems of inspiration from the notes I have made in the past. Apart from my personal thoughts, that book enables me to keep notes, pictures, cuttings, and other mementos that I come across from time to time. It is a treasury of inspiration and another prayer resource.

The bedside notebook is especially useful when I wake up realising that I have had a significant dream. Dreams have often been valuable in my Christian life, but I may easily forget them if I don't note them down. Once the details are safely recorded I can leave the notes and come back to them later. It may then seem less significant; in which case I can forget it – but my notes enable me to make that choice. Many times, however, I have returned to my notes later and seen the significance of the dream. That may involve interpretation, or it may be obvious. If the dream is significant, I then make a good copy of the details in my spiritual notebook.

Because I use poetry as a personal outlet for my feelings and insights, the bedside notebook comes in handy for noting phrases and words that gradually build up into a new poem. I may re-write a poem many times over until it feels complete – then I transfer it into another notebook in the form I want to preserve.

The bedside notebook also helps capture inspiring thoughts or to note down tasks I must remember. Once I have noted them down I am free to have an uninterrupted sleep.

At present, I continue to write my journals on paper. But there is a wide choice of apps on the market, for use on tablets and/or smartphones. Conventional books have the advantage that you can stick things in them. But you can add photos to an electronic journal, no doubt including photos of the items you may have pasted into a paper journal.

There's no 'right' way to keep a journal. It is a very personal commitment and expresses individual personality. I know people who frequently include sketches in their journal. Not having that skill, I don't do that. Your journal will be expressive of your personality; but, however you do it, make it an integral part of your prayer life.

Journaling does not have to be a chore, nor does it have to produce literary masterpieces. It is a personal record for your personal benefit. I have not yet decided what to do with my journals in the long term. Maybe it will be best to throw them away (or ask my successors to dispose of them). After all, they are personal notes, meant for my own encouragement. But, while I can still pray, journaling helps.

49. A promise to pray

A promise to pray
is a commitment to love.
I must not forget.

Samuel promised to pray for the Israelites even when they rejected his leadership (1 Samuel 12:23). Paul was consistent about praying for the churches he had founded and the people he converted (1 Thessalonians 1:2; Philemon 1:4). Jesus prayed for his disciples individually (Luke 22:32). It is obvious, from their examples and sheer common sense, that we should pray for other people, but which people? And how often?

For most of us, the obvious first choices for our prayers will be our family, our friends, and our church; they are the easy ones. Those three categories alone may produce large numbers of names, so what about the people we work with? What about charities or missions we support? What about the needs we hear about on the News? And, don't forget the less attractive prayer subjects that Jesus suggested:

But I tell you, love your enemies and pray for those who persecute you.
Matthew 5:44 NIV

A group from our church held a weekend retreat at a convent and joined the sisters for one of their regular prayer times. It all seemed normal and predictable until one of the sisters prayed for a couple who had recently been convicted as child murderers. Our group reacted with a reflex shudder (it was a case that had shocked the nation). In our heads, we knew that the sister's prayer was right, as Jesus taught. But we realised that we were being set an example that would be hard to follow.

Praying is a serious business. It involves joining hands with God in changing the world. It involves expressing love beyond our natural capacity. It calls for commitment. But, no matter what job we do, or how much free time we have, we cannot pray for everyone or everything that presents itself to us as a need. We must be selective, but we should not be selfishly exclusive.

I often receive individual requests for prayer and I invariably answer that, yes, I will pray. Knowing that my memory is imperfect, my first fulfilment of that promise is in the few minutes after making it. I pray straight away. Sometimes it is best to pray with the person there and then but, anyway, I will pray immediately and silently, thus ensuring that I keep my promise. The late Jack Leeming, a Christian friend and one who had been a leader in my youth, said "I promise to pray for someone today", and he added, "I do so, but not necessarily every day".

One prayer may not be enough and, of course, there are many people who I want to pray for regularly and often. That's where a prayer list is useful. Prayer is a spiritual exercise that can be weakened by too much formality or organisation. Even a prayer list can become a distraction from true devotion. Or it can become a burden. On the other hand, it can be helpful in prompting consistency and commitment.

An effective prayer list needs to be up-to-date and relevant. And it needs to include people and needs beyond our exclusive inner circle of friends and family.

People have been using prayer lists for centuries and, until recently, they could only have been kept on paper.

I found it useful to maintain a small notebook in which the names of the people or institutions to be prayed for could be listed and updated over time. As new issues came up, as matters were resolved, or as new subjects or people came into focus, I would rewrite my list.

What could previously be done only on paper can now be done with a digital application. Search for 'prayer list' on Play Store or the App Store and you will find many Apps designed to support your prayer times. This is a matter of personal choice. Most of these Apps are free or, at least, quite inexpensive, so it is worth trying several to find what suits you. I tried a number and settled on one called "Prayer Mate". My key selection issues were that I could easily add, edit, or delete entries (written prayers as well as name lists), that the App works well on my portable devices, that I could categorise entries ('my family', 'my church', 'my workplace' etc.), and that the App should be free of intrusive adverts or other distractions.

Don't let technology take over your prayer life; but don't neglect to pray for the people God lays on your heart.

Prayer patterns

50. Samuel listened – Joshua didn't

Samuel awoke,
hearing the same voice again.
This time he listened.
(Based on 1 Samuel 3:1-10)

One of the best-known stories in the Old Testament focuses on one of the least observed aspects of prayer – listening. Samuel was a child. He learned early. He didn't know what was happening at first, and why should he? But he remembered that lesson all through his life and became one of the most consistent leaders the Israelites ever had.

Joshua had a great apprenticeship, acting as servant and right-hand man to Moses. But he had not fully grasped the importance of listening. It's not as if he was unfamiliar with God's voice. After Moses died, Joshua successfully led the Israelites into the Promised Land, including that incredible crossing of the River Jordan. But, following their first major battle on Canaanite soil (the amazing conquest of Jericho) he forgot to listen.

After Jericho, the next place they set out to conquer was a minor city called Ai. I have no doubt that Joshua prayed before he led the people into that second battle, but he couldn't have listened to God. If he had listened, he would not have gone into battle that day, because he would have known that God was not going to give them victory. The outcome was a devastating defeat for Israel, and the reason for that defeat was that someone had broken the rules in the previous battle. God did not bless them in their attack on Ai. If Joshua prayed at all before the battle, he probably did all the talking – concentrating on his previous victory and presuming on God's continued support.

As if the experience at Ai were not enough, Joshua and his fellow-commanders repeated their error when one of the local tribes tricked them into a peace treaty. The Israelite leaders made the agreement *"but did not enquire of the LORD" (Joshua 9:14 NIV)*. Joshua was a great leader, but even the greatest men get things wrong sometimes. On this matter, based on these examples, let's follow Samuel's example, rather than Joshua's.

Ah! You may be thinking "I'm not sure if I've ever heard God's voice, so how can I follow Samuel's example?" OK, but where did your faith come from? I don't mean huge faith displayed through amazing miracles. I mean ordinary faith on the scale of a single sesame seed, such as you might find on a hamburger bun.   Where does faith come from?

> ... *faith cometh by hearing, and hearing by the word of God.*
> Romans 10:17 (KJV)

You are reading this book because you believe in prayer. You have faith in God because you accepted his word. Maybe your conversion lacked the drama of some other people's testimonies you have heard, but you believed. You have faith. You heard God speak.

Most of the time we don't need God to speak through the thunder, or the hurricane. We just need the simple assurance that we are in his will. That simple assurance is what we call the 'peace of God'.

> ...*let the peace of God rule in your hearts...*
> Colossians 3:15 KJV

The word 'rule' in that verse means much the same as our word 'referee' – the man who makes his presence known when the game rules are broken. So long as you are going the right way, trusting in the Lord, and fulfilling his will, that sense of peace continues to rule in your heart. But:

> *Whether you turn to the right or to the left, your ears will hear a voice behind you, saying, "This is the way; walk in it."*
> Isaiah 30:21 NIV

The moment you turn off the right path, you sense that something isn't quite right. It feels much like the voice of conscience but, for the believer, it is more than that. It is an awareness that may arise when the choice you are making is morally OK, but it's not the will of God for you. That sense of unease is the voice of God. If Joshua had paused before leading his army towards Ai, he would have felt that unease and sought further guidance.

Prayer is not for us to rattle off a shopping list of requests. It's not even for us to launch into other kinds of verbal prayer, such as thanksgiving or worship. It is to spend time with God. Apart from the occasions when we need to 'let it all out' (see Chapter 34), the best way to start prayer is with a pause, possibly in silence. By pausing in his presence, we allow God to speak.

Distractions

If only I could keep my mind on the subject!

Distractions

51. Lord I can't pray

Lord, I can't pray –
try as I may.
I want to, Lord, and I wish that I could
but it doesn't come out as I hoped that it would
when I come to the place of quiet devotion
I find that my mind is full of commotion.

Lord, I can't pray –
try as I may.
It's not the roar of the world outside
but the noise that I carry inside of my mind;
the thoughts, the intentions, all sorts of
distractions,
the things that I fear, the worries I bear…

Please carry my worries, ambitions, and fears
reach out in your love and dry up my tears.
Help me abandon my fear of tomorrow
and dwell in the NOW, where there's no cause
for sorrow

I think I'll stop trying to pray.
I'm here
and it's quiet,
so I'll stay.

The mind is a tool. It's not me. It's just a part of me. Athletes learn their body's limitations, respect them through good life habits and train them to achieve the best they can. Prayer is not fundamentally an exercise of the mind, but of the spirit. But the mind frequently intrudes and hinders us from developing the prayer life we aspire to. Distractions constantly interfere with our prayers – and that usually doesn't mean external distractions, but the distractions that come from inside ourselves. We have too much on our minds. We worry about things (money, job prospects, relationships etc.). We dream about things (fantasies, opportunities, revenge, wishes etc.). We fear things (phobias, risks, rejection, criticism etc.). We desire things (money, material objects, promotion, recognition etc.). And it all seems to intensify when we approach the place of prayer.

If this is your problem, take heart; you are not alone. Thomas Merton said:

"If you have never had any distractions you don't know how to pray. For the secret of prayer is a hunger for God and for the vision of God, a hunger that lies far deeper than the level of language or affection…" (quoted from New Seeds of Contemplation). Others have suffered the same difficulties as you; and they have found ways of combating the problems, as you will see in the next few chapters.

The poem that opens this chapter was written as a song for the character of Martha, in a musical about Bethany (see my book, *Little Church of Bethany*). Over the centuries, Martha has been held up as a negative example in relation to prayer. But if we put together all the New Testament stories about Martha, we see a remarkable woman whose service and witness made her a close friend of Jesus and a fine example for us all. However, she sometimes got things wrong. Don't we all? But, no matter how much we struggle, and however much we fail, we can all grow in the faith and learn from our mistakes and failures – just as Martha did.

52. Thoughts that won't go away

I just had this thought
as I started to pray;
it popped into my mind
and it won't go away

When we start to pray it's not unusual for stray thoughts to pop into our mind. Just as we settle into what we hoped would be a nice devotional experience these distractions arise to disturb our plans. But don't be too hasty. Distractions are not always bad. In fact, they may not be distractions, but directions. Of course, if it's obvious that the thought is unholy or irrelevant we will want to push it away. But some of these unexpected thoughts may be relevant and important. Where did the thought come from? Is it something that was bothering you unconsciously and that you really need to resolve?

Minds are complicated. They operate on multiple levels. Apart from the immediate perceptions that we consciously react to, there are inner thoughts about tasks and activities we may be planning, or lessons we are mulling over as a result of our reading, our conversations or items we noticed in the media. Underneath all of this, we often have inner thoughts that we are hardly aware of – the flash of worry that came from a passing expression on a friend's face, the lurking discomfort that we felt about someone we met (or about something they said), or the sense that we may have forgotten something.

Before you dismiss those kinds of thought, turn, and look at what they are telling you. Did you, in fact, pick up a faint clue to a problem that someone was trying to hide? Is there an important inspiration that you almost missed in the busyness of your day? Is there a warning that you dare not ignore? Is God trying to tell you something?

One of my sons was working quietly downstairs, while I was upstairs, concentrating on some writing. Suddenly, we heard a loud clattering noise coming from the kitchen and we both immediately rushed to the scene, leaving our work in mid-sentence. Whatever we had been doing mattered nothing in the face of an apparent emergency. We didn't have to reason out our response. Instinct told us to react instantly.

Many people like to watch birds and some of them recognise individual species just from hearing their song. But almost everyone, even if they know almost nothing about birds, recognises when a bird sounds an alarm call. By instinct, we know the meaning of the sound without having to use our reasoning powers.

Instinct guides us effectively through the 'ordinary' challenges of life and, in much the same way, those who are spiritually alive recognise when God is speaking. When the thoughts that distract you from your intended prayers are the voice of God, you don't have to reason it out. You know by spiritual instinct:

> *"My sheep hear my voice, and I know them, and they follow me."*
> John 10:27 KJV'

Useful thoughts stand out as valuable. Useless thoughts tend not to stand up to scrutiny. Don't try to reason with them. Ask the Lord if he has anything to say to you. If the Spirit does not enliven the thoughts, their irrelevance becomes obvious and they lose their power to distract.

Prayer is a two-way conversation, and we don't want to miss God's voice when he speaks. Perhaps that distracting thought that came into your mind was the voice of God...

Voice of God or hidden worry?

If it needs attention, don't treat it as a distraction. Make it the subject of your prayer. If it *is* a distraction but it's *also* a task, an idea, or an issue that you need to come back to later, jot down a quick note to remind you of it, so you can release the worry and get back to prayer.

Distractions

53. In distraction or temptation

In distraction or temptation
we're not obliged to fall –
though the phone may keep on ringing
we don't have to take the call.

Distractions can be frustrating when you're trying to pray, and it's natural to get anxious and self-critical about the problem. It's also natural to attempt to fight off the intruding thoughts. Natural, yes, but effective, no. The more you battle with them the more they intrude. The problem is that, by attempting to fight off the distractions, you are giving them your attention. The phone call imagery is helpful. Once you pick up the phone you give the caller an opportunity to engage you in conversation. If you let the phone ring it's just a noise – and, eventually, it will stop.

Leaving aside the useful distractions mentioned in chapter 52, most thoughts that assail you during prayer may be thoughts that you don't want. This is especially true in contemplative prayer, when even noble and holy thoughts are best excluded, so you can focus on God alone.

So, to quieten the distractions, don't engage with them. To engage with them is to acknowledge them. Don't fight them. Just treat them like the ring of an incoming 'junk' phone call. Refuse to acknowledge them. Don't answer the call.

The same technique can be applied to temptations.

54. When distractions come

When distractions come
I look straight over their heads
as if they're not there

When distractions come into your mind, suddenly and unexpectedly, we call them *involuntary* distractions. At that point you have nothing to be ashamed of. Just deal with them appropriately. When you follow the thoughts, you turn them into *voluntary* distractions. You always have a choice.

Treat distracting thoughts as if they are unimportant and undeserving of your attention. Look, as it were, over their shoulder, not acknowledging their presence; hardly even noticing them. Act as if you are looking for something else, as indeed you are. You are, of course, looking for God himself who, though you can't see him directly, is the one on whom your heart is fixed. By doing this you bring your focus back onto your yearning for God – your desire to love him more than anything else. And by re-focussing on your love, you overcome all else.

Let's run that through again.

All manner of thoughts come into your mind and distract you from prayer. Don't fight the distractions, which would be to engage with them. Instead, turn your mind deliberately towards the Lord, engaging positively with him. The positive cancels out the negative and makes God your sole focus. Your prayer can then continue effectively.

I must thank the unknown 14th century author of "*The Cloud of Unknowing*" for teaching me this technique, and the next chapter is based on another idea from the same source.

55. When it's all too much

When it's all too much
I fall down like a coward
and leave it to God.

If other techniques fail to banish the distractions, here's a last resort to claim victory out of defeat. Once again, the idea comes from "*The Cloud of Unknowing*".

This is a message of reassurance and encouragement. If you have struggled with distractions or temptations and tried every solution you can think of, there's still hope, and there's still power to overcome. Grace is always available to those who feel that they have failed.

You've tried to break free of the distracting thoughts and now you feel defeated. So, admit defeat. Face up to failure and acknowledge your weakness. After all, you're only admitting the truth! The battle is over and it seems that you've lost; but God will not fail to respond to your situation. Your confession brings out his mercy and grace and suddenly defeat becomes victory. The battle is no longer yours. Thank God for his deliverance and continue gratefully in his presence. Prayer can resume in praise.

Whoever conceals their sins does not prosper, but the one who confesses and renounces them finds mercy.
Proverbs 28:13 NIV

If we confess our sins, he is faithful and just and will forgive us our sins and purify us from all unrighteousness.
1 John 1:9 NIV

Distractions

56 Devices and Desires

We have followed too much the devices and desires of our own hearts...
(From the General Confession – Book of Common Prayer.)

I'm not normally enthusiastic about general confessions – not that I suppose myself to be perfect, or anywhere near perfect. No, it's because, in a church service, it's too easy to parrot the words without any real consciousness of sin. However, I am greatly impressed with the comprehensiveness and appropriateness of the words of this well-known prayer. In particular, the reference to 'devices and desires' hits the nail on the head about the sources of sin. And the same applies to distractions in prayer. Problems arise from our 'devices' (the things we are planning and scheming) and our 'desires' (the things we covet and yearn for).

Towards the end of his inspirational book, "*Mister God this is Anna*", Fynn tells the story of how his precocious 8-year-old friend, Anna, opened his eyes to his dependence on outward things – objects that he desired that were like holes in his life. If only he had this item or that gadget, life would be so much better. He recognised that, by just having these desires, he was entrapping himself and reducing his capacity to be free and complete. Wholeness comes from being able to say "I am" (reflecting God's likeness – see Exodus 3:14) and meaning "I am complete – there's nothing I really need".

The stories of the 'saints' include many examples who seem to have taken the ascetic life too far – certainly by modern standards. But self-denial has value, not the least in training ourselves to be satisfied with what we have. The more things we can do without, the less footholds we provide for temptations and distractions. We need to make it easier for ourselves to live righteously, and to keep focused on the Lord by getting rid of the things that turn us out of the way. In the epistle to the Romans, Paul puts it like this:

> *…clothe yourselves with the Lord Jesus Christ, and do not think about how to gratify the desires of the flesh.*
> Romans 13:14 NIV

Desires crowd our mind and draw us away from our centre. By attaching parts of ourselves to external things, particularly material things, we give rein to temptations and distractions. Obviously, we must eat, we need to live somewhere and we are obliged to own a range of products that enable us to live in our society. But we need to hold them loosely and to ensure that they don't ensnare us. Have what you need; but don't be imprisoned by the things that you want.

> *Where do you think all these appalling wars and quarrels come from? Do you think they just happen? Think again. They come about because you want your own way, and fight for it deep inside yourselves.*
> *You lust for what you don't have and are willing to kill to get it. You want what isn't yours and will risk violence to get your hands on it. You wouldn't think of just asking God for it, would you?*
> *And why not? Because you know you'd be asking for what you have no right to. You're spoiled children, each wanting your own way.*
> James 4:1- MSG

57. Challenges to make us strong

When we face challenges
are they –
Challenges to weaken us?
Challenges to discourage us?
Challenges to break us?
Challenges to test us?
Challenges to exercise us?
Challenges to make us strong?

However hard they are,
However many,
However severe,
However unrelenting,
The effect of any challenge
is determined
by our response.

In his helpful booklet, *The Positive Role of Distraction in Prayer*, Robert Llewelyn relates the story of a fisherman who used to keep some of his catch alive in tanks so they would be fresh on his return from a long fishing trip. But the fish in the tanks never tasted as good as the ones that were freshly caught. Then he had the idea of putting catfish in the tanks to keep the fish active. Some of the tank fish ended up inside the catfish, but those that survived the ordeal tasted better for it.

In the modern world of sit-down jobs, labour-saving domestic devices and entertainment-on-demand, health advisors are constantly reminding us of the need for exercise. Get your lungs working, put some strain on your heart, exercise your muscles... a body that is never exercised is a body that will weaken. For the same reasons, it's good for us to struggle a bit with prayer.

You learn to climb mountains by climbing mountains. Similarly, the way you mount up to the heights of prayer is to climb out of the easy valleys and face the often-rocky challenge of temptations, distractions, and trials. Distractions and temptations are inevitable, so there's no point in complaining, or in reproaching yourself unduly. Face the challenges. Deal with them. Thank God for them. Learn from them. Grow stronger in prayer.

Consider it pure joy, my brothers and sisters, whenever you face trials of many kinds, because you know that the testing of your faith produces perseverance. James 1:2,3 NIV

Journeying deeper

There must be more than this...

58. People who can teach me

The people who can teach me
whoever they may be
have views that may be faulty –
they could be as wrong as me!

When we travel to a country we have never visited before, we must go by routes that are unfamiliar. We can't expect to recognise the turns and waymarks; we must take advice from people who have been there before us. Even when we use the internet, satellite-navigation systems, or guide-books, we are drawing on other people's experience.

People make mistakes. Books and maps contain mistakes. I wrote this book and know from experience that, although I have checked the text many times – and despite the help of careful editors – some mistakes are likely to get through into the finished publication.

In the school of prayer, we may find that some of our teachers hold doctrines that we disagree with. Doctrine is of the mind. Prayer is of the spirit. Take their lessons humbly, ignoring their doctrinal asides. I can be wrong. My teachers can be wrong. None of us is right about everything. But, if I can learn from someone who, although they may be imperfect, still has something valuable to teach me, I will learn willingly and thank my God for it.

Don't allow sectarian prejudice to restrict your opportunities to learn different ways to pray. There have been giants of prayer on both sides of the Reformation divide. Roman Catholics can learn a lot from Susanna Wesley, Hudson Taylor, George Müller, John Hyde, D. L. Moody and many more. Protestants can benefit from reading the works of Saints Teresa of Avila, Ignatius Loyola, John of the Cross, Julian of Norwich, the anonymous writer of *The Cloud of Unknowing* and others. We don't all need to agree with the doctrines of these people, but we should recognise their holiness and learn what they can teach us about prayer.

The journey of prayer can be a lonely path and we need all the help we can get.

Catholic or Protestant, high church, or low church, charismatic or traditional, evangelical or whatever – most movements within the broad range of Christianity have produced women and men of prayer. Don't be trapped into the narrow confines of whatever tradition you happen to belong to. Seek God with all your heart and allow him to teach you by whatever means and through whichever people he chooses.

59. Stages of prayer

I want to progress
through the stages of prayer
whatever it costs.

Many valuable treatises on prayer speak about stages in the development of the spiritual life - particularly in relation to contemplative prayer. I have found many of those books helpful. But we must be cautious. Just as the A.C.T.S. formula can become a legalistic trap (see Chapter 26) so can these well-tried classic guides. We are individuals, each with a unique personality and a unique calling. Read books, and listen to teaching, so you can learn what other people have found helpful; but don't try to ape another person's life. Your prayer journey is just that – it is *your* journey.

In *The Interior Castle*, St Teresa speaks of seven stages in the life of prayer. In *The Dark Night of the Soul,* St John of the Cross speaks of ten stages. Others have spoken similarly, but describe different numbers and varying characteristics. There is no Bible passage that maps out the prayer journey in such definite terms, but that does not make these people's teachings wrong. They spoke from their experience and their teachings have greatly helped generations of women and men to grow effectively as prayer warriors. They all agree that there are stages, and that the pathway may be difficult. They also agree that the journey is worthwhile.

There are stages. But you won't receive a badge or certificate each time you complete one. You won't necessarily realise that you have passed through a stage except, perhaps in retrospect, at some time later. These stages are not like exam modules that you must pass before going on to the next step. You may go through some stages several times. They are more like a mountain path, which may climb to a ridge before descending a rocky slope down into a valley of grassy marshes and unexpected streams that block your way and force you to retrace your steps. You may seem to have skipped over a stage that other people found vital but, perhaps, that stage was not relevant to you. What's more, progress beyond the first few steps of prayer may be inappropriate for you, because God is not calling you that way. We are all called to pray, but only a few are called to spend most of their life in prayer. I'm not – not yet, anyway.

The journey starts at the level where we come to God simply, perhaps naively, making requests, and stumbling to discover our prayer language. If you've read this far without throwing the book down, you have probably already advanced far beyond that level. How much further you will go depends on two things – God's calling, and your determination.

If you are called to journey deeper along the pathway of prayer it will be demanding. I don't say that to glorify the calling above other ministries. Evangelism is demanding. Pastoral ministry is demanding. Teaching is demanding. Whatever ministry God calls you to will require commitment, sacrifice and perseverance. But most ministries are done in public view and involve obvious effort. Just because the ministry of prayer is carried out in private, probably in your own home, don't suppose that it will be easy. It requires commitment, sacrifice and perseverance – just like the public ministries. It involves engagement with spiritual powers. It involves a battle with your own desires and temptations. And, for all that, what you do will be invisible and unnoticed.

Everyone who takes this journey travels alone. You may be known as a person of prayer, but only God sees what you really do – and you must keep it that way. There will be stages, and it is good to read what others have written about that; but your precise pathway will be unique. God calls some people to engage themselves in a special ministry of prayer from their youth. God calls others to this ministry as they come closer to the end of their lives, maybe after many years of active service in public ministry. The rewards are always the same, just as it was for the workers Jesus spoke about in the parable of the labourers in the vineyard (Matthew 20:1-16). Whatever your background and whenever you set out on this journey, if God calls you this way, do it with your might. Your ministry of prayer is vital for the church and the world.

60. The Pharisee and the Tax Collector

To some who were confident of their own righteousness and looked down on everyone else, Jesus told this parable: "Two men went up to the temple to pray, one a Pharisee and the other a tax collector. The Pharisee stood by himself and prayed: 'God, I thank you that I am not like other people— robbers, evildoers, adulterers—or even like this tax collector. I fast twice a week and give a tenth of all I get.' But the tax collector stood at a distance. He would not even look up to heaven, but beat his breast and said, 'God, have mercy on me, a sinner.' "I tell you that this man, rather than the other, went home justified before God. For all those who exalt themselves will be humbled, and those who humble themselves will be exalted."
Luke 18:9-14 NIV

Could prayer ever be a bad thing? This story suggests that it could. The parable is about prayer but, if it has any meaning for us, we need honestly to ask if we could be the ones who the Pharisee represents.

Pharisees have often been reviled in Christian thinking – proud – rich – unjust rulers – heretics. But they were not the ruling party (that was the Sadducees). They were not necessarily rich. Neither were they heretics; in fact, they were probably the most orthodox Jews of their time. Saul of Tarsus was a Pharisee. After he became Paul the Apostle he changed dramatically in character – but not so much in doctrine, because Christian doctrine is surprisingly close to what the Pharisees believed. The Pharisee in the story *could* be one of us.

...could be one of us. It is easy to read this familiar story and condemn the Pharisee as 'one of them'. Jesus didn't tell stories just to amuse; he wanted to change attitudes.

In this case, Luke's text makes the target clear. Jesus was aiming his lesson at people *"who were confident of their own righteousness and looked down on everyone else"*. Prayer is a righteous act, but it presents an unrighteous temptation – the temptation to pride. Let's be very careful to keep our motives and actions in perspective – especially when we are praying for others.

Pharisees were disciplined people – an attitude that we would not normally regard as a bad thing. People who are engaged in active sports, like running, cycling or swimming may well impose strict disciplines on themselves to achieve progress. But prayer is not a competitive sport. There are no medals, no 'personal bests', and no winner's prizes. We are not praying to gain recognition or to boost our pride. We need humility.

But the Pharisee of this parable missed that point. His discipline led him into pride. He measured his own religious accomplishments and compared himself favourably against others. He was probably speaking the truth about his religious orthodoxy and discipline; but he was keeping the score and expected a prize. This parable is a warning for those who are making progress. The further we advance the more we are exposed to the temptation to congratulate ourselves. It's best not to keep the score on how often we pray or for how long, because it can lead to complacency and pride. The Tax Collector didn't make that mistake. Maybe he *had* been especially bad – or perhaps he was just being hard on himself. But his humility was exemplary.

God is all powerful, but he is also all welcoming. We can approach him with confidence, but this confidence comes from knowing that we are accepted and forgiven *by grace*. It is not due to our achievements, knowledge, or efforts. Confidence must not become complacency. Humility is a prerequisite for prayer. Compassion is a prerequisite for intercession.

61. I speak in tongues

I thank God that I speak in tongues more than all of you.
1 Corinthians 14:18 NIV

Speaking in tongues, or 'glossolalia', has often been a controversial subject. It was controversial in Paul's time. But he was thankful to have the gift. Writing to the Corinthian church, he made it clear that 'tongues' can be used badly. But the gift can also be used well – especially in prayer.

In meditation, we acknowledge that words are inadequate to express our deepest prayer. In contemplation, we even omit our single, special word (see chapter 62). When speaking in tongues, we *do* use words, but none that we understand. In all three prayer forms we set our intellect aside. But, in 'tongues', we engage our passions.

Speaking in tongues is a form of prayer that engages our emotions. Deep feelings are involved, even if we do not know what we are praying for. And that's an important point – we can use this prayer form when interceding for a known subject or an unknown one. We may know the subject, but we may not know specifically what to pray for or how to express the depths of our feelings. So, by praying in tongues, we allow our feelings to come out in a language that only God understands.

This may seem incomprehensible to someone who has never spoken in tongues. What value can there be in praying words that have no meaning? From experience, I can assure you that tongues do have meaning. One Sunday, in a village in Kent, I spent a few quiet minutes with the visiting speaker, who had been staying at our house overnight. We sat in the same room, each reading the Bible in silence. Then we walked down to the church together, hardly talking. During the meeting, I felt a strong urge to speak a message in 'tongues' in the expectation that the message would be interpreted. It was. The visiting speaker gave the interpretation, and it consisted of the words of a Psalm that I had been reading to myself earlier that morning. The words had been planted in my heart by my earlier reading, and I expressed them in prayer in an unknown language. The unknown words had definite meaning.

Glossolalia is not a stream of meaningless gibberish. It has form. It has tone, rhythm, and modulation. Though the speaker doesn't understand the actual meaning (other than through the gift of interpretation) the mood can be sensed from the sound. Praise is easily distinguished from pleading just by the tone and modulation of the voice – even though the words are not understood.

Tongues have meaning, but our intellect can't penetrate or interfere with it. This is a deeply expressive form of prayer that can be used in worship, praise, or supplication. Like meditation and contemplation, those other prayer forms that avoid engaging the mind, tongues are primarily for private prayer. And, like the apostle Paul, I thank God that I can use this precious gift in my prayers.

62. One word is enough

One word is enough
to fix my prayer on God
and focus on him.

Meditation. It's a practice that has become almost
fashionable in the 21st century, with books and training
sessions about 'mindfulness' gaining acceptance even
within mainstream medicine. Much of this is based on
Buddhist teachings, a fact that may worry some
Christian readers. But there is a centuries-old Christian
tradition of meditation – and there are many Christian
books on the subject.

Meditation is a form of prayer that involves stilling our
minds so we can wait quietly in God's presence. It
doesn't use words; or rather, it doesn't use many words.
One word is enough to focus on the Lord. The
anonymous medieval writer of *The Cloud of Unknowing*
recommends that we choose one word that represents
the core of our desire towards God. One word is
enough for this, just as the one word 'help' is enough
for a drowning man, or the one word 'fire' is enough to
set people running. These words are visceral. They need
no complex arguments or explanations. Our personal
prayer word should be as simple as the cry of the
drowning man – and as all-sufficient as the word 'fire!',
shouted in a public place.

The chosen word, or it may be a short phrase, will be
individual to each of us. Short is best. Ideally it should
be one syllable like, for instance, 'God' or 'love'. If it's a
whole phrase it should be a short phrase (like 'Lord
God' or 'heavenly Father'). But whatever it is, remains

your secret. It is the anchor that keeps you centred on God.

The point is not to philosophise about whatever your word may represent. This is not about theology, or any other intellect-based engagement. This is about holding your being in the stillness of prayer. Prayer of this type may last minutes or hours. Time is unimportant. It is a window on eternity when the daily routines, the realms of *doing*, are banished from our minds and all that matters is *being*.

If thoughts start to invade your mind, simply repeat your word until the distractions recede. This is no place for purpose, relevance, desire, intention, or explanation. God is all that we want. This silent time in his presence gives meaning to everything we pray and everything God calls us to do.

Although it is a sentence, rather than just one word, whole sections of the church use a short prayer known as 'The Jesus prayer' to similar effect: "*Lord Jesus Christ, Son of God, have mercy on me*". This sentence has an obvious confessional aspect, but properly recognises the sovereignty of our Lord and our humble position before him.

As you move out from meditation into intercession, you may still find the 'one word' principle helpful. Say, for instance, that you want to pray for an individual who you have not seen or spoken with for a while. You know them, but you are not up-to-date with their current needs; so, just say their name and wait in silence, holding them before God. He knows their needs – and he may even give you some insight that will direct your prayer. But, still, one word is enough.

If we don't know how or what to pray, it doesn't matter. He does our praying in and for us, making prayer out of our wordless sighs, our aching groans.
Romans 8:26 MSG

63. Dreams

God is with me all day –
and all night.
There is no time
when he cannot see me -
and speak to me.

In the rush of the day,
He directs my paths.
In the quiet watches of the night,
my dreams are open to him.

Prayer is for all of life, not just the special times we set aside specifically for communion with God. To be sure, "*he grants sleep to those he loves*" (Psalm 127:2 NIV) but sleep does not separate us from our Lord. Medical studies reveal that most of us dream at some stage during our sleep. Dreams seem to have an important therapeutic value. But they can also be part of our communion with God. That is not to say that every dream is a message from God. Most of our dreams happen without our even knowing. Most of the dreams that we do remember, however vaguely, are just a jumble of thoughts and images with no comprehensible meaning. But a few – a very few – may be important.

This should not be a surprise to anyone who reads the Bible, because dreams are prominent through both Testaments, from Genesis to Revelation. Everyone has heard the story of Joseph, popularised by the musical '*Joseph and the Amazing Technicolor Dreamcoat*', and most people know that the Christmas story includes the dreams of the Wise Men and of Joseph the Carpenter. But there are numerous other examples – notice them as you read the Bible.

Dreams do not belong in a box of their own. They are part of the broad spectrum of prayer – or, rather, they can be. Prayer is a two-way affair and dreams may be part of the conversation. Most dreams happen when we are too deeply asleep to remember them; they are completely out of our conscious range. But the kind of dreams we do recall have the potential to be spiritual battlegrounds or sources of inspiration.

The dreams that we notice usually occur in periods when we hover between consciousness and awareness, neither fully asleep nor properly awake. These are times when we are as likely to drop back to sleep as to wake up; but consciousness may kick in amidst our dreaming. At these times, we may receive significant dreams, or we may be subjected to temptations. Revenge fantasies, sexual fantasies, stories that act out our covetousness or our desire for power. That's when we can consciously step in and say "I'm not going there!" Or we can exercise the resistance techniques suggested in chapters 52-56. This is part of the battleground that is prayer. And it is an opportunity for us to execute our determination to live in holiness.

Occasionally we may have a dream that opens new understanding and draws us closer to God. How can we know when one of our dreams is significant? The answer is that we must put it to the test. The bedside notebook kept for jotting down ideas and discoveries that come to mind unexpectedly (see Chapter 48) is also valuable when we wake from a dream that seems special. By writing down the details, we relieve ourselves of the twin burdens of remembering it, and of trying to figure it out. If we have preserved the details, we can return to it later. When we do come back to it, wide awake and more able to exercise judgement, we will find it easier to see if the dream deserves consideration.

Many normal dreams consist of places, people, and experiences that we know, but the dream re-forms them into stories that we have never experienced. They act as rehearsals for novelties we may encounter in daily life. It may be that their practical purpose is to equip us to respond appropriately to novel choices and challenges we may encounter in our lives. Sometimes we meet with difficult life issues that need to be thought through carefully; but most of our dilemmas arise suddenly and without warning. If our responses to unexpected situations are based on the experiences our minds rehearse in dreams (i.e. when we are asleep) how can we be sure that our instinctive responses will reflect our ethical and spiritual values? We can protect ourselves by maintaining our 'holy habits' (see chapter 5). By doing that, we will strengthen our minds to develop our rehearsal-stories so we can handle novel challenges, choices, and temptations instinctively *and* righteously.

> *Summing it all up, friends, I'd say you'll do best by filling your minds and meditating on things true, noble, reputable, authentic, compelling, gracious--the best, not the worst; the beautiful, not the ugly; things to praise, not things to curse.*
> Philippians 4:8 MSG

Can dreams be dangerous? Yes, they can. That's why it's good to focus on them as an issue for our spiritual heath. We can't avoid dreaming. Whether we remember them or not, dreams come to all of us. They seem to perform functions that science has not yet fully explained, but which may help maintain our mental health. But dreams can be tainted with unholy images, or blessed with good ones. Dreams can host unhealthy fantasies. They can create false memories. But they can also be vehicles for revelation and inspiration. They are products of our mind, so we need to look after our minds in our conscious hours.

> *I urge you, brothers and sisters, in view of God's mercy, to offer your bodies as a living sacrifice, holy and pleasing to God--this is your true and proper worship.*
> *Do not conform to the pattern of this world, but be transformed by the renewing of your mind.*
> Romans 12:2 NIV

If you have a dream that seems to be significant, the meaning may be obvious. If it is not obvious, don't mess with it in an attempt to work out the meaning by reason alone. Dreams do not necessarily need explanation, but godly dreams need godly interpretation. If you don't receive an interpretation, let it go. Forget about it. If God wants to speak to you, he will ensure that his message gets through. Wait. Wait longer. Wait until God speaks. Interpreting spiritual dreams is like interpreting messages given in 'tongues'; it requires a gift from God.

> *"I dreamed a dream," Pharaoh told Joseph. "Nobody can interpret it. But I've heard that just by hearing a dream you can interpret it." Joseph answered, "Not I, but God. God will set Pharaoh's mind at ease."*
> Genesis 41:15,16 NIV

64. Raptures and Visions

*And that's just the beginning: After that— I will pour out
my Spirit on every kind of people: Your sons will prophesy,
also your daughters. Your old men will dream, your young
men will see visions. I'll even pour out my Spirit on the
servants, men and women both.*
Joel 2:2,29 MSG

The picture was of a hand. White and bloodless, apart
from an unmistakable wound scar, you could suggest
that it was merely a memory of some picture I may
have seen in a gallery or a book. I don't know about
that, but I do know that the image appeared in my 19-
year-old mind, unbidden and unexpectedly, during a
night of prayer in the middle of a 2-week Youth-for-
Christ campaign. It was my first 'vision' and made a
lasting impression on me.

I don't have visions very often, but I have experienced
them on several occasions. Sometimes, like that first
one, they are meant just for me – a part of my prayer
that strengthens my faith. Sometimes they are for
sharing with other people. The significant thing is that
pictures are more memorable than verbal messages.

Prayer is not a one-sided conversation. It's not just
about talking to God. Listening is at least as important.
No! it's far more important. God may not speak to you
in words, or his voice may be no more than a subtle
sense of direction or intention. You sense, without
reasoning it out, that his will is becoming clear in your
mind. There is no vision, no sound, no sense of an
actual presence, but ideas – answers – become
apparent. In traditional teaching this kind of revelation
is called a 'locution' or, sometimes, an 'interior

locution'. The terminology doesn't matter but, rest assured, that it has been the experience of many men and women of prayer. In this form, it doesn't sound very dramatic. Why should it? Do we need God to shout at us? Sometimes, possibly without any sense of emotional impact, the experience comes in the form of a mental picture, or vision.

Many people, but a small proportion of those who pray, sometimes enter ecstasies that feel like 'out-of-body' experiences. This is a spiritual experience – not at all the same as a trance (which can be induced by unholy influences or drugs). In a God-induced ecstasy, traditionally called a 'rapture', the person who receives the experience does not lose control. They may continue in the experience for quite a long time (who would willingly leave such a place of bliss sooner than they need to?) But the Holy Spirit does not 'possess' us; he enters where he is honoured and respected – and he bestows honour and respect. Paul notably entered these realms and described the experience as best he could (but in terms that showed it was beyond description):

> ... *I know a man who, fourteen years ago, was seized by Christ and swept in ecstasy to the heights of heaven. I really don't know if this took place in the body or out of it; only God knows.*
> *I also know that this man was hijacked into paradise--again, whether in or out of the body, I don't know; God knows. There he heard the unspeakable spoken, but was forbidden to tell what he heard.*
> 2 Corinthians 12:2,3 MSG

Don't seek ecstasies. To seek such privileges is to focus on an experience, rather than on God. To seek an ecstatic experience for its own sake potentially exposes the seeker to unhealthy influences. Satan can replicate ecstatic experiences, if given the chance. Don't risk deception. Physical sensations do not prove spiritual authenticity. Focus on God alone and enjoy his presence, even if your feelings remain dull and apparently unmoved. If you do experience ecstasy during contemplation or prayer, be thankful; don't over-rate it; be careful who you tell about it; and don't seek to repeat it. God sovereignly grants blessings when he will, to whom he will, and for whatever purpose he intends. Worship God alone.

Sometimes these experiences are accompanied by visions that can be recalled and related afterwards (such as the angelic vision recorded in Isaiah chapter 6). But visions can be received in quite ordinary circumstances, whilst engaging in prayer privately or in company with others. Visions, or pictures, received in prayer can be helpful in strengthening faith. 'A picture is worth a thousand words'. Treat such pictures with respect (1 Thessalonians 5:20) but don't accept them without testing their validity (1 Thessalonians 5:21). The human mind naturally generates pictures. Images that come into our minds, even in prayer, are not necessarily from God. And even those pictures that are from God may not be for sharing.

When you receive a vision, take time to sense its value and test its authenticity. Does it increase faith? Does it bring peace, or confusion? Is it consistent with Scripture? Is it relevant to your current circumstances, location, and company? Is it personal to you? Or does it hold a message for someone else? Genuine revelation will survive the test of time. If you sense *pressure* to speak it out, that may be an indication that the vision is not from the *Holy* Spirit.

The purpose of all ecstatic spiritual experiences is to glorify God. If genuine, they will usually increase faith – your own faith or the faith of those with whom you share the revelation. But revelation may come with a price:

> *Because of the extravagance of those revelations, and so I wouldn't get a big head, I was given the gift of a handicap to keep me in constant touch with my limitations. Satan's angel did his best to get me down; what he in fact did was push me to my knees. No danger then of walking around high and mighty! At first I didn't think of it as a gift, and begged God to remove it. Three times I did that, and then he told me, My grace is enough; it's all you need. My strength comes into its own in your weakness. Once I heard that, I was glad to let it happen. I quit focusing on the handicap and began appreciating the gift. It was a case of Christ's strength moving in on my weakness. Now I take limitations in my stride, and with good cheer, these limitations that cut me down to size— abuse, accidents, opposition, bad breaks. I just let Christ take over! And so the weaker I get, the stronger I become.*

2 Corinthians 12:7-10 MSG

65. Contemplation

Still waters reflect the highest peak
And echoes make solitude deep.
    Gazing,
        Listening,
            Waiting,
                Wondering,
Allows silence to speak.

Contemplation is different from meditation. Both are important aspects of prayer. Both involve silence. But they are different. Peace is more than absence of war. Both have the same outward effect. But peace has greater depths of meaning.

The above poem captures the important distinction between them by using the word 'allows'. Meditation is a powerful tool for us to achieve concentration, silence, and a sense of closeness to God. But it is a tool, which we can use at our will and under our control. Contemplation does not come from our efforts. It is a gift from God. We can't invoke it. We can only allow it.

Some experts use the phrase 'apophatic prayer' to define the wordless form of praying that the ancients meant when they spoke of contemplation. But they were not just talking about absence of words. Above all, they were talking about presence of love – and of humility. In contemplation, there is no place for pride, hatred, or self-interest. It involves the absorption of our spirit into the God who is love.

Language constantly changes, and the word 'contemplation' has recently been diminished to indicate an introspective kind of thinking, while the phrase 'contemplative prayer' is taken to cover a wide range of creative and meditative prayer styles. That's not what the great men and women of prayer meant in past centuries. So, now we must get used to the term 'apophatic prayer'. It seems a rather technical word to apply to so sublime an experience, but I relish the prayer that it defines.

But, again, we come against a word that really doesn't fit – 'defines'? This prayer-form cannot truly be defined. It is wordless, so has no form, shape, or grammar. It is imageless, recognising that we cannot see God. It is unknowing, recognising that God is beyond our understanding. But, in its formlessness, wordlessness, and unknowingness it brings us into a mysterious knowledge of God. That sounds like a paradox – and it is.

If contemplation is different from meditation, how does it differ? Compare the swan with the eagle. The swan is a beautiful creature and a familiar sight as it glides across the water, or even as it walks across the grass; but when it takes flight it flaps furiously, making a noise, and splashing as it struggles to ascend. The eagle is rarely seen, keeping out of sight and perching in inaccessible places high up on the cliff; but when it takes flight it raises its wings and calmly allows the air to lift it skyward. Meditation requires effort, but serves well for those whose calling keeps them close to the ground; and it may involve the intellect as, for example, in *lectio divina* (see Chapter 45). Contemplation involves leaning on God and allowing his Spirit to lift us up out of ourselves. Contemplation happens in the remoteness of our secret place (or some other place where we can be alone and quiet). In a healthy sense, contemplation occurs when we are removed from direct contact with the immediate affairs of earth.

Contemplation is a place of safety, because Satan, who is motivated by pride and hatred, cannot access humility or love. But it is also a place of trial, because it demands honesty, commitment, and perseverance. Contemplation places the pray-er on a mountain top which is often shrouded in thick mist and darkness; but suddenly the mist clears, giving clear and widespread views of the world that needs God's intervention. It can be a lonely place, but it is also a place of vision and strength.

Those who engage in this type of prayer should not abandon other ways. Prayer must always be an act of love. As John wrote:

> *Whoever claims to love God yet hates a brother or sister is a liar. For whoever does not love their brother and sister, whom they have seen, cannot love God, whom they have not seen.*
> 1 John 4:20 NIV

So, we pray in silence to experience the power of God's presence; and we also pray for those that we love, for those who depend on us, for those who hate us and persecute us, and for everyone who God lays on our hearts.

Jesus knew every kind of prayer, but still used words right up to Gethsemane and even on the cross.

To quote Paul out of context, but I think appropriately:

> *I will pray with my spirit, but I will also pray with my understanding...*
> 1 Corinthians 14:15 NIV

How can we bring ourselves into contemplation? In some senses, we can't. We cannot choose this way. It is a gift – an empowering – that comes to those who God chooses for this calling. But, in another sense, we can – but only as the Holy Spirit enables us. Contemplatives do not start at the deep end. They develop their prayer life over long periods, through many stages and trials and, probably, through many mistakes and wrong pathways. They will certainly have practised meditation in various forms, because meditation is a pathway to contemplation.

But, only a few of those who start this journey reach the point where they can freely engage in contemplation. And that's not a problem. This way is not for everyone. It doesn't bring special honour (*the ear is no better than the eye* – 1 Corinthians 12:16). The person who contemplates is equal to the person who shows practical mercy to the poor and needy. The evangelist who leads people into the Kingdom stands alongside the contemplative with equivalent grace and gifting. Each of us is called to act and to pray in accordance with our personality, and subject to God's unique calling for us.

If God calls you to this sublime work, accept it as a privilege and a responsibility. The church needs people who will pray unseen and unrecognised, because the mission we are on involves a battle in heavenly places.

66. The fast of choice

Is this the kind of fast I have chosen, only a day for people to humble themselves? Is it only for bowing one's head like a reed and for lying in sackcloth and ashes? Is that what you call a fast, a day acceptable to the Lord? "Is not this the kind of fasting I have chosen: to loose the chains of injustice and untie the cords of the yoke, to set the oppressed free and break every yoke? Is it not to share your food with the hungry and to provide the poor wanderer with shelter – when you see the naked, to clothe them, and not to turn away from your own flesh and blood? Then your light will break forth like the dawn, and your healing will quickly appear; then your righteousness will go before you, and the glory of the Lord will be your rear guard. Then you will call, and the Lord will answer; you will cry for help, and he will say: Here am I.
Isaiah 58:5-9 NIV

Fasting is closely associated with prayer. But it doesn't make an appearance in the biblical record until the book of Judges. Several comments that Jesus made about fasting were negative; and, outside the 4 Gospels, the New Testament makes only 9 references to the practice. Isaiah's warnings (above) match closely with comments that Jesus made on the subject. These criticisms arose because, for some prominent Jews, the practice had become an act of hypocrisy.

Despite his negative remarks, Jesus fasted. His ministry didn't even begin until he had spent an incredible 40 days in the desert, fasting and praying. For the sake of good health, it should be said that a fast of that duration is not recommended. To last that long without food requires miraculous help. The human body can withstand several days of fasting; indeed, it was normal for our ancestors to live a feast-and-famine existence, because, in hunter-gatherer communities, the hunt is not always successful.

The body can stand 1 to 3 days without food, or a longer period of partial abstinence, without harm. But it is a strange experience for people who live in a society where food is always available. As already noted, the Bible record doesn't speak of fasting in the earliest times. That's probably because a certain level of food security was needed before voluntary fasting made any sense. People who are forced to endure natural famines (as recorded in Genesis and Exodus) don't *voluntarily* choose to do without food.

On the other hand, most people in modern society, particularly in the western world, know where their next meal is coming from – or at least that there will be a next meal. In that context, our relationship with food may deserve occasional rethinking.

If you are in good health, fasting will not harm you and its purging effects may benefit your body. Whether it will enhance your prayers, is another question. Fasting is, as this chapter heading implies, a matter of choice. It is not a mandatory part of prayer, God's choice in the matter, as Isaiah and Jesus said (see Matthew 6:16-18) is that fasting should be honest, secret, humble, and voluntary. Sincere fasting is combined with attitudes of generosity, kindness, and righteousness.

When fasting has been mandated, people have been tempted to dilute its meaning, or approach it half-heartedly or in an inappropriate spirit. Voluntary, honest, sincere fasting reminds your body who is in charge. No part of us exists outside our body, which is the significance of Paul's reminder in Romans:

> *Therefore, I urge you, brothers and sisters, in view of God's mercy, to offer your bodies as a living sacrifice, holy and pleasing to God—this is your true and proper worship.*
> Romans 12:1 NIV

(to offer our bodies means to offer ourselves entirely).

Paul considered it appropriate to keep his body in submission to his will, rather than having his life controlled by bodily urges:

> *Therefore I do not run like someone running aimlessly; I do not fight like a boxer beating the air. No, I strike a blow to my body and make it my slave so that after I have preached to others, I myself will not be disqualified for the prize.*
> 1 Corinthians 9:26,27 NIV

In biblical times, when prayer was accompanied by fasting, it was usually at times of danger or extremity, such as when the Israelites were under threat from enemies (Judges 20:26, 1 Samuel 7:6) or had suffered great tragedies (2 Samuel 1:22). When Jesus delivered a boy who the disciples were unable to heal, he said "...*this kind goeth not out but by prayer and fasting.*" (Matthew 17:21 KJV – although this reading does not appear in all the early manuscripts, so is omitted from some modern translations). The elders in the church at Antioch resorted to fasting before commissioning Barnabas and Saul to their apostolic mission (Acts 13:2). These examples suggest that fasting is meant to be used occasionally and with a specific object or purpose.

The act of fasting will not prove your piety, but it may enhance your hunger for God. Hunger, however, may not be the most noticeable symptom of the experience. More prominent is the strangeness of a daily routine deprived of its normal signposts because, for most of us, our days are organised around mealtimes. The change of routine provides a constant reminder that you have set aside your day for prayer.

Fasting has a long and honourable pedigree as an accompaniment to prayer. It has lent intensity to prayer for people through the centuries, and in modern times, especially when the threats are extreme, or the opportunities are great. But righteousness comes first. Seek after holiness (in the sense of Galatians 5:22-23); then fast. Don't do it to earn gold stars or to twist God's arm. God cannot be blackmailed. Fast with joy and love. The object is prayer, not sacrifice.

Fasting is not a way of bribing God, but an aid to focusing our minds. When we sense a greater urgency for prayer, or a greater need to concentrate our praying, fasting can help. It sets the priorities, placing prayer above our bodily needs, and frees time to devote to fervent prayer.

If you choose to fast, inform the person (if any) who would normally prepare or share your meals but, otherwise, tell nobody. Fasting is between you and God. If you engage in fasting together with others, retain the same humility, and mutually agree your routine, and the time and content of the meal that will break your fast.

So whether you eat or drink or whatever you do, do it all for the glory of God.
1 Corinthians 10:31 NIV

67. Beating upon the Cloud of Unknowing

Beating upon the Cloud of Unknowing –
O Teacher
You said it was hard.
I see the darkness -
Sense the swirl of the mist -
Lord God,
I know that you're there –
Constantly unattainable,
But always desired.
So, I beat upon the Cloud,
Sensing the hopelessness,
But full of hope,
Feeling the impossibility,
But believing all things.

Lord God,
Let me know the grace
That draws back the curtain.
Though a glimpse may dazzle and frighten,
Let me take that risk
Just to know you better.

Beating upon the Cloud
Seems futile
As the mist swirls in
To fill the gap.
What sense can it make to punch the air?
But, as long as I have breath
I will beat on that cloud.

Going deeper into prayer we enter places of privilege
and spiritual power. So, they are places where Satan
would rather we didn't go. To reach those special places

is to surmount obstacles, face distractions, discouragement, and temptations. If you sense that God is calling you to these heights and depths, be prepared to travel through difficulties. However, you will not travel alone. At times, you may find it hard to sense God's closeness. Such times are testing, but a faith that has been tested is a faith that will last:

> *Consider it pure joy, my brothers and sisters, whenever you face trials of many kinds, because you know that the testing of your faith produces perseverance. Let perseverance finish its work so that you may be mature and complete, not lacking anything.*
> James 1:2-4 NIV

Don't venture into ministries where God has not called you. But, if you sense that he is calling you to a special ministry of prayer, recognise that you are engaging in a spiritual battle that calls for perseverance. Take advice from those who have trodden this road before. The spiritual classic, *The Cloud of Unknowing*, is especially helpful and, in modern translations, easy to read. Yes, easy to read, but not so easy to emulate. In fact, the anonymous writer was at pains to discourage people from taking on this ministry. He wanted to be sure that nobody got out of their depth. But the Holy Spirit has made provisions for us to enter this battle:

> *God is strong, and he wants you strong.*
> *So take everything the Master has set out for you, well-made weapons of the best materials. And put them to use so you will be able to stand up to everything the Devil throws your way.*
> *This is no afternoon athletic contest that we'll walk away from and forget about in a couple of hours. This is for keeps, a life-or-death fight to the finish against the Devil and all his angels.*

Be prepared. You're up against far more than you can handle on your own. Take all the help you can get, every weapon God has issued, so that when it's all over but the shouting you'll still be on your feet.

Truth,

righteousness,

peace,

faith,

and salvation

– are more than words. Learn how to apply them. You'll need them throughout your life. God's Word is an indispensable weapon.

In the same way, prayer is essential in this ongoing warfare. Pray hard and long. Pray for your brothers and sisters. Keep your eyes open. Keep each other's spirits up so that no one falls behind or drops out.

Ephesians 6:10-18 MSG

Journeying deeper

68. The dark night of the soul

Into the darkness of the night
With heart ache kindled into love,
O blessed chance!
I stole me forth unseen,
My house being wrapped in sleep.
Into the darkness, and yet safe
By secret stair and in disguise,
O gladsome hap!
In darkness and in secret I crept forth,
My house being wrapped in sleep.

(St. John of the Cross - translated by Gabriela Graham –
public domain)

The words of this poem may not convey much to you. Unfortunately, even the more modern translations of *The Dark Night of the Soul* fail to deliver a truly up-to-date English rendering. I hope that some modern translator will take up the challenge to give us a clearer version. Nevertheless, this spiritual classic is worth the effort of a close study.

St. John of the Cross or, to give him his original (Spanish) name, San Juan de la Cruz, was a small, but determined man and a close friend of St. Teresa of Avila. A devout and reforming Carmelite friar, he suffered much at the hands of other Carmelites who had no stomach for reform. The apparent inspiration for the original poem (which has 6 more verses) was his escape from an unjust imprisonment. But he meditated on his poem during the years that followed and wrote his famous book, which describes a profound spiritual experience that may come upon people who seek to venture into contemplative prayer.

The expression *The Dark Night of the Soul* has been picked up in popular culture and parodied repeatedly, to the detriment of the author's intended meaning. It is not depression, though it may feel like that. It is not physical or circumstantial suffering, though those who suffer may use their pain to advance spiritually. It is not an illness. It is a stage of development in the life of prayer. However, the *Dark Night* is not for everyone.

Several valuable books on the life of prayer were written around the same period as John of the Cross was writing, but they do not all speak about the experience of the *Dark Night*. On the other hand, most speak of times when God seems distant and prayer times feel dry and barren. This is essentially the same thing, differing perhaps in degree or intensity, rather than nature.

When we set out on this journey of prayer, the experience is often accompanied by feelings of joy and uplift. But, as we progress, we may begin to experience times when it doesn't seem to be going so well. We don't feel the same thrill or enjoyment. We may feel a kind of spiritual dryness. That is along the lines of the *Dark Night* that John describes. I say 'along the lines' because this is a matter of degree and, however deeply we feel this experience, it is not a badge of honour, but a springboard for humility.

This experience may make a normally devout person feel unable to pray. Some have described it as seeming as if God has put a barrier or a cloud before them, or above them, through which their prayers cannot pass. This is obviously discouraging. But the darkness is beneficial because, if we reject all input from the senses (sight, hearing, taste, smell, touch) so that we can perceive God spiritually, we are effectively in darkness. And the objective is indeed to perceive God without image, sound, or any external sense – to perceive him purely in our spirit:

God is spirit, and his worshippers must worship in the Spirit and in truth
John 4:24 NIV

Another illustration given by St John of the Cross provides a paradoxical kind of encouragement. He notes that we only see rays of light where they are reflected in specks of dust in the air. If a light beam were to pass through a room and out of the opposite window without encountering any impurities it would be invisible to us; the light would, in effect, be darkness to us. By implication, much of our sense of enlightenment comes from things that we *are* able to do something about, which God's light exposes (such as sins we can confess, or errors we can correct). But, the closer we come to him, and the more the impurities are purged out of our life, the less visible is the light that comes from him.

The very closeness of God may bring darkness. This is not as paradoxical as it sounds because, to use an illustration suggested by John himself, the brightness of sunlight can blind us. As we come close to the holiness of God, we may become painfully aware of our inadequacies, as Isaiah was in his vision of the heavenly sanctuary:

"Woe to me!" I cried. "I am ruined! For I am a man of unclean lips, and I live among a people of unclean lips, and my eyes have seen the King, the LORD Almighty."
Isaiah 6:5 NIV

The more profound our experiences in prayer, the more important it is that our hearts are humble. Deep spiritual experiences may be harmful if accompanied by pride. Indeed, over the centuries there have been movements that developed dangerous doctrines based on so-called 'higher knowledge' or 'enlightenment' and, in some cases, those doctrines led to harmful practices that risked bringing the church into disrepute. I want the best that God can offer, but I want it on his terms and in his way. If I need humbling, let it be God that brings it about.

John himself uses the illustration of the manna that the Israelites ate in the wilderness. Manna was not the product of farming or husbandry. Its production required no effort – it just appeared on the ground like morning dew or frost. Manna was a miraculous gift from God. But its taste was subtle, and some of the people yearned for the strong tastes of fish, onions, and garlic, which they had enjoyed in Egypt (Numbers 11:15). So, said John, we may be disappointed when we move from the exciting experiences of the earlier stages of prayer to the subtler rewards of contemplative prayer.

The dryness of these testing times may feel like separation or rejection. But it is part of God's pruning work to make us more fruitful (John 15:1-7). Pruning is an essential part of cultivation in the vineyard, removing the superfluous, the superficial and the unnecessary, so that the vine may bear more and better fruit. It is not punishment, but care. A vine is useless unless fruitful. Its wood cannot be used in carpentry. Its value is simply that is bears grapes.

A few years ago, at the end of December, I noted in my journal that the year had been dull and discouraging. My Christian life has usually been exciting; but not that year. A few days later, I was chatting with a friend who had similar feelings about their previous 12 months. We compared our experience to a kind of spiritual coma, then realised that it was part of a healing process. It is now medical practice in cases of severe physical trauma for a patient to be put into an induced coma. The removal of all sensory input is a therapeutic process that assists healing. It was a comforting revelation. Our times of apparent ineffectiveness had been part of God's healing and a preparation for further progress in our spiritual lives. A time of apparent spiritual dryness may be a time when the Spirit of God is working inside us to bring spiritual or emotional healing.

How can you tell if your feeling of dryness is part of this healing process or if it is something you need to worry about?

First, ask yourself if you are aware of sin that is coming between you and the Lord. This does not mean that you need to chastise or condemn yourself. Satan (the Slanderer) will try to provoke a despairing sense of guilt that has no relief. But the Holy Spirit does not *accuse* – he *convicts*, in order to lead us to confession, grace, and forgiveness.

Secondly, ask yourself if you are ill. Illness can certainly be a cause for feelings of sorrow, despair, and ineffectiveness. If sickness is the problem, you know where to seek solutions.

Finally, ask yourself if your continuing desire is to be close to the Lord and submit to his purposes. If the answer is 'yes', your dryness is a spiritual process that you may welcome as God's gift.

The *Dark Night of the Soul* is not an essential or inevitable part of the journey for every person who is called to a life of prayer. Some of the giants of prayer, whose writings inspire us, make no reference to this experience or give passing mention to less dramatic versions of the experience than John of the Cross talks about. On the other hand, we may suffer similar trials many times in varying intensity. It all depends on our personality and the path God has chosen for us. This is another example of the individual nature of our prayer journey. God deals with us as unique individuals with distinct personalities.

At each stage, we have a choice.

If this *Dark Night* is part of your experience, or if it becomes your experience, don't chastise yourself or despair of your progress. Thank God for leading you onwards, and bear it patiently in the expectation that you will come to more fruitful times. If this is not your experience, don't seek it. It is not a certificate of attainment. God will lead you according to his will and your needs. Your needs – because you are unique. Isaiah gives a graphic illustration of God's wisdom in treating each of us according to our individual needs:

> *Listen and hear my voice; pay attention and hear what I say. When a farmer ploughs for planting, does he plough continually? Does he keep on breaking up and working the soil? When he has levelled the surface, does he not sow caraway and scatter cumin? Does he not plant wheat in its place, barley in its plot, and spelt in its field? His God instructs him and teaches him the right way. Caraway is not*

threshed with a sledge, nor is the wheel of a cart rolled over cumin; caraway is beaten out with a rod, and cumin with a stick. Grain must be ground to make bread; so one does not go on threshing it forever. The wheels of a threshing cart may be rolled over it, but one does not use horses to grind grain. All this also comes from the Lord Almighty, whose plan is wonderful, whose wisdom is magnificent.

Isaiah 28:23-29 NIV

69 Holiness

without holiness no one will see the Lord
Hebrews 12:14 NIV

Prayer is about the whole of life. Going deeper into prayer means making God the centre of everything we do. Time and time again, the Old Testament prophets berated the Israelites for focusing on religious observance whilst behaving in selfish, greedy, oppressive, and generally unholy ways. God desires our worship, but it is meant to be accompanied with holiness.

> *Give unto the LORD the glory due unto his name: bring an offering, and come before him: worship the LORD in the beauty of holiness.*
> 1 Chronicles 16:29 KJV

It would be a grave mistake to seek advancement in the life of prayer without turning away from sin, holding to truth, and seeking to live in purer, kinder, more loving ways. Being a gifted healer or prophet is no proof of holiness:

> *I can see it now--at the Final Judgment thousands strutting up to me and saying, 'Master, we preached the Message, we bashed the demons, our God-sponsored projects had everyone talking.'*
> *And do you know what I am going to say? 'You missed the boat. All you did was use me to make yourselves important. You don't impress me one bit. You're out of here.'*
> Matthew 7:22,23 MSG

When we enter into the spiritual battleground of prayer (see Chapter 23), we dare not leave openings for Satan to trip us up with accusations. But, if guilt or fear assails you, take refuge in the security of the grace of the Lord Jesus Christ.

The work of sanctification is entirely a matter of grace. The Lord provides the power. Our part is to submit. We will only achieve holiness through God's Holy Spirit working in us to produce works of righteousness:

> *...it is God who works in you to will and to act in order to fulfil his good purpose*
> Philippians 2:3 MSG

But, if we are engaged in prayer, in collaboration with the Holy Spirit, we can expect that the fruit of the Spirit will be produced in us:

> *But the fruit of the Spirit is love, joy, peace, forbearance, kindness, goodness, faithfulness, gentleness and self-control. Against such things there is no law.*
> Galatians 5:22,23 NIV

Fruit is the product of life. Trees do not put on a special end-of-season effort to produce fruit. Fruitfulness is the natural outcome of their being alive. In Christ, each of us is a new creation. Our newness of life has its completion in fruitfulness.

The challenge of holiness is not a demand for effort, but for attention. Evil may try to trip us up, to catch us unawares, to divert our attention.

> *The end of all things is near. Therefore be alert and of sober mind so that you may pray.*
> 1 Peter 4:7 NIV

Prayer is plugging-in to the power of our new life.

Prayer is breathing in the power of the *Holy* Spirit.

Prayer is not just about our time in the secret place.

Prayer is about the whole of life

Beyond myself

Making a difference to more than just me.

Beyond myself

70. Praying for the nations

Why do the nations conspire and the peoples plot in vain? The kings of the earth rise up and the rulers band together against the Lord and against his anointed, saying, "Let us break their chains and throw off their shackles." The One enthroned in heaven laughs; the Lord scoffs at them. He rebukes them in his anger and terrifies them in his wrath, saying, "I have installed my king on Zion, my holy mountain." ... Ask me, and I will make the nations your inheritance, the ends of the earth your possession.
Psalm 2:1-6,8 NIV

The Psalmist personifies the nations and he's not the only biblical writer to see things that way. Verses in the book of Daniel (especially in Chapter 10) speak about spiritual forces that govern the nations and imply that Daniel's prayers had a direct effect on those powers. Few of us would make a claim to be in the same league as Daniel where prayer is concerned, but we are playing the same game; and part of that 'game' involves praying for the nations.

If that thought makes you feel out of your depth, don't worry. We can work up to this in the same way as Jesus told his disciples to work up to their worldwide mission:

...you will be my witnesses in Jerusalem, and in all Judea and Samaria, and to the ends of the earth.
Acts 1:8 NIV

He didn't expect them to start with "*the ends of the earth*" and neither need we. Start by praying for your family, then move outwards to your church, your neighbours, and your friends. As you become more confident in prayer, reach out further – as far as the Spirit leads you.

But, there are other ways. Christians are working in countries across the world, and those missions are keen to engage prayer-partners. They constantly provide information to inform their supporters, and that makes it easier to understand their needs and pray intelligently. If you feel drawn to pray for such missions, connect with them, and use their information in your prayers – but be selective.

However, praying for the nations does not just mean praying for Christian missions. Daily News bulletins bring us information about situations around the world, often in terms that stir our hearts. Wars, famines, diseases, terrorism, political tensions... where can we start, when so many needs are thrust at us? There are almost 200 officially recognised nation states in the world so there's a lot of scope for over-burdening ourselves. None of us can realistically pray in depth for each of those nations. There seems little value in praying, "God bless Upper Volta" if we don't know whether it's in Africa or Asia (it's in Africa, by the way!). So, we need to be selective, to be informed and, most of all, we need to be guided by the Holy Spirit.

If newspaper or broadcast reports prompt your prayers, don't forget that news media are fickle. They will run with a story so long as it seems to attract readers/viewers, but will drop the story as soon as something more interesting occurs. Let's not copy their fickleness. If you are moved to pray for the people affected by the story, why not continue to pray for them as long as you would wish to be remembered if you were the subject? If the location is distant from you, try sourcing a map from the internet – or an aerial view – and do an *Intercession Walk* (see Chapter 71).

Prayer is a calling. It applies to us all, but our role in the prayer-army is individual and unique. God's aim is to build a kingdom that covers the earth. We just need to take responsibility for the parts he places on our heart.

Beyond myself

71. Intercession walks

Then the man brought me through the entrance...
He then brought me to the outer court and led me around to its four corners...
he man brought me back to the entrance to the temple...
He then brought me out through the north gate and led me around the outside...
Ezekiel 46:19,21; 47:1,2 NIV

By night I went out through the Valley Gate toward the Jackal Well and the Dung Gate, examining the walls of Jerusalem...
Then I moved on toward the Fountain Gate and the King's Pool...
...so I went up the valley by night, examining the wall. Finally, I turned back and re-entered through the Valley Gate.
Nehemiah 2:13-15 NIV

If you search the internet for 'prayer walking', you will notice that most of the references are to the kind of activity that Ezekiel and Nehemiah were engaged in as they made their separate tours of Jerusalem (see above). I prefer to differentiate, what I call 'Intercession Walks' from another kind of personal prayer walk (see chapter 15). But both are important elements of prayer.

The passage from Ezekiel was a virtual walk. He wasn't in Jerusalem at the time; he was still amongst the exiles in Babylon. However, his virtual walk, in the form of a vision, was an equally valid way of focussing on an area so that he could pray for it (remembering that prayer is a two-way conversation – God speaks to us as we talk to him). In the 21st century we have facilities for virtual intercession walks that Ezekiel could not have imagined. We have easy access to maps, aerial views, and even to 360 degree photos.

Put a map in front of you, whether a paper version or an online view shown on a computer, tablet, or smart phone. Look at the area and trace a path around it, praying as you go. Consider the needs you know about, and the needs that you imagine would be present in the area. Listen to the inner voice of the Holy Spirit, who may prompt you to pray for particular issues. Praying over a map in this way need not be limited by distance. Ezekiel was focused on Jerusalem while he was still living hundreds of miles away. We can use a virtual intercession walk to pray for needs anywhere in the world. It can be part of praying for the nations (see chapter 70)

Nehemiah did his *intercession walk* on the spot, during a visit to Jerusalem. He didn't walk – he did it on a horse, which shows how broadly we can interpret this type of prayer (how about a bike?). By seeing the actual places concerned, Nehemiah could notice problems and needs, which gave him specific focus for his prayers. This kind of prayer is ideal as a prelude to special occasions, such as outreach events, or when sending invitations to special meetings, or services.

Either kind of *intercession walk* can be undertaken individually or in groups. It is a valuable tool in our prayer armoury.

72. Praying together

…they raised their voices together in prayer to God.
Acts 4:24 NIV

Most of the chapters in this book relate to our personal prayer life, but prayer is also a corporate matter. Prayer is important as a part of worship, and as a shared endeavour. A church where people meet regularly to pray together is likely to be a healthy church.

If we want our church to grow we need to pray – and growth is an essential part of a healthy church life. Prayer changes things – especially when we pray together:

> *"When two of you get together on anything at all on earth and make a prayer of it, my Father in heaven goes into action."*
> Matthew 18:19 MSG

But public prayer carries temptations. Jesus warned against using our prayers to demonstrate our superior piety (Matthew 6:5). We don't need to dress up our prayers in fine phrases. For that matter, neither should we act falsely by using language that is unnaturally down-to-earth for our personality. When praying in public or in private we should be ourselves – speak as we would normally – express our genuine desires – pray rather than preach.

When someone prays, it is normal for others in the room to respond with 'Amen', meaning "Let it be so". That means that we agree. Agreement is a key aspect of praying together; so, make sure that the things you pray for are not inappropriately controversial (don't pray for your favourite political party to win the election!). And avoid over-enthusiasm. Shouting is not necessary (God is awake!) The peer pressures that may turn a crowd into a mob can invade the prayer room, creating a false sense that may sound like faith, but is really over-enthusiasm.

Faith is a gift and a fruit of the Holy Spirit. The fruit grows out of our maturity. The gift is given for special occasions when God intends to do something remarkable. Before praying for something remarkable, make sure that you have the faith for what you are asking God to do. Then everyone can say an enthusiastic 'Amen!'

But please speak loud enough for your companions to hear. How can they say "Amen" if they don't know what you prayed for?

When we meet for prayer, we may include a variety of prayer forms. It's not necessary for us all to pray in the same way. It's not necessary for all of us to pray aloud. Some may rightly sense that their part is to remain in silence, savouring the presence of God. The meeting will benefit from that quiet influence. Don't worry that other people might think that you are failing in some way by your silence. If your prayer is genuine, it is to God.

And, of course, we should not judge one another. Corporate prayer is prayer together. It is, above all, an act of love.

> *And pray in the Spirit on all occasions with **all kinds of prayers** and requests. With this in mind, be alert and always keep on praying for all the Lord's people.*
> Ephesians 6:18 NIV

73. Prayer ministry

I am no better
than the people I pray for.
But still I can pray

*So if I, the Master and Teacher, washed your feet, you must
now wash each other's feet.*
I've laid down a pattern for you. What I've done, you do.
John 13:14,15 MSG

Ministry means service. When we pray with people to
meet their needs, worries, and concerns, we do not put
ourselves above them – we stoop, metaphorically, to
wash their feet. Prayer ministry, as part of a worship
meeting, is becoming increasingly common, and rightly
so. A sermon is not meant so much to inform as to
provoke a response. Providing an opportunity for
people to receive prayer is a helpful way of dealing with
issues that the meeting may stir up. If your church does
not yet provide a shared prayer ministry, I encourage
you to start.

Prayer ministry is best provided in a team setting. The
people who do the praying can support one another.
Having a team of women and men of various ages and
personalities enables those seeking prayer to be
matched up with the most appropriate support.
Working as a team, the prayer ministers can learn
together, pray for one another, and back each other up
in challenging situations.

Prayer Ministry is not counselling. Its purpose is to
encourage a deeper and more intimate relationship with
Jesus. The relationship between the person seeking
prayer and the one doing the praying is equal. Both
stand in weakness before God, who gives the strength,

the faith, and the inspiration that is needed. Questions are OK, but respect is paramount. If the seeker wants to limit how much they tell you, that is their right. But always listen carefully to what they do say. Always respect boundaries. Don't make unjustified assumptions.

Whatever is said in these times of sharing must remain confidential, except in cases where there may be concerns for the safety of the person seeking prayer, or anyone else they might harm. Prayer ministry is not risk-free and, for that reason, should be conducted in view of the congregation. If privacy is requested, go into a separate room and pray *in pairs*. It may occasionally happen that the person being prayed for reveals something that cannot legally be kept confidential (that is, where there is a genuine risk that the person will do something to harm themselves or someone else). In that situation, explain that you are obliged to seek help, possibly from a professional person or agency.

Be aware of the difficulties that touch could generate, and ask permission before laying on of hands. Be sensitive to the seeker's personal space. When touch seems appropriate, always explain, and ask permission in such a way that the person may accept or decline without prejudice.

Recognise any situations which are outside your experience and competence. If such is the case, draw the session to a positive close and seek advice. When the time of prayer is over, continue to remember the person you have prayed with. They have allowed you into their life, perhaps sharing intimate secrets with you. Return them the respect of praying for them on your own afterwards – and possibly asking them how they are getting on when you next see them.

People who are called to prayer ministry are not Teflon coated. As you engage with the needs, the pressures, the sicknesses, and the anxieties of the people who ask for prayer, you may feel some of the pressure within yourself. Even Jesus, when a woman in the crowd touched the hem of his robe, felt power going out from him. 'Power going out' infers some loss; we too may sense some loss of power, or even a loss of peace, after praying with someone. At such times, it is best to ask for prayer from a colleague in the ministry team. Those who pray for others need also to receive prayer.

This calling is not for everyone. But, if you are a person of prayer, you are a likely candidate, Prayer ministry is a powerful resource that supports church growth and encourages individual commitment. For those who offer prayer in this way, it is an immense privilege that brings joy, and strengthens their own faith.

Beyond myself

74. Praying for healing

But for you who revere my name, the sun of righteousness will rise with healing in its rays. And you will go out and frolic like well-fed calves.
Malachi 4:2 NIV

Well-fed calves grow fast, it is not very long before they are indistinguishable from adult cattle. So, this is not just about healing, but health. Malachi's message was to encourage the Jews, recently returned from exile but still under foreign domination, that God would bless them. But the message had unmistakable overtones that the Jewish rabbis recognised as messianic prophecy. The healer is Jesus.

God heals, and he also blesses us with spiritual growth. Let's therefore be grown-up about healing. Some people, and some sects, have laid so much emphasis on healing that they have scared people away from ever praying for healing. Other teachers have suggested that healing prayer has no place in a scientific society with effective modern medicine. Without doubt, there have been huge advances in medicine, but there were physicians in Jesus' time too. Luke, the physician, was a trusted companion of the apostle Paul. They saw no conflict between ministering to the sick with medicine *and* with prayer.

If we are 'grown up' about healing prayer, we won't fall for the extremes. God can heal through modern medicine or miracle power, or both together – and it's not our place to dictate how he should act. Healing is not given for the sake of the people who pray for the sick, but for the individuals who need relief. Healing prayer does not show how powerful or spiritual we are. It demonstrates God's love.

"But", you may ask, "don't we need special faith for divine healing?" Yes, but how much faith? Jesus said, "If you have faith as small as a mustard seed, you can say to this mulberry tree, 'Be uprooted and planted in the sea,' and it will obey you." (Luke 17:6 NIV)

Some teachers draw a distinction between miracles and healing – miracles having immediate and visible effect, and healings becoming apparent over a period. This distinction is not clear in all Bible references and doesn't need to affect the way we pray. The Holy Spirit gives the power in either case. And, in neither case can we dictate to God how he will act. We ask. He answers.

I don't regard myself as having extraordinary faith or a 'healing ministry', though I recognise that some people have been used, and are being used, to pray frequently and effectively for healing. You are probably not one of those people. Nor am I. However, healing prayer is open to all of us, and the experience of seeing someone healed is hugely affirmative to faith. On two occasions when I prayed for someone they were obviously and immediately healed, but neither example would make headline news. The first occurred when I was scarcely 30 years old, and was leading an inter-denominational worship meeting, together with a colleague. A lady asked for prayer because of a stabbing abdominal pain that made it hard for her to join in the worship. On an impulse, I told her to lift her hands in the air, which she did – and immediately let out a loud burp! We all laughed – but the pain had gone. It was wind, of course. Can we call that healing? She did.

The second occasion was more recent. As a member of the Prayer Ministry team at my local church I was approached by a friend who had a sharp pain in her neck and could scarcely turn her head. I prayed with her at the end of the service, then went home. Later that day she sent me an email reporting that she got in her car and suddenly realised that she could turn her head easily, without pain.

Two examples in all those years of praying – that doesn't sound very impressive, but who do I need to impress? In truth, there have been other examples, but no more dramatic than the stories I already related. Maybe I will have the privilege of seeing more people healed in the future, and maybe they will provide 'better' stories, but, whether that happens or not, I will continue to pray for healing. Anyway, there have been uncountable occasions when I have prayed that people would be healed, and they have recovered under medical care and treatment. Sometimes the people I was praying for had serious, life-threatening conditions and recovered under treatment. Was God involved in that?

Also, I have prayed for people who, did not recover. That is always sad, and it can be hard to face the disappointment, or even disillusion.

Through all these circumstances I have concluded that it is never a mistake to pray for healing. There is a law that says it is right to pray that people will be healed – it is the law of love.

So how do we go about praying for healing? Should we lay hands on the person? Maybe, but only with their permission. Should we anoint them with oil, as James suggested? (*James 5:14-15*) Sometimes, but not as an empty ritual. Should we act alone or with others? Be sensitive, use common-sense, and don't try to be too clever.

The most important words of advice I can offer are these:

Listen.

Listen to the person who is asking for prayer.

Listen to the voice of the Holy Spirit.

75. Prayers by the bowlful

And when he had taken it, the four living creatures and the twenty-four elders fell down before the Lamb. Each one had a harp and they were holding golden bowls full of incense, which are the prayers of God's people.
Revelation 5:8 NIV

Some people have a knack for choosing presents. As you unwrap the parcel they give you, you just know you're going to like what's inside, because they always get it right. I don't have that talent, but I've learnt that it's something to do with noticing what people choose for themselves – the colours they wear, the products they use, the trinkets they display on their mantelpiece. From time to time I've made just the right choice, and it's been a pleasure to see them (at some later date) using the item I gave them, or seeing it on display in their house. I'm happy to have given them pleasure.

What joy it will be to see those golden bowls full of incense. We will know then for certain that our prayers have been valuable, and that their fragrance has been like a pleasant incense. Not only that. We will know that we have given God pleasure, because he's kept the gifts.

The people who first read the above verse from Revelation may have been reminded of the incense that was constantly burnt in the Jerusalem temple. It was a special mixture that had been prescribed hundreds of years before (Exodus 30:43-36) and would have been in John's mind when he penned these words. Whilst we cannot now identify all the original ingredients, we can recognise certain of the aromatic resins – and they are significantly described as flowing from their host plants like tears. Those ingredients took quite a pounding to create the final mixture. The prayers to be remembered for eternity will include our most heartfelt and our most desperate cries. John (who wrote Revelation) was writing at a time of persecution, so he would know.

Prayer is not just for now. It's for eternity. The times we spend on our knees, or walking and talking with God, or screaming out to him in our times of anguish – all these prayers will become part of his treasure in the kingdom of God. Let's keep adding to that treasure store.

76. Your kingdom come

This, then, is how you should pray ...
your kingdom come, your will be done, on earth as it is in heaven.
Matthew 6:9,10 NIV

"Your Kingdom come"
Is not a dream of realms beyond the sun,
where angels sing
and all is good and God's will's always done.
No! It's a call for massive change -
"Your will be done on earth"
Let earth and heaven be rearranged;
Bring righteousness to birth.
It's not a helpless cry to God
for him to spring to action;
It's a willing offering of self
for our participation.
So now I say "Your Kingdom come"
and mean just what I say.
And say the more, "Your will be done -
Lord, start the work in me."

The kingdom prayer gets to the heart of what God wants us to pray. It gets to the core of everything that we are called to:

- *What's the point of evangelism?*
  - To build the kingdom.
- *Why should we care for the poor and needy?*
  - To build the kingdom.
- *What's the object of pastoral ministry?*
  - To build the kingdom.

We could go on asking questions like this and the answer would still be the same, because that's the destination our faith is leading us to.

When we pray "your kingdom come" let's pray it in self-commitment. Let's not dreamily restrict this to a vague concept of something God might do in the future, but as something we are going to help bring about by our actions and our prayers. Jesus told us to pray "your kingdom come" because, inexplicably, in this ultimate project for the redemption of creation, God is depending on us to work with him.

77. The parable of the tree

Reaching high,
　branching wide,
　　rooted deep.
I feed on light,
　inhaling gases
　　which, to humanity,
　　　are poisonous.
I drink from deep wells,
　drawing refreshment,
　　and I exhale
　　　the oxygen of life.
My leaves give shade.
My fruit is a gift
I give -
　Shade
　　Air
　　　Wood
　　　　Fruit
　　　　　Beauty
　　　　　Life
Multitudes live here –
I shelter them all.
I don't strive for fruit –
　I live and it grows,
　　flowing out from my being.
I don't shout.
　I don't complain.
　　I don't fight.
　　　I simply live.
When winter comes
　I rest
　　　preparing myself
　　　　to give again.

There's hope for a tree;
  if I am cut down,
    my stump will bear leaves
      and send out branches.
I may live again.
  I will give again.
    giving is my joy
      it's what I live for.
And all of this flows
  from my stillness.
I was young
  I am ageing
    I may grow very old.
But, all my days,
  I will look upwards
    arms raised towards heaven
      living and bearing fruit
        a constant prayer
          for the benefit of life
            and for God.

Blessed is the one who does not walk in step with the wicked or stand in the way that sinners take or sit in the company of mockers, but whose delight is in the law of the Lord, and who meditates on his Law day and night. That person is like a tree planted by streams of water, which yields its fruit in season and whose leaf does not wither— whatever he does prospers.
Psalm 1:1-3 NIV

Then the angel showed me the river of the water of life, as clear as crystal, flowing from the throne of God and of the Lamb down the middle of the great street of the city. On each side of the river stood the tree of life, bearing twelve crops of fruit,

yielding its fruit every month. And the leaves of the tree are for the healing of the nations.
Revelation 22:1,2 NIV

78. Conclusion

I'm not saying that I have this all together, that I have it made. But I am well on my way, reaching out for Christ, who has so wondrously reached out for me.
Philippians 3:12 MSG

Prayer has been my subject, not just in this book, but through many years of listening, reading, practising, making mistakes and enduring. But don't imagine that I am an expert, or that I think myself to be adept at prayer. I may have left the beginner's class, but I have only travelled a short way along this road. From the distance that I have journeyed, I have learned that there is much more to learn, but that the journey is worthwhile. I have related some of my experience – but not for you to copy. My journey is based on *my* personality and *my* experience. *Your* journey may include some similar episodes, but you will also make discoveries that I have never found. This book skims the surface of a deep ocean. Dive in and discover your own treasures, because no book can provide a shortcut or give you the secret key to effective prayer:

- **There is no secret key.**
- **There are no shortcuts.**
- The only way to learn it is to do it.

As for me:

"I am still digging"

Still Digging

Further reading

Still Digging cannot, by its nature, go into full detail on every aspect of prayer. There is much more to learn. This book is intended as a signpost to help you to develop your prayer life in line with your own personality and calling. For many people, this will involve finding ways that are different and even unique – though someone may have already written a book about a way that will suit you perfectly. For some people, this may mean going much deeper, in which case you will need to look for more in-depth guidance through appropriate courses, retreats, seminars, and books. The books listed on the following pages cover a wide range of prayer styles and experiences and have been helpful to me in discovering my style and developing my prayer life. Most are readily available through regular bookshops or online sources. Some are no longer in print, so they may be harder to find; but they are worth the effort. Don't expect to follow the recommendations of every book. By suggesting them, I am not saying that I agree with everything they say. We each need to read with discernment. Search out the lessons that *you* need. You are unique, so pray uniquely.

Title	Author (translator/editor)
Answers to Prayer	George Müller (A.E.C. Brooks)
Ascent of Mount Carmel	St John of the Cross
Cloud of Unknowing (The)	Anonymous (William Johnston)
Creating a Life with God	Daniel Wolpert
Dark Night of the Soul (The)	St John of the Cross (Gabriela Dunninhame Graham)
Finding Sanctuary	Abbot Christopher Jamieson
Fire of Love (The)	Richard Rolle (Clifton Wolters)
Grace Outpouring (The)	Roy Godwin and Dave Roberts
Green Leaf in Drought	Isobel Kuhn
Hearts Aflame - prayers of Susanna, John and Charles Wesley	(Michael McMullen)
Imitation of Christ	St Thomas a Kempis
Interior Castle (The) or the Mansions	St Teresa of Avila
Ladder of Perfection (The)	Walter Hilton (Leo Shirley-Price)
Lord, teach us to pray	Andrew Murray

Ministry of Intercession (The). A Plea for More Prayer	Andrew Murray
Miracles	C S Lewis
Mister God This is Anna	Fynn
New Seeds of Contemplation	Thomas Merton
Personality and Prayer	Ruth Fowke
Practice of the Presence of God (The)	Brother Lawrence
Prayer	Henry French
Prayer - does it make any difference?	Philip Yancey
Praying Hyde: Apostle of Prayer	E G Carre
Praying in Color	Sybil MacBeth
Prison to Praise	Merlin Carothers
Revelations of Divine Love	St Julian of Norwich
Short Method of Prayer (A)	Mme. Jeanne Marie Bouvières de la Mot Guyon
Spirit of Flame	E Allison Peers (biography of John of the Cross)
Spiritual Torrents	Mme. Jeanne Marie Bouvières de la Mot Guyon
The Cross and the	David Wilkerson

Switchblade

The Screwtape Letters   C S Lewis

They Speak with Other   John L Sherrill
Tongues

Union and Communion   James Hudson Taylor

War On The Saints   Jesse Penn-Lewis

About the author

Derrick Phillips became a Christian in the 1950s and initially planned to enter the Christian ministry – a plan that changed after he received an experience with the Holy Spirit and a call to evangelism as a member of *The Pilgrims* – probably the first Christian rock band. The band toured extensively throughout the 1960s, carrying the gospel into dingy night clubs, large concert halls, churches, town halls and all manner of youth venues. After leaving the band, Derrick began a career in corporate management and eventually formed his own business. He is now retired. He has served in church leadership, written, and published several books and articles on the faith and served in musical ministry as a guitarist and singer. He now lives near Bristol, where he is a member of St Michael's Church, Stoke Gifford.

Other books by this author

Little Church of Bethany

"Small village – big heart – huge influence"

In first century Palestine, a little village called Bethany was home to two sisters and a brother whose lives of faith helped change history. In 20th century Britain an 800-year-old village church went into decline, much like many at that time. But it reversed its decline and grew to become a force for change in the local community and beyond. *Little Church of Bethany* weaves together these two stories, focusing on Bethany's characters and events and showing the power of small churches to change themselves and their community.

Bethany (Ordinary Superstars)

The performance edition of the musical that preceded the above book. This version has a larger page size containing the full script and scores, including musical arrangements, plus individual part details for each character.

SOS – Stumbling Over Scripture

"A journey from fundamentalism to faith"

Fundamentalism is a risky strategy for maintaining faith. It can lead to arrogance or even cruelty and it doesn't cope well with doubts. This book records the author's 20-year journey from fundamentalism to honest faith, facing the problems and questions that cause people to stumble over scripture.

21046801R00150

Printed in Great Britain
by Amazon

DEATH
BLOOMS

YOLANDA OLSON

ACKNOWLEDGMENTS

My funny ladies that kept telling me that maybe less wasn't more this time. Lis, Linda, and Dawn—I'm pretty sure you guys are crazier than me sometimes!

Sarah Paige of Opium House. When I saw this cover, I knew immediately that you had captured my vision. This gives the story life in a dark and beautiful way. I appreciate your stunning work!

Dez of Pretty in Ink Creations for editing this. Always coming through in the clutch and saving the day. Thank you for making this shiny and neat.

Dani of Raven Designs for formatting this to twisted perfection; you the real MVP.

To the Twisted Rabbits. I don't think I've ever laughed so hard watching you guys beta read a story of mine before. You guys are hilarious and made this adventure super fun!

DEDICATION

For Bridgett, Lis, and Dawn.
#BC

PROLOGUE

It won't stop crying and I don't understand why.

I'm very good to it; I'm kind, soft spoken, and gentle with my touch, yet it whimpers and whines with blood red, tear stained eyes.

I think it wants to leave, but I've given it a much better life than it had before in such a small amount of time, that I think it will start to trust me soon.

I hope so, anyway.

I know that trust is something earned and not readily an easy reward. I know that all things take time but I want nothing more than for it to smile when it sees me. I want the tears—the terror and fear that overcomes it when I approach to be a distant memory.

Soon enough.

It's almost ready to join the others, but not until it stops reacting so unreasonably when it sees me. I'll leave it to wallow in it's own self-doubt and sorrows before I let it go with the others.

They're all much stronger and confident once they leave me and they always thank me.

Always.

Sometimes I think that maybe, just maybe, it doesn't want to leave me. I think that it reacts this way because of how kind I am with it.

I groom it, feed it, give it a warm bed to sleep in and even fresh sheets every night.

I think it may have grown attached to me as they often tend to do and the problem is that I may have grown attached too.

There's just the two of us left.

The others have met their goals and have been molded into the perfect little possessions their owners paid me to make them into.

The reason this one is different, the reason I feel so much fondness for it, is because *I* chose it. I'm receiving no compensation for the molding of it— monetary or otherwise.

I may keep it.

I may kill it.

I may kill myself.

I may kill us both.

I haven't decided yet and that's the most exciting feeling of all.

PART ONE

THE ACQUISITION

CHAPTER ONE

I've been working all night and I'm so goddamn tired, but I know that time is of the essence when attempting to create the perfect pets. I'm almost done, having already removed most of the useless parts and viscera. Since I'm self-trained in this craft, I have no care for the rules of do no harm especially not with the amount of money I get paid for these things.

I take my work seriously and I'm very passionate about producing the perfect product as requested by each suitor.

I do pretty good for myself considering that I work alone and my prices start at ten-thousand dollars depending on what kind of product is required.

Simple little things like appearance changes or body molding into some form of small animal is the easiest and quickest thing I can produce and that's usually what gets ordered more often than not.

I use the back of my hand to wipe away the sweat from my forehead, then take a step back. I'm behind on my orders because I don't need any money right now, so this is really more for fun and to keep my skills honed than anything else.

I smile and run a hand gently down the side of its face. It isn't afraid of me anymore because it has accepted its fate and I appreciate when they're like this. It makes the work easier for me and the process more bearable for them.

I don't like to hurt them, but I'd be lying if I said it didn't give me a hard-on from time to time.

The first cut is always sweet like nectar and the last stitch is the release of euphoria. It can be likened to a sexual experience if one holds that kind of perversion, but I don't. To me, this is a job and nothing more, though sometimes I do have to fight the urge to touch my creations in ways I shouldn't.

I may not be completely done for the evening, but I'm satisfied with what I've accomplished so far and decide to call it a night.

"I'll finish you tomorrow," I promise it, kissing the forehead softly.

It manages a small smile, and nods as best as it can. I appreciate them more when they're like this and that's something they come to find out sooner rather than later.

I never mistreat the pets because that's not what I'm paid to do. I recreate them from the base design I'm given and make them into something of splendor and worthy of praise by their new owners.

I smile kindly at it and pull the sheet up to its neck so that it will be as comfortable as possible when I'm gone before I head for the door.

I live by the motto usually of not shitting where I eat, but because of the amount of money that's been rolling in, I've been able to move into a much bigger place which allows me to have a workroom on the top floor of the building.

I always did like the way loft apartments looked and I saved enough money to be able to buy the entire building so I don't have to worry about nosy neighbors poking about in my business.

Figuratively and literally.

I sigh heavily as I make my way toward the lift and lean back against the cool metal, waiting for it to stop on the bottom floor. That's what I use as my general living space, while the second floor is where I sleep and conduct my business.

Just as I reach my fridge and pull out a cool pitcher of water, the obnoxious sounds of open handed, rapid knocking greets my ears and I laugh. I put the pitcher on the counter and walk over to the door, pulling it open and grinning down at Aiden James, who looks up at me with the usual mischief dancing in her narrow, chocolate-brown eyes. I like her so much because she's different. She's a little sprite of a person and her silver hair makes her look like a fairy tale creature of sorts.

"You're not ready," she points out in confusion.

"For?" I ask, raising an eyebrow and leaning against the door.

"You promised to take me to The Lounge tonight," she replies, placing her hands on her hips.

"Is that why you're dressed up like that?" I inquire, nodding at her. I let out a low whistle and she laughs, pushing her way past me.

Aiden's wearing a tight, scarlet tube

top, leather pants, and her famous stripper heels—the kind that have the huge wedge in the front and the point of death in the back. They hike her up about another four inches, but she's so tiny that I don't think it really makes much of a difference. The way her clothes cling to her body show off her figure and even though she's not supermodel thin, she's so goddamn beautiful that no one seems to care.

That and the fact that she can beat the ever living shit out of anyone that tries to do her harm or crosses her in anyway seem to make the world work out in her favor.

"Don't you look good enough to eat," I say as she sways her hips, making a show of her entering my place as she tends to do when she's feeling pretty.

"Well, the kitchen is always open for you, Gray," she replies, glancing at me over her shoulder and wiggling her eyebrows. I groan as I laugh in embarrassment. Aiden's my best friend and we tend to banter back and forth like this a lot. She always manages to say something so damn salacious that she comes out the winner while I turn eighteen shades of crimson.

"*Anyway,*" I say, desperate to change the subject, "do you wanna just hang out here? I've been working all day and only stopped a little while ago. I'm beat."

"I know," she replies, hopping up onto the counter and swinging her legs.

"How?" I ask her curiously.

"You're still wearing your gloves, Einstein," she says, reaching for my pack of smokes on the counter and lighting one. I immediately scrunch my face and mimic a high-pitched tone, to which she laughs and tosses my lighter at me.

"Get cleaned up and let's get out of here. I'm sure you can use a night out after what you've been up to," she says, crossing her legs at the ankles and placing the cigarette in between her lips. She's right and she knows it, and the way she's eyeing me tells me that I agree with her.

"Yeah, just give me a few," I finally agree, as I turn and walk out of the kitchen area.

I decide to take the stairs this time because I know how impatient she can get. I don't spend more than twenty or so minutes in the shower scrubbing away any excess fluids that aren't mine and smile slightly when I notice that the drain is a slight crimson color. I thought I had bled the piece properly, but sometimes I get so into what I'm doing that I don't really notice little things like that.

Once I'm dry and my hair is neatly combed, I walk quickly to my bedroom and drop my towel, pulling on my boxers, then my fitted black v-neck and a loose pair of dark, blue denim jeans. I head into my closet and sit on the floor as I pull on some socks and my boots, then head back down to where I assume Aiden is waiting rather impatiently for me.

"Well, damn, Gray. You sure do know how to clean up nicely," she says, from her new spot on the floor. Her head is tilted in my direction and as I slide my smokes into my back pocket, she gets to her feet and loops an arm through mine.

"Let's go get fucked up!"

CHAPTER TWO

"Penn's here," she informs me with a mischievous grin on her face. The excitement in her tone fucks with me almost immediately.

I can feel the slight tremor that quakes through my body each time I hear that name and do my best to not look like I just won the lottery, because in all honesty, I'm not entirely sure that Penn even knows I exist.

Not yet, anyway.

"So?" I reply as nonchalantly as I can with a shrug. "That's not why I came out tonight."

"Sure it isn't," Aiden replies with a sly grin.

I chuckle nervously as I reach into my

pocket for my lighter. A cigarette will help calm my nerves right now and maybe I can convince Aiden to stop fraying them by letting me buy her a drink.

"Beer or shot?" I ask her after I've lit my cigarette. I grin as her eyes light up, reflecting the bright ashen fire at the end of my smoke. Aiden's kind of a lightweight when it comes to hard liquor, which is why I gave her the option. If she passes out on the floor, I won't have to be reminded every two minutes that Penn is here and I can look like the conquering hero by carrying her out to safety.

It's a way to kill two birds with one stone, really.

"Beer," she replies, the grin still on her face.

"Bitch," I grumble as I turn and lead the way toward the bar. Aiden giggles as she follows close behind, gripping me by the sides of my waist so she doesn't get lost in the push of the ever revolving crowd in this place. I have half a mind to shake her loose and watch her struggle to get back to me, but since she's the only friend I have in this place, I decide to play nice.

A lot of people know me here by name and they've seen my face plenty of times. To me, they're acquaintances, whereas Aiden is an actual, true friend.

I reach back and put an arm around her shoulder, pulling her around me and letting her have the only empty stool at the bar.

"Get whatever you want—I'll pay tonight," I say to her as I lean on the bar and narrow my eyes at the row of bottles against the wall. I don't know what I feel like, if anything at all, but I'm sure that Aiden will manage to run through the money I brought tonight. It doesn't bother me, though. She's a good kid and being in her company always pulls me out of any bullshit my mind wants to toss at me in my quiet moments.

"Aiden!"

I turn my attention away from the bottles and glance over at the voice that's greeting my drinking buddy for the evening and just as quickly turn my eyes away again.

"Hey, Penn! I didn't know you were

going to be here tonight!" she says, reaching over and giving her friend a quick hug.

Sure you didn't, I think with a sour taste in my mouth. That's probably the exact reason she insisted we come to this place tonight; because she knew exactly who would inhabit its walls.

"What you are drinking tonight, my fine little lady friend?" Penn asks when they pull apart. I roll my eyes and try not to sigh. So much for having a fun night out with Aiden—it seems she's already being kidnapped away from me by the one person that *still* hasn't noticed me even though I'm only a mere few feet away.

I slide out of the spot between her stool and the drunken bastard on the other side of me, and head for the door. I'm not going to try and pretend to be friendly and I won't try to regain her attention, either. It's obvious who she'd rather spend her time with, and I can't fault her for it because I would pick Penn over me too if given the opportunity.

Once I'm outside, I place a cigarette between my lips, light it, and inhale deeply.

I look up and down both sides of the street, unsure of which direction I want to take home today. I always like to try a path I've never traveled before—it's pretty calming and helps with the turmoil that's constantly raging inside of me.

"You're such a goddamn drama queen sometimes," Aiden's voice greets me fondly.

I turn around, my cigarette hanging from my lips, and almost choke on the smoke. She brought Penn with her and she seems good and determined to make us speak to each other.

"Anyway," she continues with a friendly eye roll as she turns her attention back toward Penn, "this is my very best friend, Gray Talbot. Gray, this is my very big pain in the ass, Penn Harris."

I cast a quick glance in his direction, nod to acknowledge his presence, and then turn my eyes back toward the furthest stretch of pavement from where he's standing. Being this close to him makes me fucking nervous—like I'll make an ass out of myself and say something completely stupid by just trying to have a conversation and I'd rather not.

"Okay, well. I'm gonna head home," I say to them, eyes still down the street.

"Hey," Aiden says sharply, giving my arm a tug. "We just got here! You can't leave!"

I shrug as I flick the ashes from the end of my cigarette and clear my throat.

"Got another one of those?"

I grunt as I pull the pack out of my back pocket and hold it out. Penn reaches into my half-smoked pack and fishes out a cigarette, then asks for a lighter. I'm becoming agitated, but I give him one anyway. Nothing like scaring off the guy you're jonesing for to really hammer home that nothing ever goes the way it should.

"Thanks," he says after he inhales deeply. "Fuck. Menthol. That's gonna open up my lungs."

I turn and glance at him again; an eyebrow raised as he and Aiden share a laugh. I can't tell if they're laughing at me, my choice of cigarette flavor, or just laughing for the sake of filling dead air. But the smile on Aiden's face is one that I'm used to. It's the same one she gives me once I've come down from some kind of epic meltdown, which tells me that at the very least, *she's* not laughing at me. My eyes wander over to Penn, who's watching me with curiosity and a grin curving the edge of his full lips. His larger than life, blue eyes are trying to lock onto mine, but I don't look at him long enough to allow it.

"Yeah."

I don't mean for the word to sound as cold as it comes out, yet somehow, I don't think he's bothered by it. It could be the way he chuckles before he pulls on his cigarette again, or quite honestly, it could all be in my head at this point. Sometimes it's hard for me to tell the difference between reality and fantasy and that's another reason I want to go home.

I've been out in public for about as long as I can stand and since I'm not scouting, and Aiden's been swept off her feet, I really don't have any business being outside of my workshop.

"Have fun tonight," I say softly to Aiden, leaning down and giving her a quick kiss on the cheek, before I turn on my heel to leave.

"Nah, fuck that."

Penn steps forward, grabs me by the arms, and shoves me back toward the establishment door. "I have a feeling you need to get good and loaded tonight, so I'm buying. Let's get drunk."

My body stiffens under his touch and I glance helplessly at Aiden who, at the moment, is desperately trying not to laugh. Penn puts a hand on my shoulder as we stand outside the door, takes one more drag of his cigarette and tosses it, before nodding at me to do the same.

I really wanted this whole thing.

But I do as I'm directed, letting him and Aiden each grip a shoulder and lead me back toward the bar. I guess tonight started out better than this morning.

Penn Harris finally knows I exist.

CHAPTER THREE

"So, tell me something about yourself, man," Penn says conversationally as he sips on his glass of Scotch. "Aiden's constantly going on and on about you and I was beginning to think you were a figment of her imagination since I haven't met you before tonight."

"I'm an artist," I mumble with a shrug.

"You should really see his pieces one day—his work is fucking fantastic," Aiden chimes in. I know what she's doing, but if she only knew how uncomfortable I felt right now, she'd stop and let me go home.

"Oh, that's cool. So, like, what kind of art do you do?" Penn asks, setting his glass down and giving me his undivided attention.

"Um, I work with textures, I guess," I

reply, glancing down at the drink in my hand.

Penn nods and steals a glance at Aiden who shrugs and turns her eyes up toward me. "Think you'd be interested in showing him your work sometime?"

My eyes turn cold and I give her a dangerous stare. She's halfway to drunk and that means she'll be willing to talk about anything and everything—including my line of work.

"Maybe," I reply evenly. "What do you do? For a living, I mean?" I ask him before I take a swig of my Vodka. With as much as I don't want to, I'm going to have to keep talking to keep her from flapping her goddamn gums about things she shouldn't.

"Trust fund kid," he replies with an eye roll. "I get paid just to exist."

I believe it, I think letting my eyes linger on him for a moment. It's only now that I'm seeing Penn clearly for the first time. His

30

wild, light brown hair sits messily on the top of his head, and his eyes are so damn big and beautiful that I can almost swear they can see the entire fucking universe. He's tall and thin—not as tall as I am, but tall enough to be able to look me almost directly in the eyes.

But his lips are my favorite thing about him. They're so big and look so fucking soft that I think I would die if I ever felt them against any part of my body.

A smirk starts to crease his mouth and I tear my eyes away from him, turning head to toe red in shame. It's obvious he knows I've mentally fucked him into oblivion by this point, and I think he's being kind by pretending not to let it bother him.

"What do *you* do, anyway? I don't think you ever told me," he says, mercifully turning his attention back toward Aiden.

"Fight."

"Really?" he asks with a laugh as he

crosses his arms loosely over his chest, "and that pays the bills?"

She nods as she takes a swig from her beer bottle. "The bigger the guys are the more money I get, so I usually try to go after the biggest fuckers when I'm hurting for cash. Other than that, Gray is always good for a loan when I can't get a fight."

"So, the two of you are really close?" he asks, using his forefinger and middle finger to point between us. I reach up and rub the back of my neck, content on letting Aiden take the reigns on this part of the conversation.

"Didn't I tell you he's my best friend?" she asks, shaking her head at him. "You weren't listening, were you? It's okay. I get it. Gray's fucking hot so it's hard to concentrate when he's around."

My eyes widen as I look down at my drink again. I can hear the blood rushing into my ears and am barely able to make out the sound of Penn's good-natured laughter.

"Alright, it was good to meet you," I say to him, as I start to get to my feet. "Can you get her home safely? I really have to get back to my place now."

"She's just teasing you man," he says, waving off my second attempt to escape for the evening. "Hang out for a while—get drunk! Seems like you need it more than she does."

I take a deep breath and shoot back the rest of my Vodka, pull out my wallet, and drop a hundred-dollar bill on the bar top.

"That should cover me and Little Ms. Beer Slinger here. I'll see you guys around."

I stand all the way up, turn, and begin to push my way toward the door, completely ignoring Penn and Aiden calling out to me. I don't want to be here anymore and that's something neither of them can understand, so I'll leave them to get drunk and more than likely end up in bed together.

At least she'll be able to tell me what that feels like, I think glumly as I push the door open and turn left. I've been this way before plenty of times, but I figure that if I take an extra three blocks down, it'll be kind of new and give me more time to shake away the sudden cobwebs that are threatening to strangle the humanity out of me from my mind.

The longer I wander the streets, the further down I go. Into the unknown, into the darkness of my mind, into a spiral of unwarranted jealousy.

Aiden wasn't hitting on Penn and he wasn't hitting on her that I can tell. They seem to be just friends, but I'm sure if either of them get enough drinks in them, then the "kitchen" will more than likely be open for him too.

"Fuck."

I run a hand irritably back through

my hair as I keep walking, ending up somewhere between Hell and Skid Row. My eyes wander down the dark alleyways, smiling each time I hear a moan, and shaking my head when I see a pimp roll a John for his money and kick him back under the exposing eyes of the moonlight.

Each sin—each need that wasn't fulfilled is written shamefully in his eyes as he struggles to shove his little pecker back into his pants and hobble down the street, blood dripping from a small wound on the side of his forehead.

"You got a problem, motherfucker?"

I turn my eyes back toward the alley and raise an eyebrow at the pimp who's walking toward me with ill intent in his eyes and I grin.

"Not unless you do," I reply evenly, pulling out another cigarette and lighting it. I inhale deeply as I hold his eyes, and something in the way my stare meets his, makes him slightly uneasy on his feet.

"Keep moving unless you've got money," he barks at me, his voice cracking slightly.

I'm tempted to crush his neck under my boot but decide against it when his hooker comes a little closer. She's pretty, or at least she used to be, and she looks so damn young and scared of him, that it gives me an idea.

"How much for that one?" I ask, nodding in her direction.

"That one?" he asks, rubbing his chin. "That's some prime pussy right there, so the question is, how much you got on you?"

I roll my eyes and sigh, the smoke leaving my mouth like a cloud from a chimney and reach for my wallet.

"I'll give you fifty bucks and that's it," I say, holding out the money to him and securing my wallet back in my pocket.

"I didn't ask how much you would give me, I asked how much you have," he says evenly, taking a step closer to me.

"Can I tell you a story?" I say suddenly, using my thumb to rub the middle of my forehead. "I never cared for people that tried to take more than they deserve—bastards like you, give working guys like me a bad name, you know what I mean? So, the last time I came across someone who thought so highly of himself, he ended up pretty much a blood stain on the bottom of my heel. He ended up in the ICU and you know what? I *still* took what the fuck I wanted from him just to teach him a goddamn lesson in humility. So, is that where you want to go? Underneath the heel of my boot? Because believe it or not, I'm itching to take some of my pent-up aggression out on someone right now and you seem easy enough to take down. If not, then just take the fifty and let me have the girl."

By the end of my little rhetoric, I'm so close to him that he can more than likely smell the liquor on my breath and taste the nicotine staining my lips.

It's enough to back him the fuck off and nod in agreement, waving her toward me. I toss the money onto the ground as I wrap an arm around her shoulders and continue my little stroll down streets unknown to me.

"What's your name?" she asks me timidly when we're out of earshot.

"Gray," I reply curtly.

I'm not entirely sure what I'm going to do with her yet. I have no intention on fucking her because I have no desire to be in bed with someone who's being paid to be there with me.

She tries to chat with me all the way back to my loft, and I allow it. It takes my mind off of Aiden and Penn, which is why I'm so welcoming of this hourly companion.

I clear my throat as I reach for my keys and unlock the first set of doors, holding one open and letting her in first. She smiles at me, the freckles on her face seemingly glowing in the moonlight, as her flash of wild, strawberry blonde hair disappears into the stairwell.

I turn and glance down the street before I secure the door behind us. I may not have any want to sleep with her, but I do have a small desire to save her from her life of spreading her legs for random strangers at the behest of a man that forces her to do so.

And the only way to do that is to make her into something beautiful. Sometimes, pre-constructed pieces sell for much higher amounts than anything commissioned, and I think she'll be happier as a pet than she would be leaving my home to go back to that evil man.

So I'll do my best to make something wonderful out of her and she'll understand. They always do in the end.

CHAPTER FOUR

Halfway up the stairs, I let out a loud sigh and stop walking for a moment. The young hooker turns around and glances down at me curiously, but I don't know how to tell her that making her into something beautiful will have to wait another day because my workspace is preoccupied at the moment.

"Everything okay?" she asks me cautiously. I almost laugh out loud at the look on her face. She stood by and watched me back her pimp down, threatening to stomp him to death, and only now she's concerned about the man she's gone home with?

"No. I'm sorry, it's just I forgot something

important, but it's nothing that can't wait until tomorrow," I explain, forcing a friendly smile across my face.

She nods once as she turns and continues up the rest of the flight until she gets to the elevator door.

"So, is this whole place yours?" she inquires, glancing up and down the dark hallway.

"All mine," I confirm, pushing the button to open the doors.

"Wow. You must be really rich, or something, huh?" she presses curiously.

"Or something," I reply with a smile, holding out my arm toward the now open elevator doors. "After you."

"Thanks," she replies, pushing a strand of hair behind her ears and stepping in. She seems to be a bit calmer the more I converse with her and to be honest, I don't care at this point. I have no use for her anymore and I'm kind of aggravated with myself for forgetting about the pet I already have upstairs.

Once we reach my main floor, I pull up the elevator gate and let her step out first. It's at this moment that I realize I have no idea what her name is.

"So, like I said before, I'm Gray," I say, turning around and pulling the gate down. She falls into step beside me as we walk the few feet to my door and waits patiently for me to unlock it.

"Julie."

"Nice to meet you."

"Yeah, same."

I appreciate the small amount of silence she allows me as I pull the door open and once again, allow her to go first. I may not have much for humanity these days, but I'm pretty damn good at remembering my manners when I need to.

"Home sweet hell," I say to her with a

grin as soon as we're inside. She giggles and glances around the floor curiously. There's nothing in this particular space that will give anything away to my work, so I don't mind if she has a poke around, which she clearly wants to do.

"You can look around," I assure her with a nod. "Just don't wander off too far. This place is bigger than it looks and I'm not in the mood for a game of hide and seek."

She raises an eyebrow and instead of satiating her obvious curiosity of where I live, she takes a step closer to me as a wicked grin slips across her half full lips.

"What *are* you in the mood for then?" she asks in a new found, throaty tone.

I suck my teeth and look straight into her eyes. I can tell that I've unnerved her a bit by doing so, but the professional inside of her that's used to earning her money, doesn't back down.

"What I want, I left behind in a bar," I

reply bluntly, crossing my arms over my chest. "Think you can take my mind off of it?"

"I'm pretty sure I can manage that," she agrees, tilting her head to the side and slipping her arms around my waist. The width of my intertwined arms makes for an awkward embrace on her part, but I have no intention of dropping them because I'm not entirely sure yet if I'm in the mood for such a constantly misused pussy.

I roll my eyes and decide to relent.

"On your knees then," I say softly, nodding at her.

Her grin widens as she licks her lips and it takes everything in me not to shudder. Julie is not unattractive by any means, but the fact that she can go from woman to whore in such a quick flash kind of rattles me.

Before I have a chance to properly react to her switch, she's pulled my dick out of my pants and swallows as much of it as she cans. I close my eyes and pretend that she's Penn—with her full lower lip, she very well could be if I can just imagine it hard enough. I place a hand gently on the back of her head as she bobs it up and down, purposely gagging herself on me, then rubbing her saliva up and down the length before swallowing it again.

I wonder if Penn would suck me off like this or if he would let me do it to him. I take in a deep, shaky breath as she reaches up and cups my balls giving them a gentle squeeze which makes me move my hips. I pull my shirt off and toss it to the ground; she can use that to wipe her mouth off when we're done here.

When her head goes further down my shaft, my hips thrust forward forcing it further down her throat.

I lean my head back and let out another breath as she quickens her pace, my balls beginning to tighten in her grip. I can feel my

45

release coming and I find myself wondering how many times she's let a man cum inside of her mouth before.

I look down at her and place my other hand on the back of her head, interlacing the fingers, and continue to thrust my hips a little harder than before.

"Little Julie, the corner whore, fifty dollars gets her knees on the floor," I say in a sing-song tone. I grin when she begins to struggle against my hands, obviously offended by my choice of words, but I don't let up thrusting. If this is all I can stomach from her tonight, then this is what she'll give me.

"Don't stop now—I'm almost done," I grunt, pushing her head down further.

She tries to push me away but I'm too far into the moment, too close to cumming, to give her any sort of reprieve. I assume she's used to being so roughly handled anyway, and I'm not forcing her to do anything she wouldn't have finished had I not composed my little sonnet for her.

I'm so close to the edge. I can feel it. It's starting to make my body shake, my knees are becoming weak, and I'm almost done with her.

I move my hands, still interlocked, down to her neck and use my thumbs to press on her windpipe. Her struggle starts to become violent as I cut off her air, and just when I'm ready to press down and kill the little bitch, the familiar sound of raucous hand slapping against the door reaches my ears.

"Fuck!"

I push her away and let her land on her back, while I shove my dick back into my pants. Aiden's here and I'm aggravated because I didn't even get to get my fucking rocks off.

Julie whimpers and I turn and give her a deadly stare as I make my way toward the door.

"Little Julie—if you want to keep sucking dicks for a living, I suggest you shut your fucking mouth about what just happened," I warn her ominously.

Room in my workshop or not, I'm sure I can find something to do with her if she tells Aiden how rudely I just handled her. It's not that I have a thing for Aiden, because I don't, it's just that she sees me a certain way and even though she knows what I do for a living, she chooses to ignore that side of me and see me as a person and not a paid mutilator.

"Stop slapping the goddamn door!" I bark at her as I pull it open.

Aiden grins as she leans against the now open door frame. Her right eyebrow arches when she sees that I'm shirtless and glistening from sweat.

"Busy?" she asks pointedly.

"Not anymore," I grumble, running a hand back through my hair. "What's up?"

She smirks and glances behind her, drawing my eyes to the obvious thing I had managed to miss.

Penn Harris is standing behind Aiden and as they exchange a knowing glance, I wonder why the Earth hasn't opened up and swallowed me yet.

"Maybe we should come back some other time," he suggest to Aiden, turning his back to us and heading toward the elevator.

"Get rid of whoever's here," she hisses, leaning in toward me. "I'll go back and get your crush."

"How?" I ask, pulling her back toward me.

"Toss them out the window for all I fucking care. He wanted to make sure you got home safe and I think it would be a nice gesture if you let us come in," she shoots back in a hushed tone. Before I have a chance to ask anymore questions, Aiden turns around and jogs toward the elevator where Penn is waiting patiently.

I close the door to my loft and run my hands over my face. I have no idea what to do with Julie, but I refuse to let him come in and find me with a fucking hooker.

"Fuck it," I say to myself.

I walk quickly into the space I left her in and pick her up off the floor. She's still upset with me because she tries her best to pull away from me. Being much stronger than her helps my situation because I twist her arm and drag her toward the staircase.

The workshop may be occupied right now, but this bitch can ruin something for me that I want more than I even realized until this moment.

"Come on!" I grunt at her angrily, as I begin to drag her up the stairs.

"I thought you were nice," she sobs as she continues her struggle to get away from me.

I raise an eyebrow at her and smirk when an idea suddenly comes to mind. "You want me to be nice to you? Fine."

I let Julie's arm go and she begins to teeter on the step we've reached halfway to the top. Her arms pinwheel at her sides, but she still manages to lose her footing as she goes tumbling violently, landing in a heap at the bottom of the stairs.

I jog back down and crouch over her. She's still breathing but it's ragged—she won't last much longer and even though I think it would be more of a mercy to end her, I simply don't have the time right now.

I'll leave her in the dark, cold staircase to gasp for air that will never reach her lungs as I go back out and entertain my guests.

Much like pre-constructed pieces, sometimes dead ones fetch a much higher sum than the ones that I've been commissioned for.

CHAPTER FIVE

"Sorry about that," I reply sheepishly as I reenter the room. Aiden and Penn are already inside the place, the door still open, and him lingering by the doorway.

Aiden grins at me as she tosses my crumpled shirt in my direction and Penn shrugs, a friendly smile on his face.

"Did we catch you at a bad time?" he asks.

"Huh? Oh. No," I say, pulling the shirt over my head. "Just taking care of some late-night shit. Um, do you guys want something to drink? Water? Juice? Coffee?"

"Why, Gray Talbot, as I live and breathe—

those manners of yours are shining through again," Aiden teases with a chuckle.

"I guess," I say with a nervous glance in Penn's direction. "Did you guys want something?"

"Just to make sure you got here alright. You left pretty quickly and I don't know— it felt like you were in a bad mood," Penn replies with a shrug.

"I meant to drink," I tell him softly, glancing down at my boots.

"Oh!" He laughs good-naturedly as he takes a step into the room. "No, I'm pretty sure I had enough of anything to drink for one night."

"Okay," I reply quietly, my eyes wandering back up to his. I don't understand how it's possible to have eyes so big and blue, but God I wish they would look at me the way I know mine look at him.

"Do you mind if we crash here tonight, Gray? I really don't feel like doing anymore walking and you know I don't trust that Uber bullshit," Aiden states, yawning loudly.

"Um, yeah. I'll go get you some blankets and pillows. Give me a few," I say as I leave them in the room. I hear my front door finally close and the click of the lock as it's secured in place. I'm not entirely sure who closed the door, but I'm grateful for it because that means that Penn won't leave.

Once I'm up in my room, I grab some blankets and pillows from the linen closet, before I run back down, stepping over Julie's still wheezing body.

I give her crumpled body a nudge with the edge of my foot and she replies by trying to take in a ragged series of breaths.

I roll my eyes and step back out into the hallway, locking the door securely behind me. I have a feeling that if Penn found my little purchased fuck toy dying in the stairwell, he'd more than likely make a run for it.

It takes me a little bit of wandering around until I find them in the living room. Penn is sitting in my recliner, his long legs spread on either side of the bottom half, laughing at something that Aiden's saying.

"Here," I say, holding out what I offered them. Aiden glances over her shoulder at me from where she's sitting on the couch and grins.

"Thanks!"

She reaches for a pillow and blanket, tossing it at Penn, before she retrieves a set for herself.

"You know, if you stay out here with us tonight, we can make it a slumber party," she suggests with a sly grin.

"Aiden, it's almost three o'clock in the fucking morning—I just want to go to sleep," I reply with a heavy sigh.

"By yourself?" Penn asks curiously.

"How else?" I snap at him irritably. Once

again, my entire body turns crimson and I'm so embarrassed at the way I just barked at him, that I bite my lip and look away.

His friendly chuckle tells me that he didn't take it to heart. It's late, I'm halfway to drunk with unannounced guests, and a dying whore in the staircase. I haven't even gotten off yet and I'm just not in the mood to play twenty questions, regardless of who they're coming from.

"Sorry," I mumble.

"You apologize a lot," Penn remarks. "I didn't expect that from you for some reason."

"Yeah. Well. Sorry."

Aiden giggles, Penn laughs, and a small smile curves the edge of my lips. I get it, I really do. Anyone that sees me for what I am on the outside expects a hard ass because of my sleepy green eyes, my usually neat hair, and the definition of muscle to me. I'm not a muscle head by any means, I just like to keep myself strong and ready for anything I may need to capture or fight my way out of.

It's funny.

Penn is tall and thin and I'm tall and well built. No one would ever look at the two of us and think that we could be together—not the trust fund kid and the sociopathic murderer.

Considering I don't know what exactly he's into, I don't think it even matters. I just have always had this little fantasy ever since I first laid eyes on him during a night out with Aiden and have dreamed almost every single night since of being everything he's ever wanted. Penn would be able to command me to do anything his heart desired, and I would be the submissive, subservient, obedient little boy, eager to please his owner.

I guess in a way, that makes me a pet too.

"Did those hurt?" he asks, nodding at my arms and breaking the uncomfortable silence.

"Huh?" I ask, glancing down.

"The tattoos."

"Oh, no. Not really," I reply with a shrug. "I've felt worse than a needle."

He nods again and cuts his eyes toward Aiden who's watching us both from the couch. She's laying on her back now, pillow behind her head, and blanket pulled up to her chin, a thoughtful expression on her face.

"I punched him once," she explains, turning her face toward Penn. "That's what he means by that."

Penn grins and I rub the back of my neck. It's starting to get so hot in this fucking room that I almost feel like I'm beginning to suffocate.

Gray Talbot, with a crush so severe, can't

stand to be around him whenever he's near, I taunt myself mentally.

"Stop sulking and bring your big ass over to this couch," Aiden instructs, sliding her legs off the side.

I shake my head and snicker quietly, but I do what she asks me too. At this point, I could curl up on the floor and fall asleep, but her offer is nicer because it will give me somewhere comfortable to lay my head down for the evening.

"Want my pillow?" Penn asks, as I lie down on the opposite end of Aiden.

"Nah, I'll be alright," I reply as I pull my shirt off again and toss it on the floor. Aiden lets go of her blanket and allows me to pull it halfway up my body before she brings her legs back up and turns onto her side, curling her tiny body into a ball.

"Thanks, though," I add, realizing that I hadn't said it yet.

"Cool," Penn replies with a nod as he

pulls the lever to bring up the bottom half of the recliner and situates himself on the piece of furniture.

"Good night, guys," Aiden says tiredly, with another loud yawn.

"Good night," Penn replies, closing his eyes and taking a deep breath.

"Night," I offer quietly as I turn my eyes toward the high ceiling and stare.

There's no way in hell I'll be able to go to sleep knowing he's only a few feet away, so I'll just have to do my best to fake it until morning. When they're both gone, I'll take Julie up to the top floor and then take a nap.

CHAPTER SIX

I wake up to the sound of hushed conversation with the occasional chuckle here and there. I don't know what time it is, but I feel like I may have slept longer than I should have because my body feels much more rested than it normally does.

I wonder if Julie died yet, I think with a wide yawn as I stretch my arms over my head.

"It's about time you woke up! Breakfast is getting cold—get over here!"

Aiden?

I turn onto my stomach and glance over the top of the couch arm, narrowing my eyes to gaze into the kitchen area. Yeah, that little frame and wild bed hair definitely belongs to Aiden. I had almost forgotten she came over last night.

But that means—

My mouth feels like cotton when I remember that Aiden didn't come alone. A tall, thin figure moves around her and meets my eyes as best as I can tell. I turn around immediately and lay on my back again, rubbing the sleep away, wondering if I look presentable enough to even sit up, let alone go join them.

"I made western omelettes, home fries, and bacon—hope that's okay," Penn calls out to me.

Beautiful and he can cook.

I wave a hand over my head in thanks, not making a move to leave my spot on the couch.

A loud sigh escapes from Aiden as well as the unmistakable sound of her hands hitting her legs, followed by her footsteps toward me. She hops onto the couch, straddling me, and gives me chest a gentle push.

"Get the fuck up and get over there. The man cooked for you," she hisses.

"He cooked because he was hungry," I reply, gently pushing her off of my lap. When she lands on the floor with a dull thud, I turn on my side and grin at her. "Did you let him eat-in while I was asleep?"

"Fuck off, Gray," she grumbles getting to her feet and swaying her hips, making it halfway back to Penn when I realize I need her help. I sit up and run my hands back through my hair, before I glance at them and notice that his eyes are still on me. He's watching me with a curiosity I can't quite place and it's making me slightly apprehensive.

"Hey, Aiden," I call out to her. She turns around, halfway to Penn, and arches her eyebrows at me. I motion for her to come back because I need her to do the one thing I know I don't have it in me to do.

"What's up?" she asks with a sigh.

"Get rid of him," I say to her softly, lowering my eyes to the floor.

"Gray," she says as patiently as she can, crouching down and taking my hands in hers. "It was *his* idea to come last night. Even though I told him that you would be okay, he insisted. He said he didn't like that you left in a bad mood and he wanted to make sure that everything was okay. I didn't want to come—Penn did."

I smile and scoff.

Aiden may be a pain in the ass, and she may make me crazy sometimes, but there will never be a better friend than the spitfire in front of me.

"Does he know?" I ask, raising my eyes slowly to hers. Aiden's never been able to lie to me and when she tries, her eyes tell me everything I need to know.

"No. I haven't told him," she promises, shaking her head.

"Do you … do you think I have a chance?" I continue, biting my lower lip.

"I don't know, honey. And you won't know unless you get off of your ass and *try*."

She's using her gentlest tone to try and persuade me to be a man. Normally it works, but I don't know if I can do this. I don't even know if Penn is into cock or if he's into pussy or both, because I don't have the balls to even bring it up. How does one even ask that? I'm pretty sure, *hey can I suck your cock* wouldn't exactly go over well with a guy like him.

"Okay," I finally relent. She smiles as I get to my feet and stretch my arms over my head and laugh when she pokes my sides. It's my soft spot—the one place that can always make me laugh and she only does it when she wants me to be in a good mood.

Even though work has been great, and

my pieces get better and better, I've been a miserable bastard and it worries her.

I follow her into the kitchen and thank Penn quietly when he hands me a fixed plate. I'm starting to wonder if he thinks I'm something of a child because I could have done this myself, or if maybe he's just being kind.

Penn pulls himself up on the counter and turns his attention back to Aiden and they continue whatever conversation they were having that woke me up.

"Yeah but I'm not the one that got up on the bar and damn near stripped myself naked," Penn teases her.

"What?" I ask. My fork is halfway to my mouth and I'm staring at Penn, waiting for him to repeat himself.

"Nothing, man. She was just having fun," he replies, crossing his arms over his chest.

"And were you going to protect her

if someone tried to harm her? Were you going to make sure that nothing happened to Aiden if there were one too many people crowding her?" I snap at him.

His eyes widen for a moment, as he rolls them toward Aiden then back at me.

"I can take care of myself and you know it, besides, I wasn't *that* damn drunk," Aiden quips, giving Penn a playful shove. "You'll have to take that with a grain of salt. Gray is just really protective of me even though he knows I can take him if it ever came down to it."

I walk over to the counter and put my plate down. My stomach is sour because of how I just barked at him and I don't have an appetite anymore.

"Want me to make you something else?" he asks.

"No. I'm sorry for snapping at you," I reply quietly, turning my eyes toward his body.

"Stop apologizing—we're fine. I would probably be the same way if I were in your shoes when it comes to little Miss Toughy here," he says, waving off my anger.

I nod before I turn and begin to walk away from them, but as Aiden lets out another loud sigh, Penn reaches over and grabs my shoulder.

"I heard some groaning last night from the stairwell. I took care of it for you," he whispers, his breath hot on my ear.

CHAPTER SEVEN

Aiden is in the shower now.

I'm sitting on my couch staring at Penn who's back on the recliner, his long legs splayed on either side, a wide grin across his full lips.

"Why do you look at me like that?" he asks, tilting his head to the side.

"Like what?" I ask defensively. The reality of his question snaps me back to the moment because even though I've been silently staring at him, I've been a million miles away in a world of my own.

"Like you want to eat me or something," he replies with a chuckle.

"Sorry."

He rolls his eyes and sighs. I can tell that my habit of apologizing is becoming something of a nuisance with him, but it's just in my nature.

"We're gonna have to snap you out of that. Saying you're sorry is fine but saying it so damn much is kind of annoying," he says, cutting his eyes back toward me. The way he's looking at me now, from the corner of his eyes, the grin again prominent on his lips is actually terrifying and exciting all at the same time.

I shift in my seat and hope to God he can't see that the look he's giving me has made me hard because that's something I won't apologize for.

"How long have you known Aiden?" he asks, reclining the chair and stretching his long arms over his head.

"Um, for a while, I guess," I reply with a shrug. "Have you ever been to one of her fights?"

"Can't say I have," he replies in a semi-bored tone.

"She's amazing—fucking phenomenal really because you'd never expect someone that damn tiny to be as savage as she gets when she has an opponent," I gush proudly.

"What kind of fighting does she do, anyway? Boxing?" he asks, crossing one of his legs over the other.

"Bare-knuckle."

"No shit?" He looks at me and lets out a low whistle. "I didn't think that little shit had it in her. I've been to some of those fights—bet a shit ton of money on them, too. I've never seen her at one though."

I shrug again.

"I don't like her doing them, so I give her money to keep her away from it. She has a ten-oh record, but the last one was brutal. Big motherfucker—knocked out some of her teeth so I paid for them to get fixed," I explain.

"Are you guys together?" he asks suddenly.

"What? No! She's just my friend," I reply defensively. "No, I've never felt like that about Aiden. *Ever.*"

"Hm," he says with a nod.

"If you're interested, she's wide open," I offer softly. I can feel every ounce of confidence that I don't have seeping through the couch onto the floor. He's asking too many questions about her to not want to fuck her at the very least.

"I'm not. I do have a question though."

I raise my eyes toward him and wait.

"Why did you have a girl in the stairwell?"

I let out a heavy sigh.

"I came across her and her pimp last night when he was beating up one of her

Johns and rolling him for his money. I felt bad for her, so I paid for her company for the evening. She fell down the stairs, so I left her there," I reply with a shrug.

"Did you fuck her?" he asks, the ends of his lips curving slightly.

"No."

"You're lying. Know how I know? You looked like the aftershock of a sweaty fuck last night when we got here," he says with a laugh.

"She gave me head."

"Was it good?"

"I was getting there," I confess uncomfortably.

Penn laughs and clasps his hands behind his head. But the longer he sits in silence, the more curious I become about something.

"Hey, how did you get into the stairwell

anyway?" I ask arching an eyebrow at him.

"Aiden snores. She woke me up, I was bored, I looked around, I heard the groans. I realized the door was locked so I picked it. I'll buy you a new one."

"What did you do with her?" I press.

"That's a surprise for another day," he says with a smirk. "Don't you look all sweet and innocent?"

His sudden change of subject confuses me until Aiden's wet, bare feet slap the floor on her way into the living room.

"What are you two talking about?" she asks, rubbing her damp hair with the towel. She's wearing a pair of my basketball shorts and is in her bra.

"I was just telling Gray that you snore like a goddamn bull in your sleep," Penn explains.

"Shut up! No I don't!" she yells, tossing the towel at him. He laughs and catches it before it hits him and throws it back at her.

"Whatever," he replies, stealing a glance at me and grinning again.

I clear my throat as I lean back against the couch cushions. "Listen, I've got a long day ahead of me, so..."

Aiden rolls her eyes. "Come on Penn. The great master has to get back to his work and he can't concentrate with an audience."

They both get to their feet and she tells me that she'll bring my shorts back some other day to which I agree. I don't mind when she takes my clothes—she probably has an entire closet full of my shit and I know I'll get it back one day.

I walk them to the front door and hold it open as they walk through; Aiden first, followed by Penn. Just as I'm about to close the door and head back upstairs, Penn turns around and pops up the collar of his jacket before he smooths it out.

"I'll see you around, Gray," he says,

glancing at the staircase door behind me.

I feel uneasy, sick. There's something not right about Penn and coming from me—that means a hell of lot more than it would coming from anyone else.

Penn has secrets that I need to find out because if he's willing to hide one of mine, he obviously has the upper-hand in whatever game he seems to have just initiated.

CHAPTER EIGHT

"I just don't get it, you know? How he can be so okay with what he found or how he could just get rid of it without telling me what he did and act like it was just another day in his life," I muse with a sigh. "He's not like me—he looks much too delicate, too fragile to be able to do the things that I've done, but he seems to have the same disregard for inferior stock like I do. Of course, he could just be fucking with my head like everyone likes to do for some reason."

I shift on the stool and cross my arms over my chest, the sound of the thick, plastic apron squeaking slightly as I tighten my arms.

"Do you think I have a chance? I think I'm okay looking enough to at least blow him, don't you?" I ask.

A muffled grunt is the reply and I'm not entirely sure why I expected conversation. The pet I've been working on had its mouth sewn shut two days into the transformation because it wouldn't stop screaming and crying. Lately, though, I've been thinking of undoing the stitching because its become much more compliant, but I can't. Part of the order was for a quiet one and the only way I could think of making that happen was to seal its mouth permanently.

"Can you at least nod or shake your head when I ask you this next question?" I beg, glancing at it. It nods and waits. "Okay," I say as I blow out my breath, "would you want me? If circumstances were different, I mean. Like would you fuck me?"

It blinks rapidly a few times, obviously shocked at my question, but I can't help it. I have no self-confidence these days and that's why I throw myself into my work. While it's true that I have the traits of someone who gives no fucks about how anyone perceives me, how I perceive myself is important, and it's just not there anymore.

"Would you?" I ask it again nervously. I bite my lower lip while it ponders my question, taking me in as best as it can from the table it's strapped to, before it looks back up into my eyes and nods once.

I let out a huge sigh of relief and smile. Before I acquired it, it was so beautiful. I watched it for days and nights on end wondering why someone would want something so magnificent to be transformed into a pet, but that wasn't up to me and the money had already been transferred so I took it and began my work.

I don't think it hates me like it used to, and I don't think it minds when I'm around anymore. Even though it knows that comes with more modifications and with some pain, I do my best to be quick and always attempt to dull the senses of my projects before I make any nicks or cuts.

I may be nothing more than a man, but when it comes to my work, I'm God and they know it. I can make them into anything that's desired and I can destroy them just the same.

The alpha and the omega.

"Okay, well," I say, getting to my feet, "since you've been honest with me, I'll leave you alone for a few days. You're not due for completion until the end of next week anyway so we have some time."

It closes its eyes and straightens its head again. It has nothing left to offer me right now because its upset that I won't finish it tonight. I understand that, but I'm a perfectionist and we do have time, so it will have to figure out how to deal with working on my schedule.

I take the apron off and hang it on the door on my way out. I only wear that when I plan major modifications, and since I've had my little confidence boost, I don't think I'm in the mood for work.

I'd rather lounge around or maybe see if I can find Julie. It would be interesting to know where in the building she is or at the very least what Penn has done with her.

I lock the door to my workshop and walk down the hallway toward the elevator. I'm so lost in my own little fantasy world where Penn and I are a thing, that when the elevator doors open, and I step in, I find myself wondering if maybe Aiden would give me his phone number.

Not that I'd ever use it, I think with a sigh as I push the button to take me to the second floor.

As I make my way down the hallway toward the door down below, I find myself staring at the back of Aiden, who's hand slapping at the door.

"Hey," I call out curiously.

She turns around and even in the dim light I can see that's something's wrong. I can see the tears streaming down her face, black from the mascara that she wore the night before and smeared on the back of her hands.

"What the fuck is going on?" I ask walking over to her quickly.

But when she collapses into my arms, I see that the tears aren't from sadness, they're from laughter and she's shaking much too hard to tell me what's gotten to her. I push open the door and take her inside, walking her over to the couch and sit her down, my arm wrapped loosely around her shoulder.

Patience has never been one of my virtues unless it's when I'm working and Aiden's hollow laughter—her gasps for air, are starting to grate on my nerves.

"Get a grip, kid," I say to her through grit teeth. "You sound like a dying seal."

Aiden pulls away from me, lays on her back, and places her feet on my chest. I hold my arms out to my sides and raise an eyebrow. At this point, I'm starting to think she's lost her goddamn mind, until she taunts me.

"You'll never guess what I found out?" she asks, in a sing-song tone. She wipes away the tears again and tilts her head to the side.

"What?"

"He's coming back," she declares, her eyes wide with joy and terror alike.

CHAPTER NINE

"Who is?" I ask, moving her feet off of my chest.

"Max," she replies, rolling her eyes, "who the else would I be talking about?"

"Oh," I say, in realization. I get her mania now. Max is the big motherfucker that knocked her teeth out and almost put her in the hospital. "Okay, and?"

Aiden sighs and sits up, pushing her hair behind her ears. "And I've got another chance to show him what's up and redeem myself from last time."

I eye Aiden wearily. Max Boothe is about six-foot-three and is two-hundred fifty pounds of solid muscle. The fact that Aiden even survived the first round was a fucking miracle in itself and she wants to fight him again?

"What if I say no?" I ask counter.

"Then you say no. You're not my father, uncle, grandfather, brother, husband, or boyfriend. I don't need your permission to fight anyone," she huffs, getting to her feet and moving over to the recliner.

"How much is it worth?" I ask, doing mental calculations in my head. Those bare-knuckle fuckers make bank when they win, and I know that Aiden has every intention of winning, but I also think I have enough left to bribe her out of doing it.

"More than you've got," she replies with a smirk. "This is the rematch of the century and people are coming out for this one by the dozens—lots of money getting tossed at us for it."

"You already agreed to it?" I ask her

incredulously. How the hell did she find the time to do this since this morning? I sigh. Considering Aiden is a big draw just herself, it wouldn't surprise me if she had an organizer waiting for her when she got home this morning.

"Yup, and the cock du jour is putting a ton of money on me winning," she states proudly.

I wrinkle my nose at her. Sometimes she says the craziest shit and it usually gets a laugh out of me, but I don't find the humor in this.

That reminds me.

"Aiden? Penn says he's never seen you fight before, but I could swear that I saw him at one of your bouts. Am I crazy?" I ask, running a hand over my face.

"Well, that's obvious. You *are* crazy, but you're letting your crush take over your senses," she says, pulling her legs underneath her. "Honestly, I don't know if he's ever been to one of my fights. That's not how I met him, remember?"

I let my breath out in a huff and fall back against the couch cushions, my arms at my sides, and nod.

"I know."

"Does that bother you still?" she asks softly.

"No."

"You're lying."

I can feel the agitation rising in me, so I decide to change the subject.

"What's the biggest bet going right now?" I ask, letting my eyes drift toward the ceiling.

"I think it's Penn's," she replies with a laugh.

"How much?"

"Five thousand."

Fucking trust fund kid.

"Okay, well, let me know when the fight is, and I'll come," I say, finally relenting. There's nothing I can say or do that will make Aiden walk away from that kind of cash.

"It's on Thursday night."

"Aiden, it's fucking Sunday," I reply, staring at her.

"You know that's one of the many things I like about you, Gray—you're so goddamn smart," she says with a laugh.

I grit my teeth and tear my eyes away from her again. Aiden's not being cruel to me and she's not mocking me. She's always been kind to me and she'd never say anything that she knows will afflict my soul further than it's already broken, but sometimes, the things she says does manage to hurt—even if it's just a little sting.

"I know what might make you feel better," she says as she leans forward on the recliner and smiling at me.

I grunt.

I don't know what she's offering but she knows if it's anything other than her friendly company, I'm not interested.

"Wanna shape me up?"

A small smile plays across my lips as I feel the anger and hurt leave me almost immediately.

"Get off your ass and get into the bathroom, you little shit. Let's make you presentable."

Aiden laughs and gets to her feet, then walks over to where I'm sitting and pulls me off the couch.

"Can I buzz you?" I ask her playfully as I rub the top of her head.

"I need to go short for this fight, but not *that* short," she replies, laughing again.

I smile as she throws an arm around my

waist and let her light up with excitement all the way to the bathroom. I have to start thinking of Aiden as the tough girl she is because she won't hesitate to remind me or attempt to put me in my place.

I'll still do my best to talk her out of it and if that doesn't work, then I'll take her place. I've never been in an organized bare-knuckle fight, but I refuse to let her get hurt again the way she did before.

Besides, maybe if Penn sees what I'm capable of, he'll tell me what the fuck he did with Julie instead of making me wonder where in the building she could possibly be.

CHAPTER TEN

It's Monday, mid-morning, and I've spent all of this time holding the punching bag at Aiden's place while she lays into it.

The fight between her and Max is inevitable, but with her snazzy new 'do, she seems to have renewed focus on getting in as much training as she can before the event.

I have an idea that will help her. Nothing that will be considered cheating, just something that might save her jaw this time from some painful dental surgery. Once I get home tonight, I'll get started on it, but first I need her to stop hitting this thing and give me something that I'll need for it.

"Wanna take a break there, champ? I think this thing is leaving an impression in my chest."

Aiden laughs and gives the bag one last good punch before she stands straight up and runs a gloved hand back through her hair.

"Can't have that. Wouldn't want you to have to explain to Penn how that happened," she teases with a mischievous smile.

"Give it a fucking rest already, Aiden," I grumble, heading out of her workout room. I walk into the living room where I left my bag and Aiden's girlish giggles follow me all the way there.

I roll my eyes.

She's obviously not going to be happy until either I fuck him, or he tells me to fuck off. Aiden throws herself onto her patchwork couch while I pull the contents of my bag out. I can feel her eyes on me, the curiosity burning a hole into my back while I get to my feet with my stuff.

"Do you have a mixing bowl or some shit you don't mind tossing?" I ask her, walking toward the kitchen.

"All of them!" she calls out and I laugh.

As I reach for a big, orange plastic bowl I find myself wondering when the last time was that I've ever seen Aiden cook anything.

It doesn't take me very long to mix the plaster and when I call out to Aiden to move her ass, she comes into the kitchen quickly.

"What is that?" she asks, wrinkling her nose.

"Open your mouth," I say softly, holding up the small block.

"For what? I'm not putting that in my mouth, Gray," she replies, shaking her head vehemently.

"Just open your goddamn mouth, Aiden," I bark at her. "I'm trying to save some money on another round of unnecessary dentistry."

She scowls at me and crosses her arms over her chest, a pout prominent on her pretty face, but she relents, and does as I ask her to.

"Bite down hard," I instruct her. I need a deep enough cast to be able to mold her a set of mouth guards that I know will hold under the pressure of a hit from Max.

Drool slips down the side of her mouth and she attempts to whine, tapping her wrist.

"About forty-five minutes. I can't wait to enjoy the silence," I reply with a sly grin.

She mumbles angrily through the block, but I reach over and place a hand gently on either side of her face. "If you fuck this up, we have to do it again. Stay still."

Her eyes widen in disbelief, but she leans against the counter and turns her eyes toward the clock on the wall. It won't really take forty-five minutes, but with her training, she has to learn discipline, and this is my way of making her relearn it.

Plus, I really am looking forward to the silence. The longer she keeps her mouth busy, the less I have to hear comments about Penn.

The ringtone from Aiden's cell phone starts chiming from her bedroom and she sighs, wiping the drool from her chin as she carefully makes her way to retrieve it. She returns a few moments later, the phone still ringing, and holds it up, a curious look in her eyes to show me the caller ID.

I lean down and narrow my eyes because she's so goddamn tiny, it's hard for me to see it from up here.

Penn.

I roll my eyes and start packing up what's left of my provisions, intent on getting away from her teasing, when she grabs my arm and shakes her head. I raise an eyebrow and reach for the phone, sliding the answer button just in time to hear the line click dead.

"He hung up as soon as I answered," I mumble, handing it back to her.

He probably knew it was me. Probably felt my fucking heart beating through the phone at the possibility of hearing his voice again.

I reach over and roughly pull the mold out of her mouth.

"Ouch, Gray! That fucking hurt!" she says, reaching up to rub her jaw.

"Yeah, well it's not as bad as what's coming your way and you know it," I mumble unhappily. I hold up the mold and look it over. "That's good enough. I'm going home; I'll be back tomorrow, and I'll have your mouth guard."

Before she can object or even ask me what the problem is, I march into the living room and grab my bag, heading for the front door.

"Later, kid," I say to her softly without so much as backwards glance.

Aiden doesn't understand, but she will soon enough.

CHAPTER ELEVEN

"I really hate my life sometimes. It hurts just to be alive and breathing, but I don't want to end things just yet either. I know it may sound corny, and I know that you probably think I'm nuts at this point, I just kind of feel like shit has to get better, you know? It can't very well get any fucking worse."

I reposition its legs on my shoulder, making sure that it has some comfort while I feed it. This isn't a pleasant time for either of us but the only hole that I can get some nutrients into is its rectum, so I have enemas that I fill with as much good stuff as I can, liquefy it as much as possible, and squeeze the bag empty into her. It may sound strange, but the ass is one of the places on the body where there are so many veins that anything placed into it—alcohol, drugs, nutrients, etc., get absorbed much quicker than being consumed the normal way.

The bag is almost empty, but while I have its attention, I decide to keep talking.

"Would you hurt yourself if you were me? I know—no one really knows how I feel except for myself, but do you think I'm worth the time? To be alive, I mean. Or am I just wasting space on this stupid fucking planet?"

It grunts in response.

Always a grunt, never words.

And yet I find myself still longing to converse with it. I sigh and give the bag one last final squeeze before I ease it out and place the legs back down.

"Hope that helps," I tell it with a kind smile as I toss the bag into the metal barrel near the table.

It nods and spreads its legs gently so that I can fix the restraints I use to hold it back in place. Its such a good pet and I hope that its owner will love it as much as I do.

I *do* love my pieces.

Even though if not in a way that most people feel love, but I'm proud of each of them and I want them to thrive in their new homes.

They know if they're ever mistreated that they only need to come back and I'll take care of them. It hasn't happened yet, though, but I like to give them the option.

"I'll be back tomorrow night, okay?" I say to it, running a hand over its hair. "It'll be over soon, and you'll be out of here. Off to your new home—I promise."

It tries to smile but the stitching is so tightly done that it can't. I appreciate the gesture though, and in return, I place a gentle kiss on its forehead.

"Sleep tight," I say to it softly as I replace the blanket and then pull my gloves off. I toss them into the trash can near the door and stretch my arms over my head before I walk out of the room, flipping the light switch on my way.

As I make my way down the stairs, I find myself wondering about Julie again. It's been a couple of days and the smell of decay hasn't reached my nose yet, so whatever Penn did with her, he must have done it well.

But what was it?

I could do the reasonable thing and ask him, but I'll more than likely stumble over my words or snap at him like I'm apparently prone to do when he's around. Either way, I'd end up looking like an asshole and that's not exactly how to woo someone.

I sit down on the third to last step and look at the spot on the floor where Julie once laid no more than a few days ago. She wasn't dragged, because the blood pooled into a dried puddle. Maybe he lifted her, but if he did, why wasn't there any blood on his clothes? Is he a fucking magician? The great Houdini reincarnated?

I let out a sigh and lean back against the stairs, cracking my neck and closing my eyes.

I never used to be like this. I used to have so much confidence that I could suck the energy out of a room just by stepping into it. I don't know where I lost it and I want nothing more than to find it again, which is why I spend almost all of my time with Aiden.

Even though she's nothing I would be interested in romantically, she helps me be a human being. I could spend my time just cashing in on pieces left and right and never having to worry about making another one for ten years, but she makes me go out and coexist in a world that doesn't see me hiding in plain sight.

And I love her for it.

One of the many reasons Aiden will always hold a special place in my heart, and one of the many reasons I know I have to protect her from monsters like me.

She knows what I am, and she doesn't care. She tells me she knows that I have to work to survive and to keep my head on straight and she's even offered to help me from time to time, but I always decline.

I can't put her in that kind of danger.

There's always a new kid on the block that wants to be bigger and better than me, and if they saw how close we really are, they would hurt her to get to me.

That's when the last shred of humanity I'm hanging onto would be clipped off. Like the wings of a fallen angel, hurtling down to Earth, at the speed of sin, and crashing into the goddamn ground, ready to rise a bigger monster than anything ever before.

And I *refuse* to let that happen.

A chuckle escapes me as I hear a

knock on the door. It's Aiden—I can tell by the way she's knocking, even though its a little softer and not as fast as usual, but I just chalk it up to her being tired.

I get up and walk out of the stairwell, swinging the door closed behind me, and jog over toward the door. One thing I love about her is her curiosity, and I know she's probably here because she doesn't want to wait to see her mouth guard. Unfortunately for her, it's still setting, but I don't mind having her over for some mindless chatter while it works.

"Were your ears burning?" I tease as I pull the door open.

But it's not Aiden on the other side of the door and the reason the knock wasn't quiet her makes sense now.

"What are *you* doing here?" I ask, closing the door slightly and staring curiously at my unannounced visitor.

PART TWO

FOLIE D'UN

CHAPTER TWELVE

"Sorry," Penn says with a laugh. "I was trying to get a hold of Aiden and this is the only place I could think of to look for her."

"Maybe you should have tried *her* place?" I reply evenly.

Penn smiles and rubs the back of his neck, glancing down the hallway. "So, she's not here then?"

"No."

"Okay," he turns to walk away, but hesitates, cutting his eyes back toward me. "Um, can I come in for a sec? There's something I want to talk to you about."

I stare at him, trying to see if his words can be found in his eyes, but I see nothing, so I relent and nod.

"Yeah. Sure, man," I say, taking a step

back and opening the door the rest of the way.

"So, what's up?" I ask Penn once he's standing inside of my home.

He grins at me like a mischievous child. I can't tell what he's up to and he knows it, which makes his grin widen just a little bit more.

"Did she tell you that she's going to fight again?" he asks, crossing his arms loosely over his chest.

"Yeah."

"How do you feel about that, Gray?" he presses, tilting his head slightly to the right.

"How the fuck do you think that makes me feel?"

Deep breath. Stop being an asshole.

"Sorry."

"Yeah, I know," Penn replies, rolling his eyes. "Listen, I'm not here to piss you off, I'm here because I want you to know you're not the only person that cares about her getting hurt. She's a good kid, and I want what's best for her too."

"Mm," I grumble in response.

The silence between us is putting me on edge, and Penn seems to take notice because he drops his arms to his side and glances around the room.

"Did you find her yet?" he asks curiously.

"Huh?"

"The hooker. Did you find her?"

"No. Wait; is she in the building?" I inquire, following his gaze.

"I think you would have had to spray the place down by now to get rid of the smell," he replies dryly.

"So, where is she?" I ask, glancing back at him.

"Hm."

He uses his long forefinger to tap his chin and then suddenly snaps his fingers, causing me to jump.

"Let's talk about something else," he suggests. It's obvious that Penn is enjoying this little game of his but there's only so much I can take before I throttle the fucking answer out of him.

I let out a loud sigh and run a hand irritably over my face before I stare at him.

Penn doesn't seem to be too bothered by my obvious annoyance.

"I actually didn't come looking for Aiden," he says sheepishly.

"Then why are you here?" I ask a little louder than I mean to.

"I'm—"

"Sorry, yeah, I know," he cuts me off. "So, what would you say if I told you that Aiden told me something that might piss you off."

"Like what?" I ask him gruffly.

"Like how you feel about me," he answers quietly, the grin returning to his lips.

I'm going to fucking kill her. She doesn't need to worry about Max Boothe, because I'm going to snap her fucking neck.

"Yeah, well," I say with a shrug.

"Well, maybe I'm interested," he replies softly.

"What?"

I look Penn straight in his eyes and they soften as he takes a small step toward me. "I've never been with a guy before, you know? But I'm pretty sure I could get down with you. I see the way you care about Aiden, and I see the way you watch me when you think I'm not looking. The thing is, I look at you the same way too and only Aiden seems to have noticed," he confesses nervously.

My body trembles slightly and I do my best to control it.

This can't be real.

There's no way in fucking hell this is anything other than my mind playing a trick on me.

Right?

"I'm kinda hoping you haven't changed your mind since Saturday otherwise I'm going to feel like a fucking idiot," he says with a slight tremor to his laugh.

"No, I haven't," I reply quickly. "But I'm not used to getting the things I want either."

"And you want me?" he asks with a smile.

"Yes," I whisper softly.

"Thank God," he says, leaning his head back and letting out a relieved sigh. "Okay, so, show me where you sleep."

I lower my eyes to my feet and shuffle them before I finally pull up the courage I thought was lacking and start walking down the hallway. Penn follows closely behind me—I know it because I can smell him now even though I couldn't before.

It's intoxicating and maddening at the same time. He smells like cinnamon with just a hint of cranberry and for some reason it makes the world come into focus.

For the first time in a long time, I can see shit again clearly.

When we enter my room, I shuffle to the inside wall and lean against it, bending one of my legs and watch Penn.

He walks in and looks around curiously. I'm not entirely sure what he was expecting it to look like, but it's very simple. A large platform bed sits in the middle of the room against the wall. A few factory size windows line the wall directly across from me and the dressers that hold my clothes for the most part. Everything else is in the closet. I don't like clutter. I like order, so I keep things as simple as I can.

Penn spins in a slow circle, his long legs twirling around before he drops down on the edge of my bed and glances at me. He leans back on his hands and begins to chew the inside of his mouth as he watches me for a moment before motioning for me to join him with a jerk of his head.

I let out a sigh and walk over to Penn, taking the empty spot to his right and lean forward, my arms crossed over my knees. I never realized just how much I liked his long legs until now. For some reason they're making me smile and he chuckles when he notices.

Penn sits up and places a hand on my leg, sliding his hand down to take mine in his as he leans over and places his chin on my shoulder.

"Your move," he whispers into my ear.

I'd be lying if I didn't say just the feel of his hands, the knowing that he wants to be with me, gives me an instant hard-on.

I turn my face slowly toward his, our lips just inches from each others and I wait.

I want him to kiss me first because that's how I'll know this is real and not just some fucked up fantasy in my head.

"Okay, my move then," he says with a low chuckle, moving his face forward.

In this moment, the world can explode around us and I wouldn't even fucking notice. The rivers could run dry and the heavens could rain fire, but nothing would be able to steal this away from me.

When Penn pulls away, I let out a deep breath and he chuckles again.

"I'm sure we can do better than that," he says, getting to his feet and holding a hand down toward me.

I take it and let him pull me up from the bed, trembling like someone who's feeling the touch of another for the first time, and that's when I realize something.

I'm nervous.

I never thought that when this moment finally came, that I would be nervous. I thought we would just fall into each other's arms and that nature would take its course, but it's nothing like I imagined it would be.

To have Penn this close to me—to have felt his lips against mine, the hunger that he kissed me with, it's completely destroyed every fantasy I've ever had about being with him.

His hands feel so goddamn soft as he slides them underneath my shirt and uses his fingertips to pull my shirt up over my head. Penn tosses my shirt to the side and leans down to kiss my neck, my bare chest, then gently suckles one of my nipples. Using his teeth, he grabs hold of it, before using the tip of his tongue to circle it just once.

"You're shaking," he whispers, looking up into my eyes. "Why?"

"You make me nervous," I reply with a low chuckle.

Penn's lips curve into the grin that drives me fucking wild as he takes a step back, his hands firmly on my hips as he looks deeper into my eyes. "I thought this was what you wanted?"

"It is," I tell him a little too quickly. "From the first time I laid eyes on you, it's all I've wanted."

"Then relax," Penn says gently as he tilts my head up and kisses my neck again. "I'm not going to hurt you—unless you're into that kind of thing, that is."

I chuckle and when I feel his lips curve into a smile again against my skin, I shudder. It's an involuntary tremble, but the way it feels is indescribable.

"Or do you want to be fucked gently?" he inquires, his lips trailing down my neck to my chest again, but this time, he doesn't stop there. He continues his way down my stomach and drops to his knees, his hands on the waist of my pants. I look down at him and see him grinning up at me. His eyes are wider than normal, bluer than anything I've seen before, and as he runs a hand up and down the apparent bulge in my sweatpants, I swear to God it takes everything in me not to cum right here and now.

"Tell me what you want," he says, gripping me tightly in the palm of his hand. "And I'll give it to you."

"I want you to make me beg you to

fuck me. I want you to make my body ache for you and I want you to use me when you finally feel that you've prolonged it enough. I want you to be gentle and I want you to hurt me. I want everything you can give me and more," I confess between shuddering breaths. Penn sits back on the heel of his feet as he reaches up and pulls the drawstring on my sweatpants, then lets them fall down to my ankles.

"Commando," he remarks with a laugh, putting his hands to his mouth. "I'm not entirely sure I can get all of that into my mouth, but I'll be damned if I don't try."

Before I have a chance to say anything, Penn wraps those beautiful, soft, full lips around the head of my cock and licks the tip. His hand is firm on my shaft and he slowly begins to stroke the length while swirling his tongue around the only part he has in his mouth.

"Oh my God," I breathe, leaning my head back and placing my hands firmly over my face. It feels so much better than anything Little Julie was capable of and considering that she used to get paid to fuck, that's saying something about the way he uses that mouth of his.

Penn slowly moves his lips to meet his hand and takes in a little more than half of my dick. It's more than enough for me to feel his touch but knowing that he wants to take as much of me down his throat as he can, is already making me grit my teeth.

I place a hand on the top of his head and ball up a fistful of hair. Penn's lips curve on my dick and I know he's smiling. I think it's because he's finally getting me to react the way he would have expected and if that's what he wants, then I'll give it to him.

"A little more, please," I beg him, thrusting my hips forward.

He pulls back and spits on my cock, looking up at me with those eyes of his, his hand slathering me with is saliva, as he jerks his head to the right to move his hair out of his face.

"I thought you wanted me to use *you*," he remarks, arching his eyebrows salaciously.

"I do," I reply, my chest heaving. He's already got me aching to feel his mouth around my cock again, so he seems to know how to play this game better than I thought.

"Then shut up," he remarks with a sly grin. "Let me take care of you, Gray. You deserve it."

Penn's mouth is wrapped around my dick again and it's taking everything I have not to grab the back of his head and throat fuck him. The man of my dreams is on his knees in front of me and I'm a fucking wreck trying to control the primal urge to knock him onto his back and gag him viciously with my cock.

But as quickly as he's back to sucking me off again, he's done. Penn pushes my body away and gets to his feet, pulling his shirt over his head and tossing it to the side. I can see his lips glistening with what he managed to take from me on his lips and when he kisses me again with such fucking earnest, I can taste myself.

"My turn," he says, reaching down and

unzipping his jeans.

I reach down and push them to the middle of his thighs and drop to my knees. I want him to force his cock into my mouth, I want him to make me take all of it and I want him to cum in my throat. I want to feel his juices sliding down into my body and let it plant a seed that no one will ever be able to take from me.

"Show me what I've been missing," he says, licking his lips and putting his hands on his hips, but the moment I reach in and pull his dick through the fly of boxers, he pushes me roughly away.

"What the fuck?" I ask, looking up at him in confusion.

"Come on—you're a tough guy, you can take a little roughhousing," he teases with a half smile.

I shake my head and laugh as I reach for his dick again, but Penn pushes me away like he did before and reaches down for himself.

"Open your mouth," he commands softly, and I do as I'm told. I kneel in front of him, my mouth open and watering at how close he has the head of his dick to my lips, yet he doesn't let me taste. Not right away, instead he begins to tug on his dick while I watch, moans of pleasure escaping him from time to time. When his breathing becomes labored, when his hand begins to move faster, I finally understand what he's going to do.

"Do you want it?" he asks between labored breaths.

"I need it," I reply as quickly as I can, opening my mouth again, and using the tip of my tongue to lick him gently. Penn moves his hand faster and lets out a low chuckle at my boldness. The game he's playing right now is that I can't touch him unless he tells me to, but there's only so much temptation I can take before I act out, and he seems okay with it.

Penn gets so fucking close, almost to the point of cumming, when he stops and grunts.

"Nah. I'd rather not—not this time, anyway," he says with a wicked grin. I raise an eyebrow at him, feeling absolutely betrayed that he won't let me taste his seed even though he knows how badly I'm craving it.

He leans down and kisses me viciously, grabbing a handful of my hair in a tight fist, before he pulls away and places his forehead against mine.

"Get on the bed, Gray."

A genuine grin creases my lips as I do as I'm told. I move all the way back against the headboard and slide down onto my back, getting as comfortable as I can while I wait for Penn.

"You know, I gotta tell you," he says, leaning down to pick up his pants. He bites his lip as he fishes around for something then drops them again when he finds what he wanted. "This is fucking crazy." He brings the square foil to his mouth and rips it open with his teeth, tossing the wrapper to the side. "But I should probably tell you, that if I end up enjoying this—and I have a feeling that I will, I can be rather insatiable. Think you can handle it?"

He punctuates his question by sliding the rubber onto his hard cock then climbing on the bed, hovering just above me. He purses his lips for a moment, then tilts his head to the side.

"How many guys have you been with?" he asks curiously.

"A couple," I lie.

This isn't the time to tell him that the major reason I felt so damn bad for Julie is because before I found my calling as an artist, I supplemented my income by fucking old men for money.

"Liar," he whispers, leaning down and kissing me gently. When he pulls away from me, he grins again, then reaches down for his cock. He lifts one of my legs over his shoulder and gently begins to push into me.

It burns and that's new to me. I'm never the one that gets fucked, I'm usually the one doing the fucking, but if this is how he wants me, then goddammit, I'll submit to it.

I grunt and grit my teeth as he fills my hole then begins to gently thrust his hips.

"Oh my God," he breathes. "You're so fucking tight."

I let out a moan and arch my back as Penn begins to thrust a little faster and reach down for my cock. I begin to jerk off while he thrusts his hips, but he pulls my hand away, replacing it with his own.

I've never felt anything like this before and I don't know if I'll ever have the chance again, but everything feels the way it *should.*

He grunts as he pushes harder and just when I think I can take it anymore, he mercifully pulls out of me. But the mercy is short lived as he commands me to get on my stomach.

I do it with an eagerness I never knew I could feel and as he puts a hand on either one of my hips, I take a deep breath and grit my teeth while he slides back into me again.

Penn slaps my ass and I grunt in response. He leans forward and takes a fistful of my hair again, arching me back toward him, then kisses my neck, running his teeth along my skin.

"Fuck," he groans into my ear before he shoves me forward again and keeps fucking.

Violently.

Viciously.

Like it's everything he never knew he needed, but I did.

"I'm gonna cum," I say through grit teeth. Penn reaches under my body and begins to tug on my dick again, while he rams into my ass. He knows he's the reason, and he wants me to know it too.

A few more thrusts, a few more tugs, and I make a mess all over my bed sheets, a loud, euphoric moan escaping me. Penn laughs as I fall forward, and he pulls out of me again.

"That didn't take very long," he teases, as he lies down next to me.

"Sorry."

"For fuck's sake, Gray," he sighs.

I look at him, trying to even my breathing again, and grin. "Old habits. Did you finish, or do you need me to finish you off?"

Penn laughs as he reaches down and pulls the rubber off of his half flaccid dick. "I finished almost as soon as I started fucking you," he confesses sheepishly.

"Then why didn't you stop?" I ask handing him some tissues from the box next to my bed.

"What kind of fuck would I be if I didn't

make sure that you got happy ending too?"
he asks with a sly smile.

I let out a low chuckle as I reach for more tissues to clean myself up then hold my hand out for his. I toss them into the garbage can under the nightstand and let out a satisfied sigh.

Maybe things are better than I thought they were and I just couldn't see it. As Penn leans down and grabs the blanket, pulling it up around us, I fold an arm behind my head and grin nervously as he drapes an arm across my waist and yawns.

Maybe this doesn't have to end the way I thought it does.

CHAPTER THIRTEEN

I wake up the next morning, a smile on my face and feeling like more of a man than I have in years. Last night was the most amazing experience of my life and I know damn well that nothing will ever come close to topping it. I stretch my arms over my head and yawn, turning my head to the side and become confused when I see the space next to me on the bed is empty.

What the fuck?

I prop myself up on my elbows and swallow the sigh of relief when I see Penn sitting at the very edge of the bed, hunched over, preoccupied with—to be quite honest, I can't see what he's doing, but I feel better knowing that he didn't take off like I initially thought.

"Morning," I say to him softly.

"Hey," he replies, still hunched over, and offering me a quick glance over his shoulder.

I shake my head and drop onto my back, running my hands over my face, and sigh loudly. Maybe last night didn't mean as much to him as it did to me, and I wouldn't be surprised if he's having second thoughts about it.

"Buyer's remorse?" I ask, my voice muffled by my hands still on my face.

"Huh?" he asks.

"Nothing," I reply glumly. I push the sheet off of my naked body and sit up, as I glance around the floor for my sweatpants.

"If you're talking about last night, the answer is no. Fuck no. I'm actually kinda hoping we can do that again sometime," he states with a chuckle, his back still turned to me. The paleness of the color of his skin— the absolute flawlessness of the surface, with the exception of the scratches I left on his back, makes me want to touch him again. Just to feel how soft he is one more time before he gets out of my bed.

"Got it!" he says triumphantly, casting me a grin over his shoulder.

"What were you doing?" I ask curiously, craning my neck to see if I can figure out what had him so damn preoccupied.

"Hang nail. I hate those," he replies, holding out the palm of his hand to show me. The proud look on his face almost reminds me of how Aiden looks when she wins a fight, but this is different. He fought with himself to destroy a piece that no longer quiet fit and I can relate to that more than to fighting someone for the cash and glory of it all.

I smile at him, then look back down on the floor again, finally locating my sweatpants. I extend my leg and drag them over with my foot, before I reach down and shimmy them on, Penn's gaze is on me the entire time. I can feel his eyes on me the way one can feel the ripple of a tide gently rolling against the skin. It has the same cool and calming effect if he doesn't know it yet.

I walk into the bathroom and look at

myself in the mirror above the sink. I've done something I once thought was the most impossible and absolutely fucking unattainable—I've spent a night with Penn Harris and I can't wait to tell Aiden all about it.

She's going to be so damn proud of me, I think with a chuckle as I turn on the faucet and splash some warm water onto my face. The sudden sound of the toilet lid being snapped upright makes me jump and I end up choking on some of the water.

"Sorry," Penn says with a laugh. I reach for a hand towel that sits on the rack above the hamper and give him a dirty look before I dry my face. "What? I thought you heard me come in."

He clears his throat and begins to piss into the toilet. I'm actually kind of taken aback by it; not because it bothers me in the sense of manners, but because he's willing to do something so personal that damn freely in front of me. He must feel my eyes on him because he slowly turns toward me and arches his eyebrows.

"Does this bother you?" he asks curiously.

"No. I just … never had anyone, you know … uh …"

"Take a leak when you're around?" he finishes with a laugh. "Sorry, but when I have to go, I don't care if it's the Pope standing next to me," Penn shrugs. "Though I do need that sink now."

He takes a step toward me after he flushes the toilet and uses his hip to gently nudge me out of the way so he can wash his hands. I watch him for a few seconds before I sigh and walk out of the bathroom. Not because I'm still trying to wrap my head around him peeing in front of, but because I hear the unmistakable "knocking" of Aiden James at the door.

"Do you want me to sneak out before you let her in?" Penn calls out to me quietly. He's standing just inside the bathroom door and half of his body is hidden in the room. I take him in again for a moment—the length of his limbs, the frailty of his body, the white of his skin and almost feel like fainting from being so overcome with his fucking beauty. His eyes are so wide with innocence right now and I know he's only asking because he doesn't want Aiden to make me feel uncomfortable by asking me a thousand and one questions about why he's here.

"No," I reply, shaking my head slowly. "But maybe get dressed?"

Penn grins and slaps the bathroom door happily as he turns off the light then makes his way quickly back to my bedroom. Once he's out of sight, I walk the rest of the way to the door and pull it open.

"You have *got* to learn a different way of knocking, kid," I tell her, shaking my head and leaning against the door frame.

"Well how else would you know it's me?" she quips, sticking her tongue out at me.

I smile.

Aiden smiles.

Silence.

"Do I get to come in or is there a special password to get in now?" she asks in exasperation.

I suck my teeth and chuckle, stepping back to let her in. Aiden gives me a curious look as she steps past me and raises an eyebrow.

"Whatcha hiding from me, Gray?"

"Nothing."

"Liar. I can tell you're lying. Your damn upper lip always twitches when you lie," she states, putting her hands on her hips and narrowing her eyes.

"What are you doing here?" Penn asks, stepping into the room. He raises an apple to his luscious lips and as he bites into it, I can see the flow of juice running down his chin. His steals a glance at me, giving me a subtle wink, as he licks it away then turns his attention back to Aiden. He's dressed in the same clothes he came in last night and they're so wrinkled from me tearing at them that he looks like he's been pushed through a dryer.

"Whoa! What are *you* doing here?" she shoots back at him, looking from me to Penn, then back again.

"My place is being fumigated today.

133

Remember? I told you," he says casually as he takes another bite of the apple.

"Where'd you sleep last night?" she asks, her eyes narrowing again.

"Here, obviously. Gray let me crash for the night."

"Yeah, but where exactly?" she presses.

"That's none of your fucking business, is it?" he asks, his lips curving into the same dangerous grin that he seduced me with last night. "Where did *you* sleep?" he counters.

She takes a step back. It's almost as if he moved her with his tone and the fact that he doesn't want her asking questions she knows she'll more than likely get answers to at some point. Maybe he's just embarrassed about what happened between us last night. Maybe he had a moment of weakness and he regrets it now.

Maybe I shouldn't have expected anything less.

"Calm down," she says, holding up her hands. "I just didn't expect to see you here, is all."

"Likewise. What do you want?" he asks evenly, crossing one of his arms over his chest and staring at her. *Crunch.* Another lick of the lips, another glance in my direction, another flutter in my heart.

Aiden rolls her eyes at me, then shakes her head, "I don't need a reason to come see my best friend."

"Can you two stop bickering? I haven't had any coffee yet so I can't join in on the fun," I intercede dryly as I turn away from them and head to the kitchen. Penn chuckles as he falls into step beside me, Aiden following close behind.

"I'll get it started. I'll make some breakfast too," Penn offers as he picks up his pace and passes me.

"Thanks," I call out to him. He nods, without looking back and when I stop walking, Aiden bumps into my back.

"What's up, kid?" I ask her curiously. "I told you I'd come by later."

"Did you guys do it?" she asks me with a childlike giddiness flashing in her eyes. She looks so hopeful that I might answer her the way she wants me to, or answer her at all, that I'm afraid she's going to fall over from all of her excitement.

I roll my eyes and sigh, "Why didn't you wait for me to come over?"

I decide to side-step her question, not because I'm not dying to answer it, but because I feel like it would be an invasion of Penn's privacy.

"Fine," she says with a pout. I smile down at her and put an arm around her shoulder, leading her into the kitchen where Penn is already busy at the stove. He glances over at us when we walk in and smiles, then turns his attention back to his task.

"Anyway, I know you said you were coming over later, but I wanna see what the hell you made out of an impression of my teeth."

"Did you get a haircut?" Penn asks suddenly. His face is scrunched up and I can't tell if it's curiosity or if he's not impressed with the job I did on her head.

"I sure did. Gray gave me a new 'do. Like it?" she asks, primping her shorter hairstyle. I shaved the sides almost down to the skin and cut the top down enough where she can push it back but not be at a disadvantage of it getting into her eyes when she fights Max again.

"It's not bad," he finally says with a shrug. Aiden makes a face at him and he turns his back to us again.

"What's his fucking problem?" she asks me quietly.

I shrug and walk over to the coffee machine. I'm not in the mood for much right now except for a nice, piping hot cup of java.

"Want one?" I ask Aiden, who nods. "How about you?" I ask, nudging Penn. He glances at me from the corner of his eye and winks again, making me blush.

"Sure. Thanks."

I hand Aiden a mug full of coffee and then slide the next one toward Penn, before picking mine up and walking to the living room. She takes the hint and follows me; sitting on the end of the couch I've settled onto. She curls her legs up underneath her and waits for some kind of juicy gossip, but my lips are sealed for now.

"Does this mean I don't have to swing by your place later?" I tease as I take a sip of my coffee.

Aiden rolls her eyes and laughs, "I mean if you don't want to help me train, that's fine. You know I'm more than capable of doing it myself, Gray."

I shake my head and set my mug down on the floor next to me, giving her a disapproving look. She knows that I won't let her go into any fight alone, let alone one of this magnitude. Both of these maniacs are going to be attempting to redeem themselves, and I want this little shit to make it out in one piece.

"Keep that up and you're next and last fight is going to be with me," I say tossing a small pillow at her. Aiden grins as it flies past her head and then takes a sip from her mug.

"Are you gonna show me that thing you made or not?" she asks curiously.

"Later."

"Promise?" she asks, narrowing her eyes at me.

"I promise," I confirm, leaning my head against the back of the couch and smiling at her. Aiden loves to see my pieces when they're done, and I appreciate her feedback and critical eye when it comes to some small detail I may have overlooked. In a weird and wonderful way, it's Aiden's version of training me. I help her with her strength and discipline, while she helps me be a better artist and allows me to keep holding on to that last thread of humanity I have.

"Breakfast is ready," Penn announces as he walks into the living room. I turn toward the sound of his voice and smile when he hands a plate to me, then one to Aiden before he goes and takes his place on the recliner. *I wonder why he likes that spot so much?*

"Thank you," I say to him. Aiden already has a forkful of pancakes in her mouth, but she points from me to Penn with her fork and gives him a thumbs up. "Aiden says thank you as well," I translate with a laugh.

Penn chuckles in response as he pulls the lever to recline the seat and turns his eyes toward the ceiling. I turn to my meal of pancakes, scrambled eggs, and sausage, folding a leg under myself and begin to indulge. If last night doesn't lead to anything more than the bliss we shared, maybe I can pay him to cook for me and Aiden every now and then.

"You're not hungry?" I ask Penn between bites.

He shakes his head, his eyes still on the ceiling, and crosses his arms loosely over his chest.

"I usually don't eat as soon as I wake up—it fucks with my stomach when I do," he explains before giving me a suspicious look. "What's upstairs?"

My eyes immediately cut to Aiden. My heart is racing, and I don't know if I have it in me to lie to Penn, so I hope my best friend can pull me out of this fire before the flame is even lit.

"It's where Gray keeps all of his monsters and dark secrets," Aiden replies sarcastically with an eye roll. "And if you think his silences can be scary, you should see what happens when he spends time up there. Why don't you take a walk to the elevator and go on up? See what you can find out when something that obviously is none of anyone's business is just one floor above your head."

A small smile forms across my mouth and I have to turn my face away so that Penn doesn't see it. In her telling him the somewhat truth, she makes it sound so damn outlandish that he probably thinks she's sassing him.

"Give him the keys, Gray," Aiden continues, nudging me with her foot.

"Maybe if he sees the Boogeyman for the first time in his life, he'll learn it's not nice to poke around in people's private affairs."

"Good Lord," Penn remarks, rolling his eyes at her. "All you had to say was that it's off limits instead of babbling like you just did."

She gives him a toothy grin then turns back to her food. I glance over at Penn who's now busy picking his fingernails and sigh. I don't want these two to go at each other, but I know the tension of her being here right now is getting to all three of us.

"Pussy," she teases him.

Penn raises an eyebrow at Aiden, then stands up and walks over to the couch. He holds out one his pale hands, the long fingers extending toward me. "Give me the keys."

"The keys?" I echo nervously through a mouth full of food.

Aiden may have underestimated this one.

"Yes; the keys. To upstairs," he says again.

I glance desperately at Aiden. I need her to stomp out this little fire she began, and I need her to do it fast.

"Penn, I never thought of you as the gullible type," she finally says with a laugh. Her foot brushes imperceptibly against my leg to let me know she has every intention of keeping him down here with us. "It's just storage. Gosh. I wonder if you believed me if were to tell you that I was born with two heads and a dick."

He purses his lips, takes a step over toward Aiden, and leaning down. He's so goddamn close to her that she ends up recoiling a bit, stealing a confused glance in my direction.

"Be nice to me," he tells her softly. "You may have him wrapped around your finger, but I'm not him and it'll take a hell of lot more than a few cuddles and your sharp wit to make me fold under whatever delusional hierarchy you live in."

She screws her face up at him and I'm wondering how it is that I ended up a casualty in their little tiff.

"No offense," he says, glancing at me quickly and grinning. "I just know from the little bit of time I've spent with the two of you that you'd move mountains for Aiden."

"That doesn't make me anything less than a damn good friend," I say softly, looking down at my half empty plate. "Excuse me."

I leave them in the living room, ignoring their protests. The way they just treated each other, the way I just got dragged into it, made me lose my appetite and I wonder how much weight I'll end up losing if I keep these two around. If it's not my nerves turning my stomach sour, it's their newfound negativity toward each other that does the job.

I empty what's left of my breakfast into the trash can, then turn on the faucet in the sink and proceed to clean off the plate.

"Hey."

I ignore him.

For the first time since I've fantasized about being someone good enough for Penn Harris, I ignore him completely.

"We were just kidding," he says, coming to stand next to me. I continue to wash the plate, then the fork, then the base of the sink. Anything to keep from having to look at him right now. "Gray," he continues, placing his chin on my shoulder. I can feel his breath against my neck and it makes me stiffen slightly. "Don't be angry with us. That's just how me and Aiden talk to each other—don't be mad, okay? Please?"

In a world where shit doesn't make sense, where only last night things became clear to me, the scent of cinnamon and cranberries starts to invade my senses again. Penn Harris is actually begging *me* for something and that doesn't make much sense to me.

"I'm not," I reply, turning off the faucet and turning around. I lean back against the sink, my fingers drumming along the stainless steel base and give him a tight smile. He moves to stand in front of me and places his hands loosely on my sides and I shake my head. "Aiden's going to catch us."

"Then let her catch us," he replies with

a scoff. "I don't care if she knows, and I'm sure she's going to find out sooner or later, anyway. I just want to make sure that you're honestly not mad at me because all I can see is the prospect of having another night together flying out the fucking window and swan diving to a painful death below."

I roll my eyes quickly and glance toward the couch on the other side of the room. Aiden's curiosity hasn't gotten the best of her like I thought it would have by now. Instead, she's rearranged herself and the only thing I can really see from here is the top of her head as she lazily changes channels on the television.

"I have to finish getting her ready," I say to him quietly, looking down into his eyes.

Penn nods in understanding as he lets his hands fall down to his sides and chews his lower lip.

"How much time do you guys need?"

"We'll see you at the fight."

He looks at me for a moment, almost as if he's trying to figure out if I'm playing some kind of game, but when I clench my teeth and begin to drum along the top of the sink again, he nods.

"Give her hell."

Penn leans forward and tries to kiss me, but I turn my face toward Aiden, reminding him that she's still here. He sighs and shakes his head, making his way back toward her.

I can hear him tell her that he'll see her in a few days and that he knows she's going to do great. I can hear him tell her that he's proud of her for getting the balls to do it all over again and I can hear him tell her that she's lucky to have a friend like me.

"See you crazy kids later," he finally calls out as he makes his way to the door. He laughs at something Aiden says, pausing in the doorway for a moment, then turns his gaze toward me. I haven't moved. I'm still in the same rigid spot with the same rigid soul waiting for him to do something else to attempt to get me to ask him to stay. I give him a solemn nod, and he lets out a sigh as he turns and walks out.

There will be plenty of time for fucking and maybe a little more later.

My main concern right now is making sure that I still have a best friend in a few days.

"Alright, kid. Get up—we've got shit to do," I call out as I start walking toward her. Aiden glances over the armrest of the couch and groans as she turns off the TV, but she manages to pull herself up to her feet. She knows as well as I do that she's going to need every last bit of help I can give her to be able to last another dance with Max.

CHAPTER FOURTEEN

"Jesus fucking Christ, Gray! Are you trying to kill me?" Aiden asks, as she drops to her knees. I smile down at her and raise an eyebrow.

I reach down and wipe the sweat off my bare stomach and size her up. Aiden's wearing one of the sports bras she left here before and some kind of tight workout shorts. Since she's more than dressed for the occasion, I plan on making her do some work.

"When did you become such a weakling? You used to be able to pass me up and down these stairs."

"Yeah; *one* flight! Not the entire goddamn building," she shoots back, giving me a dirty look.

"Well, little lady, I just want to make sure that you're at pique condition and I've only got a few days to do it. Once you catch your breath, meet me outside," I say, wiping my face with my towel, then slinging it over my shoulder. "Bring those two big water bottles from the fridge too, okay?"

Aiden mumbles something under her breath that I can almost make out and I laugh as I head back down the stairs. She knows that if I'm asking her to step out of the building, things are about to get fucking messy.

I have an idea, a plan of sorts to make her stronger than ever before, and even though she'll look at me like I've lost my goddamn mind, she'll know she has no choice but to agree.

Everything I intend to do—every moment of pain she will feel, every tear that I will have no choice but to ignore, and every mercy I'll withhold will be for her.

Once I'm outside, I take in a breath of the fresh air that's eluded me for the past couple of days and smile.

Things seem to be looking up.

Aiden is taking her training seriously so far. Penn seems to want more than just a one-night fuck, and I'm almost done with my new piece.

Another ten minutes of feeling the sun on my face and Aiden finally appears.

"Here," she says, holding out one of the bottles of water. I smile at her and jerk my head to the left. She rolls her eyes and follows me as we walk around the building. She doesn't know what I'm up to, yet she understands that she can't say no.

When we reach the back, I take a huge swig of water and tell her to do the same. She uses her towel to clean off the sweat from her face while I place my bottle down and pick up a pair of sparring gloves.

"Put these on," I say tossing them at her.

"What the fuck, Gray? Are you gonna make me hit the building now?" she asks, wrinkling her nose in confusion.

"Nope," I say, leaning down and swooping up a second pair. As I begin to pull them on, a look of horror and realization falls over her.

She gets it now.

"I'm going make you hit me," I tell her softly, getting into a fighting position. "And I'm going to hit you back. I'm sorry if I hurt you, but you know this is the only way."

"You … you want me to fight you?" she asks uncertainly.

"I want you to put me down, Aiden. I'm not going to make it easy for you, but neither is he—now get ready to knuckle up," I say in a serious tone.

Aiden shakes her head as she secures the gloves on her hands and mirrors my position.

I extend one arm out to her and she briefly hits my fist before she steps back and begins to circle me, like a predator ready to kill their prey, and I couldn't feel more proud of her.

"Show me what you've got," I tell her, and she lunges forward, landing a hook to my ribs. I stagger for a moment on my feet because I forgot just how strong this little shit is when she's in fight mode, but as she takes her second to be smug, I jab her right in the jaw and she stumbles on her feet.

Aiden grunts angrily.

She knows that I'm not here to play a game—she knows that she *has* to fight me or take a beating instead.

"Come on," I taunt her, furrowing my eyebrows and stepping around her as she lunges at me and misses. I've never known Aiden to miss one of her swings—ever. She doesn't want to hurt me even though I told her to, so I'm going to have to teach her a lesson.

I take a deep breath and move toward her quickly, bobbing and weaving to either side, confusing her with my speed and hook her right in the stomach when she least expects it.

She lets out a pained cry but takes the opportunity of me being so close to uppercut me and I almost lose my footing again. I spit some blood onto the pavement and motion for her to attack me again.

That's the only advantage she needs. She takes a step back to size me up and then the next thing I know, she's coming at me like a hurricane, landing fist after fist to my chest, ribs, stomach, and one last blast to my face to knock me onto my back.

I land with a dull thud and grimace when I feel the dirt and small rocks crush into my bare skin. Aiden walks over and glances down at me with a tired, yet triumphant expression on her face.

"You okay?" she asks between bated breaths.

"Never better," I reply, putting my gloved hands over my eyes and laughing.

"Are we done now? Can we just hang out for today or do I have to mess you up again?"

I peek through my fingers at her, then reach up quickly, and yank her down onto the ground next to me.

"Ouch!" she yells with a laugh. "I'm gonna end up hating you before this is all said and done, Gray."

"Yeah, but at least you'll be in one piece too," I reply, glancing at her with a grin.

"You let me win, didn't you?"

Yes.

"No."

She rolls her eyes and turns over onto her stomach, pushing her hair out of her face. The look she's giving me tells me that I'm in for an interrogation, and I may indulge her considering she's been doing such a good job with her training.

"So …" she says, her voice trailing off, and her cheeks turning red. It amazes me that wanting to ask me about my personal life always has this effect on her, when she's always so open about her dalliances all the damn time.

"Yes, we had sex."

"Oh my God, Gray!" she squeals. I appreciate her enthusiasm for me getting laid, but she's so goddamn loud that I end up having to cover my ears in an attempt to get the ringing to go away. She sits up and crosses her legs underneath her; with wide eyes and a huge grin she begins to press me for details.

"How was it? Was he good? Who fucked who? Or did you take turns? Oh my

155

God, tell me everything!"

"'Who fucked who?'" I echo her, raising an eyebrow in amusement. "Have I ever asked you something as asinine as that before, Aiden?"

"No, because in my cases it's always been obvious," she replies with a grin. "With you, one can never tell. Though if memory serves correctly, aren't you a pitcher?"

"'A pitcher,'" I repeat with a laugh as I shake my head. "Sure, kid. Whatever."

Aiden giggles nervously, "Sorry; I didn't mean to sound offensive, I just don't really know how it works is all."

"Same way as it does with you, except there's no snatch," I reply, tilting my head to look at her. She wrinkles her nose at me in response and my grin widens. "Anything else you'd like to know?"

"I already asked what I wanted to know most, and you ignored it," she replies dryly. "Oh wait, did you go down on him?"

I prop myself up on my elbows, letting the dirt and pebbles dig into my skin and snicker. "He did me. I didn't go down on him, but he went down on me. Yes, it was good—honestly, it was fucking amazing, and the only reason I didn't say anything when you barged in earlier asking questions is because it's not just my business that I would be telling you and I don't know how he's dealing with this yet. He seems to be okay with it, but I don't know exactly know Penn Harris outside of my random moments of salivating for him, which is why I kept hushing you up."

"Would you like to know about him?" she asks as she uncurls her legs and stretches. Aiden leans back on her hands and crosses her legs at the ankles and gives me a questioning glance, and I nod. I know she can't tell me his entire life story, but anything would be nice at this point.

"He's pretty strange, which I'm sure you've noticed by now. Well, maybe you haven't," she corrects, rolling her eyes, "all you probably see is that face. Not that I'm judging you for it—what's the point of spending time on chasing someone you're not attracted to, you know? Anyway, he doesn't really do shit except for go out and party with his friends. He's clean though— addiction wise I mean. But then again, depending on how you two interact the next time I see it, I'm sure he'll already have his narcotic of choice picked out. A little bit of advice though, Gray?"

I sit up and nod, waiting for Aiden to continue.

"Okay," she begins with a heavy sigh. "He can get really weird around the rest of the Trust Fund Brigade, so if you see him at the fight on Thursday night, it's best to let him approach you first. Otherwise, if he's not completely comfortable with what happened last night, he'll do his best to make you feel like you're two feet tall. It's his defensive mechanism."

I chuckle as she gives me a sympathetic smile.

It doesn't bother me as much as it should because I should have expected it all things considering. I sigh and get to my feet, content to let my inquiry into the life of Penn Harris die a slow, painful death, and extend a hand down toward Aiden.

"Now what? Are you gonna make me try to lift the damn building off its foundation?" she grumbles, taking my hand and letting me stand her up. I let out a laugh because she looks so damn conflicted and worried about what's next on the list for today, that I kinda wanna pinch her cheeks and tell her to stop pouting.

"Actually, I was going to take a shower then a nap. But I mean if you want to keep going, we can," I reply with a grin.

Aiden lets out a sigh of relief and loops her arm in mine as we pick up our bottles of water and help each other undo the sparring gloves. She seems to be in a much more complaint mood since she knows that she won't have to worry about me running her ragged—at least not for the next few hours.

"Besides," I say as I open the door to the building and let her in, "I can always just kick your ass for real later."

Aiden rolls her eyes and sighs, as she disappears up the staircase, stomping all the way up to the second floor like a young child having a tantrum.

CHAPTER FIFTEEN

Aiden and I are lying in my bed together, cuddled up, and I'm amused at how easily we can go from brutalizing each other to being like this. She insisted on stripping the bed sheets first and made me take them down the washing machine, which I would have done eventually. I just liked having that damn cinnamon and cranberry smell staining the bed sheets. While I was down starting the washing machine, she was in my room putting new sheets on the bed.

"How long were you planning on laying around in that?" she asks, glancing up at me and wrinkling her nose.

"For fuck's sake, Aiden; you make it sound like I'm the only person in the world that's ever slept in sex sheets before," I reply as I close my eyes and let out a yawn.

"You know how long it's been since I had sex sheets?" she gripes, giving my side a poke.

"Ow," I complain with a laugh. For obvious reasons my body is still sore, and the little comeback I have planned is only going to make it worse. "Tell you what—the next time I fuck in my bed and get them all nice and sweaty, I'll let you roll around in it for a while, okay?"

"Oh, shut up," she grumbles, giving me a firm shove in the ribs before turning on her side, facing away from me, and pulling the blanket up to her neck. "I really hate you sometimes."

"Hush," I say, spooning up behind her and placing a hand over her mouth. "It's sleep time now."

Aiden gives me one last, subtle elbow to the stomach to let me know that she's still as in charge as she can be, and I chuckle.

It's strange the way I feel around her. It's much different than the way I've felt around anyone else, but it's nothing more than knowing that she genuinely loves me as the person I am, and not the false perception that I wear day in and day out. She sees the monster and she loves it.

It's almost as if she can feel that I'm thinking about her because she reaches for one of my hands and interlaces her fingers with mine, then moments later, she falls asleep.

And I'm not too far behind her.

When I finally wake up, Aiden's gone from my bed and I sigh. It's becoming something of a habit, it seems, to fall asleep with someone in my arms and wake up absent the person.

I sit up and rub my eyes, before shoving the blanket off and going on a little voyage to find her. I doubt she left because she would have woken me up to tell me that she was heading out.

That's something Aiden's always been good for—never abandoning me.

One of the many reasons the little shit will never get rid of me, I think with a grin as I head into the kitchen area, but she's nowhere to be found.

"Huh."

I glance into the living room and she's not there either—that's when I notice that the door is slightly cracked open. I'm feeling a little frantic at the notion that maybe she *did* leave without telling me after all.

I walk quickly toward the door and pull it open, stepping into the hallway and looking up and down the corridor.

"Aiden?" I call out, my voice cracking slightly.

"I'm upstairs," the faint reply comes.

What the fuck is she doing up there?

I let out a heavy sigh and head toward the staircase, taking the steps two at a time, until I reach the landing and head into my workshop.

"What are you doing?" I ask her curiously, stepping into the room.

She glances at me over her shoulder, a smile on her face, and shrugs. "I just wanted to see what you were working on this time."

I walk over to the table and saddle up next to her, nervous that she'll find something wrong with the piece, but if she does, she hasn't said it yet.

"What do you think?" I ask, chewing the inside of my cheek.

"I actually really like it. I can see where you're going with this—it's not done yet though, is it?" she inquires as she tilts her head and lifts the sheet gingerly. Aiden cranes her head and narrows her eyes so she can see what the body of it looks like, then smiles again. "You're almost done."

"Yeah. I've been a little delayed the past few days, but it's not due for a while, so I'm actually ahead of schedule," I reply, scratching my head. "I'm gonna need your help to finish it completely. You up for it when the time comes?"

"Of course! I'm surprised that you think you even have to ask me that," she replies, nodding her head enthusiastically.

I grin at her and she nudges me before she turns and walks out of the room.

"You'll like her. She's nice and gentle too," I tell it softly. It looks at me and nods as I secure the sheet underneath it's neck.

"I know I've said this to you a hell of a lot more than I should lately, but I swear it's almost over."

It closes its eyes and that's how I know it wants to be alone.

I understand how it feels and I wish it had a friend like Aiden or a lover like Penn. Because maybe if it did, maybe it wouldn't be so resigned to knowing that the end is closer than I've been telling it.

CHAPTER SIXTEEN

I wave at Aiden as she switches her hips painfully down the side of the building. I think it's kind of amusing that even after the hell I put her through today, her need to be the center of every man's attention is still prominent in the way she walks.

Even though I know that's just the way her body moves, it makes me wonder how many times it's gotten close to getting her into trouble when I'm not around.

I shake my head and step back inside once she's safely out of view. I don't have anything else planned for the remainder of the evening. The piece really can't be finished at this point without Aiden and I don't want to bother her about that until after the fight.

I've pushed Penn off until the night of, and from what Aiden tells me, I'll be lucky if he even acknowledges me again when the time comes.

Fuck it.

I decide the best thing to do is just pick up around the place and call Ernie to come get the trash out of the dumpster.

I like Ernie, though he's a bit of an oddball. He runs one of the local morgues and I pay him a good amount of money to have whatever is left over from my art incinerated in his crematorium.

I start on the bottom floor because that makes the most sense. I don't really do much down here, but there's still some dusting to be done. Once that's taken care of, I decide to head up to my workshop. That particular part of the building is never really dirty or unkempt, but the barrels still need to be rolled outside and the trashcans still need emptying.

Ernie always brings me new barrels and shit when we trade out the garbage so I'm never at a loss for what I need.

Plus, it's just nice to be able to talk to someone every now and then that isn't Aiden. Even though I love her to death, sometimes the same conversations with the same person can become rather monotonous.

I don't bother checking on my project before I leave the room. The condition hasn't changed in a couple of days because I've been too starry-eyed and destitute to work on it. As long as it's breathing—and it still is—that's the only thing that matters.

With a whistle, I drag the barrels and garbage to the elevator and take the slow ride down to the second floor. In a weird way, I'm hoping that maybe Penn didn't listen to me and that he'll be waiting, but it's not a disappointment either when I don't find him in the hallway.

I guess he has more discipline than I do. Request to stay away or not, I would have been knocking on his door by now— just to see his eyes for a few moments.

But he's much different than I am that way. While I spent most of my time in the same spaces as him, I would steal glances like a young boy in love, while he would spend his time not realizing it.

Or so I had thought until last night.

A smile crawls across my face as I begin to dust the living room. This particular spot has never seen so much goddamn use except for the past few days when I've had more company than I can usually deal with.

With a happy sigh, I turn to the recliner and think about how it seems to be his favorite part in my home. I lean down and inhale deeply, hoping to find his scent still lingering, but it seems to have climbed onto Aiden's skin and left with her.

It's okay.

In a few days, everything will be normal again and he'll come back. At least I hope he does. I don't know if just the taste that I was given the night before would be enough to satiate my need for him.

Maybe just one more time if that's all I can get.

I walk around and head to the couch, picking up the pillows and punching them a couple of times before they're to my liking, then set them back down again.

Nothing spectacular ever happens on this damn thing so I know it doesn't need any special attention.

I stretch my arms over my head before I head toward the back of the space and proceed to pick up the bathroom. When that's done, I don't even bother with my bedroom.

The bed smells like two of my favorite people right now and I'd rather not fuck with that.

I pull the garbage bags down the hallway then get to work in the kitchen, deep-washing as much of it as I can. I'm not a germaphobe by any means, but I like to keep a tidy home when possible.

Was this place neat when they came over the first time?

I sigh as I finish sweeping the floor. That's going to fucking bug me now, but I'll ask Aiden tomorrow when I see her.

I empty the trashcans and place new bags into them before I wash my hands and call my buddy to swing by.

"I'm already outside, Gray. Tuesday nights seem to be garbage nights for you."

I laugh and disconnect the call, picking up all of the bags and walking into the hallway again. I press the button for the elevator then step inside and turn the key that will keep the doors open while I haul everything inside.

It never takes me long to do and before I know it, I'm downstairs and stepping into the crisp, night air, bags in hand, being greeted by the strange man that I sometimes see as my friend.

Mostly he's a business associate, but he's so damn kind that I can't help and hope that he thinks of me as a friend too.

"Hey, man!" I call out to him, a grin on my face.

Ernie nods as he takes a drag on his cigarette. He looks a little nervous; paranoid even, and it slows my walk to a halt.

"What's going on man?" I ask curiously.

"Um, I ... I found something in your dumpster when I was loading the shit into my truck. I was kind of hoping I could keep it," he says, shuffling his feet against the pavement.

"Huh?"

My face wrinkles in confusion as I drop the bags and walk over to the dumpster, lifting the lid and peering inside.

"Oh shit," I say, the blood draining from my face.

Ernie comes over to stand next to me and peers inside again before he purses his request.

"Can I keep it? I'll be discreet—you know you can trust me, man."

Little Julie, the corner whore, tossed into the dumpster. Fell down the stairs and lies your reward.

CHAPTER SEVENTEEN

I take a deep breath as I step back and give him an even stare. No wonder I could never find her or why the smell of her decomposing body never reached me. Penn hid her in the fucking dumpster.

I finally nod, and Ernie lets out a deep breath. "Get rid of it," I tell him softly.

What he plans to do with her body is none of my fucking concern. What I plan to do with Penn for being so goddamn careless is another matter.

Ernie helps me load the rest of the trash into his truck, but when he reaches into the dumpster to retrieve Julie, I turn away from him and bid him farewell.

"See you next Tuesday?" he calls out.

"Like clockwork," I reply over my

shoulder.

I'm sure the rats and bugs have gotten to her by now and I can't stand to see what's become of her.

I wait just inside the door to the building like I always do, arms crossed firmly over my chest, and wait for the beeping sound of Ernie's truck. Once that's done and he pulls past me, I nod at him again as he waves then I go back upstairs.

I'm so fucking angry right now that I'm having trouble seeing straight. This man that I gave myself to—that I let fuck me so violently because that was his pleasure, could have gotten me sent to fucking jail for the rest of my life all because he wanted to play a game of hide-a-whore.

At this point, I don't know how to feel about him anymore. Did he know that this could mean my downfall, or did he just think that when people die you throw them away in the trash? Why the fuck did he think this was okay to do?

I toss myself down onto the couch and reach for my cellphone, dialing Aiden's phone number. It rings once, twice, three, four times before she finally answers.

"What's up?" she greets me tiredly.

"You said Penn was strange. Does he not have a grip on fucking reality?" I bark into the phone.

"What? Did something happen?" she asks, her tone picking up and becoming curious.

I don't know how to tell Aiden the truth. She knows what I do because I like her feedback and help with my art, but I don't want her to think of me as some kind of mindless killer.

I take a deep breath and let out a long sigh. "I'm sorry, kid. It's nothing major, I just think I'm going through withdrawals."

Aiden giggles, "Was his dick really that good? I mean it's only been a day, Gray."

I chuckle slightly, feeling the anger starting to slip away momentarily. I swear, if Aiden had been born with a dick instead of a pussy, I would have married her by now.

"Best I had in a while," I reply quietly. "I'll let you go. I think I just need to sleep and I'll be okay."

"Hey, before you go," she says, "what's on the agenda for tomorrow? Do I get to kick your ass again?"

I roll my eyes at the ceiling and laugh. "Nope. Tomorrow is yoga and stretching. Then maybe, just maybe, if you're not a whiny little pain in the ass, I'll take you out to dinner. Sound like a plan?"

"For sure!" she replies enthusiastically. "I'll see you in the morning, Gray!"

"Later, kid," I reply softly before I disconnect the call.

As soon as I hang up with her, I kick myself for not asking for Penn's phone number, so I send her a text then set my phone down next to me, rubbing my face with both hands.

I may have told him that I would *see* him at the fight, but that doesn't mean I can't talk to him beforehand.

Aiden replies almost immediately, and I stare at the information. Maybe I won't call him because it would make me feel awkward to try and explain how I got his phone number, so I decide to send him a text instead.

A few, very painful minutes pass by before the phone vibrates on the couch next to me. I don't look at it right away, instead bringing my legs up, and stretching out comfortably onto my back first.

Hey.

It's a simple reply and for some reason it's not what I was expecting. Granted, I don't know what the hell he would say, but I was hoping for something a little more substantial.

I found her, I text back.

Took you long enough lol, is the reply.

Give me break. It's only been a couple of days.

I'll give you a break. ;)

My entire body burns crimson and I'm actually relieved that there's no one here to see how hard I'm blushing right now.

Anyway, I just wanted to let you know that she's gone now.

Where to? Anywhere fun?

Just gone.

Tell me!

To where all little dead whores go.

You're being boring.

The message stings to read, but I don't think he means it in a cruel way. Until I get to know him better, I just have to brush it off and take it as just words with no meaning.

I'm going to sleep now.

Alone? ;)

Yes. Goodnight.

Dream of me.

I have no doubt that I will.

I toss the phone onto the couch, ignoring whatever message he's just sent through. If I read it, I know I'll end up staying awake all night just to fucking talk to him and I have to get some rest.

Tomorrow is a new day and I have to get back into workout mode with Aiden. Penn can wait until Thursday and so can I.

Can't I?

With a loud groan, I reach for my phone and smile at his reply before I take a deep breath and send one back.

I yawn widely as he sends another one

179

back and then me in return.

Aiden is going to fucking kill me when I show up dragging ass or she may be grateful for the fact that I'll more than likely be too tired to do anything. I guess I'll find out in the morning.

CHAPTER EIGHTEEN

It's Thursday afternoon and I've been staring at myself in the bathroom mirror for the past hour. Wednesday's training was partially uneventful because I ended up staying awake until four in the morning texting Penn, but it wasn't too bad considering it was meant to be an easy day anyway.

Aiden did everything I told her to with a fire burning in her belly that I had never noticed before, then I treated her to dinner. We didn't talk much because we knew at that point today was inevitable. She still hasn't shown any signs of regretting her rematch and I've done my best to stop trying to get her to at least postpone the fucking thing.

In a way, I don't want to go tonight. I don't want to see what could potentially become of Aiden if she doesn't take this as seriously as she should. Sometimes, when she realizes that she has the upper hand, she'll start fucking around with her opponent, but Max Boothe is the one person that almost took her fucking head off when she got too cocky with him.

"Goddammit," I whisper to my reflection, as I finally get my ass into gear. I turn around and turn on the shower, testing the water to make sure that it's just above what I can handle. Whenever Aiden has a fight, I tend to scald myself a bit so that I'm numb to whatever injuries she sustains, if any.

I spend another hour under the hot water, meticulously washing myself until I can't take the heat any longer. The more time I spend doing things that shouldn't take as long as I'm making them take, the sooner I'll get to going to pick up Aiden and drive her to the forum.

I have her mouthpiece and even though I know it may not entirely be within regulations, if it's not allowed, I'll pull her out of that fucking fight before it even begins. The organizer likes bare-knuckle blood and I like not having to pay for expensive dental surgery. Worse case scenario, I'll just take him inside and suck his dick to change his mind, but I refuse to let Aiden's teeth get knocked out again.

I step out of the shower and wrap my towel around my waist as I go back to the sink again.

I take a moment to compose myself. My nerves are fucking shot, and I haven't even left yet.

I let out a heavy sigh as undo my towel and wipe myself off thoroughly. I go through my daily ritual of rubbing lotion on my body, towel drying my hair and making sure it's neatly brushed, then walk to my bedroom to get dressed.

I've decided on a loose pair of black jeans and a white tank top. The reason I choose to dress like this is in case I decide to step in for Aiden at the last moment, I need to be comfortable and relaxed.

When I'm dressed and ready, I sit on the edge of my bed, head in my hands, wondering how the hell tonight is going to play out.

Will Aiden win again, or will Max be her undoing? Will Penn acknowledge me, or will he decide I don't exist again?

I know I shouldn't think of anything other than Aiden's well-being, but goddammit it. My mind has been so fucked lately that it's hard for me to understand what's important and what's not anymore.

"Are you praying?"

I jump and gasp in shock.

As I pull my hands away from my face, I see Aiden standing in the doorway, leaning against the frame, her arms crossed and watching me with an amused smile.

Sometimes I forget that she has keys to this place because she barely ever uses them.

"Jesus Christ—you almost gave me a fucking heart attack," I grumble at her, trying to regain my composure.

"That would be counterproductive,"

she replies, sticking her tongue out at me.

"What are you doing here, anyway? I thought I was going to pick you up?" I ask her, raising an eyebrow curiously.

"Yeah, I know," she replies with a heavy sigh. Aiden comes over and sits next to me on the bed and gives me a nudge. "But I haven't forgotten how you get before one of my fights and I want to make sure you're okay."

I chuckle quietly and smile at her. She worries about me more than she should, but that's just the sign of an amazing friend and I feel like I don't deserve her sometimes.

"I'll be okay when it's over," I tell her softly.

"Good," she says with a nod. "Now show me my fighting gear."

I laugh and get up from the bed and walk over to the closet. I have it on the top shelf where I left it to set after I was able to pry the mold out of the rest of the plaster.

I retrieve the small box and walk back over to Aiden. I decide to be playful in the moment because I think it's something we can both use, so as I stop in front of her, I drop down on one knee and open the top.

"Aiden James, will you do me the honor of keeping all of your teeth in your mouth?" I ask with a grin. She laughs and swats my shoulder, then reaches for the mouthpiece.

"Wow, Gray. This is bad ass," she exclaims in appreciation. I grin proudly as I sit back onto my ass and cross my legs in front of me. They're not as stylish as I would have hoped, but they'll get the job done. Aiden takes out the top part and slides it into her mouth, securing it in place, then does the same with the bottom half.

She sucks her teeth—more than likely to get used to the subtle, metallic taste, then gives me a toothy smile.

"These are more comfortable than I thought they would be," she manages to say. I laugh as she wipes the saliva from her mouth and chin and shake my head.

"As you can see, they're not exactly great for talking with though," I explain with a grin.

She reaches up and pulls the guard

out of her mouth then places it back into the box.

"Well, I'm ready when you are, Gray," she says brightly, but I can see the sudden glimmer of nervousness in her eyes and it kills the smile on my face.

I get to my feet and look down at Aiden who's also standing now and sigh.

"Ready as I'll ever be."

CHAPTER NINETEEN

The parking lot is almost full when we get there even though we're still a half an hour early. As we get out and start walking toward the crowd of people waiting for tonight's melee, a cheer erupts from them. Most of them are happy to see Aiden and I bet that the ones that are shouting her name are the ones that placed a massive amount of money on her winning tonight.

But there are also the ones that are jeering. The ones that don't know what she's capable of and only see a small figure of a woman and a mountainous man of an opponent. They're the ones that think she's more than likely going to be brutalized tonight, but I know she'll show them.

Win or lose, Aiden always has a way

of making sure people remember her. I can see the barrel fires the closer we get and the unmistakable form of Max Boothe looming in the distance between them.

"I'll get you registered," I say to Aiden, placing a hand on her back and handing her the mouthpiece box.

She smiles up at me before she turns her attention back to the crowd of people, then disappears into it.

"Hey, man," I say to Gordon. He's the main organizer of these fucking things. A homely old, fat bastard that makes his living off of the blood and tears of others. "Aiden's here."

He nods and crosses his arms as best as he can over his swollen belly and watches me carefully as I sign her in. I shudder at the though of having to blow this bastard to get the mouthpiece past him, but I'd do anything for Aiden.

"So, listen. Because of last time I made her something to protect her teeth," I say, as I finish signing my name on the sheet. "It's nothing that'll give her an edge. It's just something to make sure she doesn't lose anymore of them."

"I'll check them out before the fight starts," he says evenly with a nod.

"Cool. Thanks."

I turn my back to him and crane my neck as I walk back toward the crowd. I can't find Aiden at the moment but that doesn't mean anything. She usually likes to spend time talking to her adoring fans before shit starts to get too messy.

"What's up Gray?"

I grit my teeth. I know that voice because it haunted my dreams for as long as Aiden was in the hospital. I turn slowly and have to fight the urge to beat the shit out of Max the closer he gets to me. When he stops in front of me, he looks down at me and smirks.

"Ready to watch your little girlfriend get her ass handed to her again?"

"Actually I am. But you're not my type, so I wouldn't exactly call you my girlfriend," I reply, looking him up and down. "Maybe next time, if you beg me hard enough, I might let you suck my dick."

His friends laugh, as does anyone in earshot of our conversation, but Max's face flushes red with anger. He probably wants nothing more than to beat me into the ground and I'd gladly take him on to get Aiden out of this shit.

He takes a step closer to me and my body tenses as I clench my fists at my side. I know I can't take him down because I'm a realist, but I also know where to hit him to hurt him and I wouldn't hesitate to take the chance to cripple the big buffoon.

"You just co-signed her next trip to the hospital. Except this time, I'm going to make sure she doesn't fucking make it out," he seethes, his eyes boring into mine.

"Yeah, well, we'll see, won't we?" I respond with a grin. I'm wearing the visage of confidence when I actually just died a little bit on the inside.

What the fuck did I just do?

Gordon just finished inspecting Aiden's mouth-wear and has thankfully approved of it. Since I made it out of dual-laminate, I know that it would protect her when she needs it but not do damage to Max's fists. Even though that's not something I would normally give a fuck about. She's standing in the middle of the cleared space, facing Max and ready to fight for her honor.

I've tried in the past twenty minutes to get her to let me step into her place, but she refused to the point of almost reducing me to tears.

Max is standing opposite to Aiden, his hands on his hips, staring down at her dangerously and I feel so fucking alone watching from the edge of the circle.

As Gordon starts going over the rematch and the rules, I notice Aiden is trying to catch my eye. When she finally does, she almost imperceptibly jerks her head to the left and I allow my eyes to follow her direction. My body trembles slightly, but only once, and then I turn my attention back to the center of the circle.

Penn's here.

I can almost hear Aiden's excited voice in my head. Just like it was the first night I met him, and she made the introductions and now we're both here watching, hoping that she'll be okay.

In the two seconds I looked over at him I was able to see that he's standing with his friends and when he stole a quick glance in my direction he saw me looking at him, which caused him to almost immediately cut his eyes back toward Max and Aiden.

I shake my head and cross my arms over my chest, praying that this will start soon because the faster it does, the faster it will be over with.

"Alright, shake hands, and let's get this going," Gordon finally says loudly.

I run a hand over my face as Aiden extends a fist and Max waves her off. He raises his fist and Aiden does the same, and as Gordon gives the go ahead, I feel faint.

I don't know if I can watch her fight him again, but I refuse to leave her alone. She may have a shit ton of fans here, but I know

I'm her only true friend besides Penn that gives a shit about her right now, so I can't leave.

As they begin to circle each other slowly, I damn near jump out of my skin when someone nudges me. I glance over to my left and roll my eyes when I realize it's Penn. He nods at me but says nothing else since his friends are on either side of us now.

"Aiden's your girl, right?" one of them leans over and asks over the roar of the crowd.

"What?" I ask, turning my eyes back toward the center of the forum. Aiden and Max are circling each other like predators and I seem to have missed who threw the first swing. I assume it wasn't Aiden, because had it been, she would be on him still piling on as many hits as she could get.

"Aiden?" he shouts into my ear. I wince and give him a dirty look causing him to back up a bit. "I was asking if she's your girlfriend."

"No," I reply evenly, turning my

attention back to the fight. Max steps forward and puts power behind a swing that Aiden manages to dodge again. She moves quickly and lands a number of hits to his torso before she bounces back away from him. I smile when I see her eyes. She's damn determined to make it out of this in one piece and I know she's looking forward to the payday too.

I take a deep breath and rub a hand over my face when Max quickly regains his footing and swings at Aiden again, this time clipping her—just barely, in the face. It's enough to make her stagger slightly but when he moves on her again, she manages to skitter out of the way and land a hook to his ribs.

"He's gonna fuck her up when she gets tired of running around," one of Penn's friends says gleefully.

"Shut your fucking mouth," he snaps at him before I have a chance to react. I hold Penn's eyes for a moment and nod in thanks, when the crowd erupts again.

Aiden's managed to climb onto Max's

back and she's wailing on his head, blow after blow, until he violently grabs her by the arm and throws her off of him. She lands roughly on the pavement and he moves quickly, leaning over her, and smirking.

"It was fun while it lasted," he taunts her as he reaches down and grabs her by the throat, lifting her up. Aiden's dangling a couple of inches off the ground as Max scans the crowd. When his eyes finally land on me, a malicious smile dances across his lips as he begins to beat her violently.

She's like a sack of meat hanging from a hook in a slaughterhouse getting tenderized and I don't know if there's anything I can fucking do about it. If I intercede, she gets disqualified and she'll hate me forever. If I don't, he'll probably kill her, and I'll lose her regardless.

Aiden coughs up blood onto Max's face which causes him to drop her to the ground. While she's down, holding her sides, he angrily wipes away the mess before he does something that seals his fate as the loser in the fight.

His anger takes over him and he ends up kicking her so hard in the fucking ribs that causes the entire crowd to gasp at once. My mouth drops open as Aiden lets out a scream of pain and before he has the chance to land another kick on her, I spring into action.

"Motherfucker!"

I run at him and lower my head, landing my shoulder in his stomach, and taking him down as violently as he dropped her. Max doesn't have a chance to defend himself or react because I'm so overcome with rage that my body has him pinned to the ground.

Fist after fist. Blow after blow. Each moment of worrying about how Aiden would survive this fight is behind my rage as I keep hitting him in the face. His nose breaks, blood spurts out of his mouth, and that's still not enough for me.

I want to do more than just harm him. I want to fucking kill him for what he did to her. He had no intention of fighting fairly—he wanted to humiliate her and put her out of commission, but as God is my witness, I'll fucking kill him first.

"Gray, Gray!"

Penn's frantic voice is in my ear and I can feel multiple pairs of hands on me attempting to pull me off of Max. I'm losing the will to hang on to him, but not because my rage is subsiding, but because there are more people trying to drag me off of him than there probably are checking on Aiden.

It takes about five men to finally pry me off of the unconscious Max, but he's still breathing and that's still too good for me.

"Fuck him. We have to get Aiden help," Penn says, stepping in front of me and blocking Max. My eyes begin to come into focus again as he fills my view.

"Oh fuck. Aiden," I say, staggering on my feet.

I turn around and push my way through the people that are crowding over her, scoop her off the pavement, and cradle her in my arms. She cries out from the pain of broken bones, and I turn around frantically. I don't know how to get her out of the crowd without hurting her more, but Gordon comes over, declares her the winner by disqualification, and tells the crowd to move out of our way.

I nod at him in thanks, tears streaming down my face, as I move as quickly as I can toward the parking lot. The crowd is following me, people are calling out to Aiden. Some are congratulating her, others are taunting her, and the entire time, she's in my arms shaking violently hoping for the pain to stop.

"I've got you now. It'll be okay," I say to her softly. Aiden looks up at me and forces a smile through her tears then closes her eyes, her body going limp.

It's in this moment that I realize my worst fear may be coming true. The one thing that could send me into a downward spiral that I won't be able to climb my way out of.

I think I just lost my best friend.

CHAPTER TWENTY

I haven't seen Aiden in a couple of days. Penn had me follow him to some stranger's house, telling me that he's a good friend of his family and that he can fix her up. Turned out the guy is a big time M.D. and he seems to help Penn and his friends out a lot.

I didn't put up an argument when I left her there. They both assured me that she would be in good hands and that she would make a full recovery, but that I had to give him the time and space to work on her.

As I lie on the floor in my living room covered in sweat and my mind racing in a thousand different directions, I can't help but wonder if she's getting better. I want to call and check on her even though I know I'm not allowed to, and it's not like it would matter since I don't have the doctor's phone number anyway.

A knock on my door gets my attention but I don't move from my spot. There's only one person I want to see right now, and I know she's not better yet; she can't be. Not after the way Max left her.

"Fuck off," I call out.

The knock comes again; harder and louder.

"I said fuck off!" I shout at the top of my lungs.

"Open the fucking door," comes the muffled reply.

I let out a laugh and roll over onto my stomach, push myself to my feet and sigh heavily. Once I get to the door, I run a hand back through my hair, then pull it open and lean against it.

"I have Aiden's money."

I look into Penn's eyes, then lower my gaze to the fat envelope in his hand. With a nod, I take it from him, then attempt to close the door again, but he pushes it open.

"Um. She's doing a lot better," he offers

nervously. "Doc says she's healing up pretty fast."

"Thanks," I say with a nod, attempting to close the door again. But Penn's persistent in his visit and he uses his foot to prop the door open.

"Are you okay? I mean, I haven't heard from you in days and when we went our separate ways the other night you looked absolutely fucked."

"I watched my best friend get beat to a goddamn pulp, so you'll have to excuse me if I wasn't as friendly as you hoped," I reply through grit teeth. "Now, if you don't mind, I really want to be alone."

Penn looks like he's been slapped in the face, yet I don't find it in myself to care at the moment.

"Yeah. Sorry. I'll uh … I'll go then," he says quietly, turning away from me and walking back toward the elevator.

Great. Now I feel like shit twice over.

"Wait. Penn? Do you want to help me with something?" I ask, leaning out of the door. My piece is due soon and I can't put off finishing it any longer, but I know I can't do it without help.

"You sure I'm not intruding?" he asks curiously, taking a step back in my direction.

"Positive. Come on, I need your help."

Penn grins widely as he enters my home and I'd be lying if I said I didn't give a shit about what his reaction will be to my work.

"What do you need help with?" he asks.

I walk back to my room and toss Aiden's payout onto my dresser. When I turn around, I damn near walk right into Penn, who's smiling at me wickedly.

"Not that," I mumble nervously.

"Oh."

His face drops and a small smile creases my lips. He looks so damn disappointed right now that I kind of feel bad.

"Maybe after?"

"Cool," he says happily. "So, what do you need help with?"

He crosses his long arms over his chest and I take a deep breath. I've never been apprehensive about what I choose to do for a living, and I wouldn't be surprised if Aiden's already slipped during a conversation, but I just don't know how he'll handle actually seeing my work in progress.

"I need to finish my project. I have to take it to the owner tomorrow night," I explain.

"I'm not very artsy, but I'll do what I can," he replies enthusiastically.

God, I hope he can keep a fucking secret.

"Alright, let's go," I say with a nod, motioning for him to follow me back into the hallway. I press the button for the elevator doors to open and once we step inside, Penn sighs heavily.

"What's the matter?" I ask him curiously. He sighs again, tilts his head to the side, and as the elevator begins to crawl to the third floor, he grabs me around my waist and shoves me back against the wall.

"Whoa, there," I say with a quiet chuckle, holding my hands up. "I surrender."

Penn smiles, leans forward and brushes his lips gently against mine but he doesn't kiss me.

"Just giving you something to think about for later," he says softly. "Is it working?"

That should be a give-in at this point. I'm sure he can feel my hard dick pressed against his body, but Penn seems to be the kind of person that needs verbal confirmation.

"Obviously," I reply, moving his hand to my dick. Penn lowers his eyes down to the prize in his hand and bites his lower lip. "But not right now," I say as soon as the elevator doors open. "Now, we have work to do."

Penn grunts, a sulking expression on his face as he follows me to the workshop door. I don't open it right away, though, because I need to prepare him for what he's about to see.

"Do you remember when you asked me what kind of art I do, and I told you that I work with textures?" I ask him, shuffling my feet nervously. Penn nods and waits for me to continue. "I'm very proud of the work I do and if this isn't something you can handle then tell me as soon as I show you the piece and we can part ways right then and there. I won't force you to help me with something you may not be able to handle, but I also expect that you'd be able to keep my little secret."

He grins mischievously and tilts his head to the side. "Took you long enough to find that chick. I'm pretty sure I'm good with secrets."

My eyes soften as I return his smile with an even stare. I don't have it in me to admonish him for thinking that this is anything like the Little Julie situation. What's inside is alive and going through a transition that no one other than Aiden has seen. It may be harder on him than he may understand, but if he's willing to help me, he needs to be able to keep the secret.

I run a hand over my face before I relent and turn back toward the door, unlocking it and pushing it open.

"Welcome to hell," I say over my shoulder as I lead the way into the room.

CHAPTER TWENTY-ONE

Penn is looking at it like it's the most beautiful thing he's ever seen. His eyes are wide with child-like innocence and his mouth is slightly open as he walks around the table, taking in every stitch, every new modification, and the possibility of what it's going to become.

"What do you need me to do?" he finally asks after he's taken it in. He places his hands on either side of its head as it watches him with curious eyes. Penn is looking down at it, runs a hand over the side of its face, then turns his attention back to me, eager for instruction.

A little *too* eager for my liking.

But I'm still grateful for the extra pair of hands.

"First, you need to put on some gloves. You'll find them on that table over there," I say nodding to a long, wooden table full of tools and devices that sits alongside the back wall.

Penn quickly goes over and locates the pair I mentioned, slipping them on, as he walks back toward us. I'm smiling down at it and its looking up at me with a kind smile dancing in its eyes.

"Do you … uh, do you love that thing?" Penn asks me curiously.

"I love all of them," I reply softly, looking up at him again. "Someone has to."

He gives me an amused look before he shrugs, "So what are we doing?"

"We're finishing it," I say, moving away from the piece and walking toward the table. There's a rather large rucksack sitting in the middle with the final parts that will make this everything the owner required it to be, and while it will hurt it for the most part, I'm hoping that with Penn's help, we can move quickly.

I pick up the heavy bag and go back to

the metal table.

"Fuck, can you grab that power drill for me? There should be two, actually," I say to Penn as I drop the bag onto the floor and begin to unpack it.

He nods and moves quickly, returning with the necessary tools we'll need to get these fucking things screwed into place.

"I wish I had something to give you that would dull the pain, but nothing will help this time. We'll move fast, though. I promise," I say to it softly as I place the handmade, metal hooves onto the table.

"How do I do this?" he asks, patiently holding out one of the drills toward me.

"You have to slide it on—rest it on the ankle bone, then use one of the bolts to get it into place. That's where the drills come in," I say to him quietly as I fidget with my own drill. I press the button and it comes to life, briefly causing the pet to let out a frantic moan.

"I know, believe me, I know. But we all have to feel real pain at some point in our lives to become the beautiful things we're destined to be," I tell it as I move down toward the end of the table and slip the other hoof on.

Penn looks at me and waits. It honestly surprises me that he hasn't asked anymore questions or even backed out of doing this. Maybe he knows that I need him as much as it does, or maybe he just has no regard for human life.

Either way, he's a godsend right now.

"Aiden's gonna be so pissed at me," I say to no one in particular with a soft chuckle.

"Why?" Penn asks.

"Because she was supposed to help me finish this," I explain, shaking my head woefully. "Alright. On three. Ready?"

"Yeah."

"One." It whimpers, and I try not to make eye contact with it. "Two." We both power our drills on and line up the bolts with its ankle bones. "Three."

"That was fucking amazing," Penn

exclaims with a huge smile on his face. We've finished securing the hooves now and I've been cradling its head, trying to help with the pain and show it that even though it's a completely transformed into a pet now, that I hope it can forgive me.

"Can you give us a minute?" I ask him irritably. Its tears have almost subsided, but I know the pain will last much longer because I chose to not sedate it this time.

Penn looks stung. Like I reached over and slapped him, but he has to understand that gloating in front of a pet is something I don't do, nor will I tolerate.

"Sorry. I'll clean up the mess," he offers quietly.

I nod at him as he begins to put the drills away, the bag slung over his shoulder on his way back to the table.

He leaves the room once he's done and I can hear the echo of his footsteps as he jogs down the stairs.

"He's new at this, but I think he did a good job, don't you?" I ask it softly. It closes its eyes tightly, tears streaming down the side of its face, and manages a small nod.

"It'll go away soon—the pain doesn't last forever. I'll help you take your first steps before I turn you over and if you don't like your new owner after some time, you can come back to me."

Penn returns a few moments later with a hand towel and a bottle of antiseptic. Without a word, he quickly goes to work washing the outside of the hooves and getting as much into the cuff as he can, careful to do his best not to hurt it.

My heart fills a little more for him because of how gently he's caring for it in his own way. I think he understands now that even though its not quite human anymore, it deserves to be treated with a modicum of respect. It needs to be loved just like anything else in this world—and it deserves it more than most.

When he's done, he leaves the room again, and I follow not far behind him. Of course, I've kissed my finished product gently on the forehead as I always do in parting after I've worked on it and tell it that tomorrow, I'll deliver it where it belongs.

By the time I make it back down to the second floor, Penn is walking back down the hallway from the bathroom and gives me a nervous look.

"Sorry if I pissed you off up there. I really was only trying to help, and I didn't think being proud of what we did would make you mad," he explains with a sheepish grin.

"Why were you so comfortable doing that? And getting rid of Julie?" I finally ask, giving him an inquisitive stare. At this point, I don't think secrets between us should be a thing and I'm hoping he agrees.

Time will tell.

"Huh? Oh," he begins with a laugh. "Did you ever hear about those places that you can go where you can pay like x amount of dollars and shoot someone in the head or some shit? Well, last year, me and a bunch of my buddies went overseas and found one. It's not so bad after you pull the trigger—it's more of a rush than anything else, know what I mean?"

I stare at him, unblinking, shocked by

his revelation and doing my best not to show it.

"Not really," I finally manage to say.

"Well, you've killed too, even if it was by accident, that chick? She didn't fall down the stairs, I bet," he says, the grin widening on his face.

My face turns red and he nods knowingly. "It's okay. If I was going to narc on you, I already would have done it."

"Right," I reply evenly.

I sigh and look away from him. My mind wanders back to Aiden and how she's holding up, but something tells me that even if I ask Penn, he won't tell me.

"Hey, so. Didn't you promise me something?" he asks, taking a few steps forward and sliding his arms around my waist.

I chuckle and drape mine around his shoulders, peering into his eyes and wondering if maybe this is something more than just randomly fucking.

"Can I ask you something?" I ask with a smile.

"She's fine. I called the doctor before I came over," he replies, leaning forward.

I pull my head back and shake my head. "It's not about Aiden, but thanks for the update."

"Then what is it?"

"Before Aiden told you that I had a thing for you, did you know?"

Penn's lips curve into a dangerous grin as he raises his eyes back to mine. "Maybe. But like I said, I've never been with a guy before and my friends aren't exactly the understanding type, so I always knew that I would have to act like you weren't there even though you were."

"Oh."

That makes sense. Rich, little bastards that fly around the world shooting people in the head for fun can't handle one of their own having a same sex relationship.

I guess it's just fucking after all.

"Fuck them," he says dismissively. "They're usually so coked out, they wouldn't know a good thing if it hit them in the face with a brick—but I do. And while I may have to keep this from them, I ... I want what you promised me. I need it really. You're like a fucking drug that I hadn't tried yet, Gray and from the first taste, I've become hooked on you."

"And what happens when you decide you need rehab? What then?" I ask him quietly.

"There's no cure for you. And if there is? I don't fucking want it," he breathes, stepping forward and pressing his soft lips against mine.

I close my eyes and lose myself in his kiss. I didn't realize how desperately I need him until I felt him pressed against me again and I'll do everything I can to never have to let go of him.

CHAPTER TWENTY-TWO

His moans bring an animal out of me that I never knew existed. I'm gripping his hips tightly and fucking him as gently as I can even though I want nothing more than to destroy him. His ass is as tight as I thought it would be and the sound of flesh against flesh—the scent of sweat and desire is fucking maddening.

Penn reaches back and grabs one of my wrists tightly. His nails digging into my flesh make me smile and I fuck him just a little harder to let him know it.

"More," he gasps, through grit teeth. I oblige, lean down against him, and bring one of my feet up onto the bed and thrust into him further than I had been before.

Just when I can tell that he can't take

anymore, I pull out of him and begin to tug on my cock. I need to cum right now and I don't want to do it inside of him. Not just yet—he hasn't earned that.

My breathing becomes labored as Penn lays on the bed in front of me, trying to regain his composure. His body glistens in the moonlight and I can see the smile on his face. I lick my lips and keep rubbing my dick until I shoot my load over his perfect ass.

"Fuck," I moan loudly.

"You should have let me do that for you," he chuckles softly.

"I'm not done with you just yet," I tell him, pulling him up and laying down on the bed. "Climb on and show me what you've got."

Penn grins as he moves on top of me, holding my dick in his hand and gently easing it back into himself.

"Holy shit," he breathes, his eyes closing tightly, before he places them on my shoulders. He leans down, mouth open against mine, and I lick his lips. The feeling of his tight hole gripping my cock is an amazing sensation and I honestly hope that he's enjoying this as much as he seems to be.

He moves slowly at first, raising and lowering himself on my cock. I know he needs to get used to the feeling, so I don't rush him. If anything, the pace he's moving at right now is almost enough to make me cum again, but I grit my teeth and hold onto to it.

"Oh fuck," he whispers, his forehead against mine as begins to move faster. I grin and push him back so that he's forced to take as much of my dick as he can, and he leans back as he begins to bounce up and down.

His eyes are closed tightly as he moves faster and harder. I keep one hand firmly on his hip and use the other to being to pull on his cock. I want him to cum with me inside of him, because in a way, that makes him mine.

Penn lets out a loud moan as I keep tugging on his dick and I'm ready for it.

I know he's going to cum and I want him to. I want him to do it for me so fucking desperately.

"Come on; you know you want to," I say, tugging a little harder. He grunts, and I know that I'm hurting him a bit, but I don't care. I need this right now and it's the only thing that will keep me fucking sane until I can see Aiden again.

"Oh shit!"

Penn finally cums, and I can't help but laugh when he settles back against my bent legs. I tug on his dick a couple of more times to make sure I've gotten it all then glance down at my stomach.

"Really?" I tease him.

"Sorry," he says with a laugh as he climbs off of me and lays next to me. I roll my eyes and shake my head.

I let out a content sigh and glance at him, licking his cum off of my hand when he looks at me. Penn grins and reaches down for my still hard dick and gives it a gentle tug.

I close my eyes and take a deep breath

as he rests his head against my shoulder and keeps moving his hand up and down my shaft. It won't take much to make me cum right now because I've been holding another load since blowing the other one on him and he knows it.

He snakes his tongue out toward my nipple and flicks it against it gently enough to make my body shudder as he keeps jerking me off.

I turn my face toward his, my lips in his hair and my breathing becoming labored again.

Penn moves his hand faster.

I open my mouth and begin to gasp against his hair.

Penn moves his hand slower.

He knows what he's doing and it's fucking driving me crazy which seems to be his endgame.

"Oh God," I grunt against the top of his head.

Penn moves his hand faster again.

And this time, he gets what he was after. I cum so fucking hard that the room spins for a moment and it takes me a little longer than normal to even my breathing out again.

"Jesus Christ, you're so fucking good at that," I say with a tired laugh.

"Well, not to brag or anything, but I practiced on myself for years as a kid," he jokes, glancing up at me and laughing.

I grin and sigh, turning my eyes toward the ceiling. A thought crosses my mind suddenly and I'm wondering just how far Penn is willing to go with me.

"Are you busy tomorrow?" I ask him.

"Not really. Why, what's up?" he asks, sitting up and reaching for the blanket. He pulls it up over my stomach and across his lap and glances down at me.

"I have to walk the pet around the building a couple of times to make sure it can be sturdy on it's new feet, then I have to drop it off later in the evening," I say slowly.

"Want some help?"

I look up at him and nod.

"Okay, then that's tomorrow planned," he replies, running a hand back through his sweat slicked hair. "If you want, we can swing by Doc's place and check on Aiden too afterwards."

"I would love that," I reply softly.

He nods and lays back down, turning his body toward me, yawning loudly. "I'll call him after we take care of the other shit then."

I don't say anything right away. I'm sure he knows that it means a great deal to me see my best friend—to know that she's okay because of being there with her and not just getting a report on her condition.

Penn's breathing starts to become even and when I can tell he's not awake anymore, I finally say what I know I should have when he could still hear me.

"Thank you."

PART THREE

ALL GOOD THINGS

CHAPTER TWENTY-THREE

When I wake up the next morning, it's not to an empty bed. It's in the arms of the man that I think I'm falling in love with. Having never known what that feels like, I'm not entirely sure if that's what's happening or if my crush is just growing into some out of control feeling that I've never experienced before.

I can't love him and Aiden at the same time, can I? Does a man like me really have enough room in my heart to love two people in completely different ways?

My heavy sigh stirs Penn next to me, but if it woke him up, he's not letting on. I turn my face toward him, burying my nose in his hair and inhale deeply. I know I have to go upstairs and start getting the pet ready to go to her new owner, but I want to take the smell of Penn's body with me.

Aiden would laugh if she could see me right now. Not in a cruel way, more of an "I told you so" kind of way. She tried for years to keep me upbeat after I decided to kick the male escort thing by doing even the smallest things.

Taking me out for ice cream, walking down the beach to take in a sunset, randomly showing up with little presents to make me smile—hell, she even tried to set me up on a few blind dates, but I never went. Then one night, she talked me into taking a break from being a hermit and took me to a movie.

That's where I saw Penn for the first time.

That's when I felt my heart race and the blood rush into my ears for the very first time in my life, that's when I knew what it felt like to truly want something. Aiden saw it on my face as soon as Penn walked away from her when they were done chatting at the box office and she understood at that moment she had finally produced the one thing that she knew could keep me from falling into a hellish despair of my own making.

Ever since that night, she tried her damnedest to get us both in the same places again, but when I caught on to her, I stopped her in her tracks. I told her that I didn't need or want anything that I didn't already have, but Aiden knew I was full of shit.

I had managed to do okay for myself until she dragged me out to The Lounge. It was easy enough to do since she didn't tell me that she knew Penn would be there, and to be quite honest, I had almost forgotten about him until that point.

Penn Harris with the magical big blue eyes and soft, full lips.

I chuckle as I pull away from him and gently ease myself off the bed. I don't want him to wake up until he's ready—it will give me some time alone with the pet and a chance to figure out if I should take it outside or just up and down the hallway to learn to walk again.

After a fair bit of looking around, I manage to locate my boxers on the floor and slip them on, casting a glance over my shoulder on my way out of the room. *Yeah, he's definitely asleep still,* I think with a small smile.

I stop in the kitchen and grab an apple, then make my way to the elevator. I'm eager to see how it's healing today and maybe see if it'll let me feed it. Sometimes, they can get temperamental after completion and don't like me touching them again, but this one seems to be different from what I can tell. Of course, I could be wrong about that, but there's only way to find out for sure.

I lean against the wall of the elevator as it ascends to the top floor of the building and rub the fruit against my chest before I bite into it. It would be nice if I could share some of this with it, but I don't want to undo the stitching since that's healed up so nicely. Also, it doesn't seem to mind the way I do feed its body. This piece has been the easiest of all the ones I've worked on so far which only makes me feel worse about not sedating it before we attached the hooves last night.

I walk out of the elevator and push the door open to the workshop. There's no reason to keep it locked now since the only two people I give an actual shit about have been in here.

"Good morning!" I call out to it cheerfully as I approach the table.

I turn the hanging lamp on over the table as I tend to do when my pieces are finished to give them a once over before I begin prepping them for the move to their new home.

It doesn't greet me with warm eyes like it usually does, instead it follows my movements with a solemn, and somewhat pained stare. I pull the sheet completely off of the piece, letting it fall to the floor and run my hands down its thigh and stop just below its knee where the fur I hand sewn into it begins.

I'm very proud of the job I've done on it. The order placed was particularly specific at to the type of fur it wanted for this piece, and I was able to get an amazing deal on some faux fur at the local craft store. I'd never hurt an animal to recreate something like this—or at all for that matter. They don't deserve to be mistreated any more than small children do, so I tend to always work around requests like this and still produce what's requested to the highest quality that I'm capable of. The end product is always so well done that the owners don't think anything of it.

The finished product looks exquisite and the owner will know that this is money well spent. What they choose to do with the pet once they have it in their possession really isn't my concern, but I always do wonder about them sometimes.

It can be chalked up to absence making the heart grow fonder and being proud of one's work.

I walk around to the other side of the table, biting into the apple again, with my back to the door and raise an eyebrow.

"Fuck."

I let out a sigh when I notice that a patch of fur seems to be coming displaced.

"I'm not going to sew it again, so don't worry," I tell it as I flip the small square of material. "I'll just glue it—it'll do the same job."

Just as I'm ready to walk away from the table, I feel a pair of arms slide around my waist from behind and a chin rest on the back of my shoulder.

"You know what sucks? Waking up to an empty bed when it wasn't that way when you went to sleep."

I close my eyes and lean my head back slightly. Penn's voice is so soft and destitute, and I know how he feels. I've felt that way so many times in my fucking life but never with someone I care about so goddamn much.

"Are you … are you not wearing clothes?" I ask suddenly.

"Nope," he replies with a laugh, his hands snaking their way into the waistband of my boxers.

I shake my head and pull away, then

turn to face him. "Not in front of it," I say softly. "Besides, I was pretty sure I wore you out last night."

Penn tilts his head to the side and grins, "Did you miss the part where I told you that I can be insatiable?"

I laugh and give him a gentle, but firm shove. "Go put some damn pants on."

Penn gives me a dirty look before he turns and leaves the room. Once he's out of earshot, I put a hand gently on its forehead.

"I'm sorry about that. I hope you know that I would have never allowed that in front of you. He's the guy I've been telling you about," I explain with a smile.

It closes its eyes and jerks its head away from my hand and I sigh. I don't want it to leave my home hating me, but I don't think there's anything to be done about that now. It was the pain it felt—the affliction of knowing that I was trying too damn hard to impress Penn in front of it and hoping that it would be able to bear the brunt of what we had done together, and it hates me now because of it.

I head over to the table and get the crafting glue so I can fix the patch that's falling off. Maybe since this won't cause it any pain, I might win some favor in its eyes again even though I know I'm going to lose it once I get it on its new feet.

Once I have that set, I place a hand firmly down on its leg and count to ten. I let out my breath in a rush as I pull my hand away and give the fur a tug. *Well at least that worked the way I wanted it to.*

I bite into my apple again and smile when Penn walks back into the workshop. He's wearing my sweatpants which are baggy on his thin frame and I actually kind of like that look on him.

Penn walks right up to me and takes my face in his hands, but I pull back and chuckle.

"I haven't even brushed my teeth yet," I say softly.

"Considering I had your dick in my mouth, I'm pretty sure that a little morning breath isn't going to bother me," he replies with a smirk.

"Hm."

I take another bite of my apple, chewing slowly as I stare into his eyes and take him in carefully. Penn really is beautiful in his own, weird way and something tells me he knows it, but I wonder if he thinks that all I need is sex to keep me interested in him.

He moves his face forward again and I raise the apple to stop him. "Not until I've brushed my teeth."

"Whatever," he mumbles walking away from me. He stops at the table and looks down at the pet's ankles and leans down closer to inspect them. "Looks good. No infection."

I take one last bite of the fruit before I toss the core into the garbage can and nod. "And today, we learn how to walk again."

Penn moves away from the table when I reach it. I begin to quickly undo the restraints and pull it up to a seated position. He reaches for it and holds it firmly around the waist while I undo the leg restraints and I smile at him.

"Thanks."

"You're welcome," he replies kindly.

I reach under its arms and place one around my shoulders, hoisting it up from the table and Penn helps me steady it on its new feet before he goes on the other side of it and puts its other arm around his shoulders and we begin to help it take slow steps toward the door.

Together.

CHAPTER TWENTY-FOUR

Three hours.

That's how long it took us to get the pet moving on its own, but patience goes a long way when you have someone by your side. Penn did a wonderful job of keeping my nerves calm each time she fell, and he would help her up each time until she was finally able to make her way to me unaided.

Its laying on the couch now recovering with Penn watching over it, allowing me to get dressed and call its new owner. I set the meet for the usual place and head back to the living room, running my hands back through my hair.

"Okay, I'll be back in a couple of hours. See if you can get a hold of that doctor while I'm gone?"

As I move toward the pet, Penn sidesteps in front of me and gives me a curious look.

"Don't you want me to go with you?" he asks.

I smile at him and place a hand gently on the side of his face, shaking my head. "You've already done enough. I don't want to put you in danger by having any of them know what you look like."

Penn lets out an incredulous sigh and gives me a critical stare. "Do I look like a pussy? You really think I give two shits of anyone seeing me with you and … what the fuck is that exactly, anyway?"

"Satyress."

"What?"

"It's the same thing as a satyr, only it's the chick version," I reply with a shrug. "I do what I'm paid to do."

"So … shouldn't it have horns?" he asks, glancing curiously at it.

"Move the hair back," I tell him with a smirk. Penn raises an eyebrow and walks over to the couch. I sit on the recliner and pull my smokes out of my side pocket, tapping one on the pack, before I light it.

"Holy shit," he says with a laugh. "How the fuck did you do that?"

"I had to scalp the fucking thing, but yeah. Those come out to play whenever the owner wants them to. It was just something I wanted to try," I reply with a shrug.

I lean back in the recliner and take a drag of my smoke as Penn walks back over to me and straddles me, a grin on his face.

"Did anyone ever tell you that you're good with your hands?" he asks.

I roll my eyes and laugh. "Yeah, you just did. But really, I have to get going so that I'm not late dropping it off and I want to see Aiden when I get back."

Penn sighs heavily and pins my shoulders back. "You're not going without me. I'll hide in the backseat or some shit if you need me to, but you need me to get into the doctor's front door and I'm sure you don't want to waste more time having to come back to get me when we can just go straight there."

He's got a point there.

"Alright, go put your clothes on. I'm gonna load it into the car and I'll wait for you," I finally relent as I gently push him off and get to my feet. I walk over to the couch and pick it up, cradling it against me like I had done with Aiden not too long ago, and walk out the front door as Penn disappears down the hallway toward the bedroom.

It doesn't take me long to get it secured in the backseat. I lay it across so that it can be comfortable and as soon as I climb out, Penn walks out of the building and disconnects his call.

"Aiden's looking forward to seeing you, so she knows we're coming," he says, walking around to the passenger side of the car and climbing in. "Let's get this over with so we can head over there."

Just as I suspected, the owner was elated with the final result. So much so that he ended up handing me a thick envelope he insisted I take as a bonus when I tried to decline it.

Penn did a good job of staying in the car while I delivered the Satyress, even though it took some sweet talking and promises of another night in bed together if he just stayed fucking put.

Once I got back to the car, he offered to drive, and I let him. I figured it would be a lot easier than asking for directions, and an hour later, here we are.

Standing outside the doctor's house and I'm giddy with excitement knowing that my best friend is inside waiting for me.

When Penn pulls in front of the house, he has to stop me from jumping out before he finishes parking the car, but he's being kind about it. He doesn't seem jealous at all that I'm more excited to see Aiden than I ever have to see him.

"Ready?" he asks when he turns off the car.

I nod in excitement, and he laughs as we both get out of the car and head up the walkway together. Penn knocks on the door, giving me a nudge and a grin and I can tell by the amused look in his eyes that I must look like a little boy on Christmas.

He knocks again, a little louder this time, and the door finally begins to open slowly.

"Hello?" he asks curiously when no one appears in sight.

That's when the door swings open the rest of the way and I let out a sound that I never knew I was capable of.

Aiden grins up at me, her face still a sick shade of yellow and purple, but I'm so fucking happy to see she seems okay that I let out something strangled that sounds like a laugh and a sob.

I reach for her and wrap her up tightly in my arms, burying my face in her shoulder and she starts to laugh.

"This one is such a crybaby," she jokes to Penn as she returns my hug. "Not to tight there. My ribs are still a little sore."

"I'm sorry," I say, pulling back and wiping the tears from my eyes. "Oh God, Aiden."

I begin to sob, and Penn reaches over to

rub my back awkwardly as Aiden steps out onto the front stoop with us. She reaches over and greets Penn with a hug before sitting down on the gravel step, pulling me down next to her.

"It'll take a hell of a lot more than what he did to put me out of my misery," she says proudly, putting an arm around me.

"Gray beat the shit out of him. I don't know if you saw that," Penn says with a nervous laugh.

It's not because Aiden is finally back in the picture—that's not what's bothering him. The reason for his awkward demeanor right now, is because he hasn't seen me like this yet and it's probably putting him off.

I don't give a shit.

Aiden is alive and as well as she can be right now and that's all that fucking matters anymore.

I laugh and use the back of my hand to dry my face. I look up at Penn who's standing in front of us, one of his feet up on the step, trying to find a way to fit in.

"If Penn and his friends hadn't pulled

me off, that would have been the end of Max Boothe," I add, smiling at him.

"Well, I would imagine that prison orange doesn't look good on you," he replies, rolling his eyes.

Aiden nudges me, then rests her head on my shoulder. "You two been getting along alright while I've been gone?"

"We've been hanging out," I reply.

"And?" she asks, glancing up at me.

"Fucking," Penn offers.

I look up at him. I'm actually shocked that he would admit that in front of her, but she doesn't seem bothered by it. If anything, she says the most Aiden thing that she's ever said.

"It's about goddamn time!"

I steal an embarrassed glance at her and she starts laughing. Penn chuckles and lowers himself down onto the pavement between my legs and glances over at Aiden.

"I have a feeling that was your plan the entire time. That's why you talked so much about him, isn't it?"

Aiden moves away from my shoulder and grins at both of us. "Gray needed someone to love him the way he deserves and even though you're a weird little fucker, I knew he liked you, so why not? Just call me Cupid."

I shake my head and roll my eyes.

I can't recall a time in my life when I've ever felt this genuinely happy before. Granted, me and Penn have a long way to go, but I have a feeling that Aiden will be there helping us along, every step of the way.

PART FOUR

THE GRAND DESIGN
(PRESENT DAY)

EPILOGUE

I still haven't decided if we deserve to live yet, but I know that what I've done here will make me incredibly happy—in life or in death.

"You know, when I first started down this road of making custom pets, I never though it would go this far," I tell it, leaning on the table. "I don't know why I decided to do this. I guess it was a way to not feel lonely anymore and make some extra cash in the process. Then I met Aiden—sweet, little Aiden who could destroy damn near anything with a single punch. I thought that would be enough because of how much she's always loved me, but then I met Penn and I experienced a different kind of love. It got to a point where I knew that the two

248

of them co-existing, each holding half of my heart, would never work the way we all wanted."

I take a deep drag off my cigarette and sigh before I continue. "I never wanted this to be the way it was, but when I almost lost Aiden to that last fight of hers … fuck, the world fell out of focus. Even nights spent in Penn's arms, with as amazing as it always felt, left half of me empty."

I can hear it struggling against the restraints and I chuckle. "You can't get away from me no matter how hard you try, so just let me finish what I have to say."

A moan.

A loud grumble.

Silence.

It makes me sad to know that I'll never hear her laugh again, or the sound of his moans when we're fucking each other, but the mouth is always the first thing I take care of.

I can't stand the screams once a project realizes it's going through a transformation and I only made that mistake the first time.

I sedated them to the point of death, then carried them one by one up to my workshop, knowing full well what would become of them.

The strangest thing is how calm I felt once I began to suture them together. The blood flow was much more than I expected from him, but I chalked it up to his thin frame. She didn't produce much blood and I think that's because of how much she had lost in the fight.

And now, she never has to fight again. No one will ever hurt her because I'm saving her.

He woke up first, but he didn't understand what was happening until she struggled against him. That's when they both realized that they would be mine forever; joined in a thing of beauty that I know will eventually love me more than I can bear, but I look forward to suffocating in the moments we'll share together.

"I didn't think this would work. Did you know that? Did you believe in me when I started working on you? See, you're special because you're *mine* and no one else's. You're one of a kind and the most beautiful thing I've ever created, and we can be happy if you just give this a chance."

I finally turn around to face it again and smile shyly. One part is taller than the other, but those are the pieces I've been dealt to work with.

I reach a hand down toward it and lose myself in the moment. I can't help but kiss those beautifully full lips again. The way the big blue eyes widen in terror as I get closer makes me grin because it will just have to learn to deal with life this way.

I walk around to the other side of it and bite my lip happily. A pair of familiar, narrow brown eyes are watching me in disbelief— in unimaginable terror and I purse my lips for a moment.

"Don't look at me like that. This is all your doing, you know. I was happy with just you but then you pushed me toward him and I … I can't be without either of you. I need you both. One to love the side of me that no one else will, and one to love my body. It's best this way and you know it."

I let out my breath in a rush and toss the cigarette to the floor, crushing it under my boot as I walk to the end of the table and pull the sheet off of it.

The stitching is healing nicely, and my own personal pet seems to be complete. I didn't make any major alterations to it, only joined them together so that I could have both halves of my heart in one vessel.

It's so beautiful that it's fucking maddening.

"Maybe we don't deserve to live," I say quietly, as I pull the sheet back up to its waist.

"Do you think we should die together? I really would like to give us a chance."

The half with the blue eyes shakes its head vehemently and the half with the brown eyes begins to sob.

I let out a chuckle and walk over to my workbench, glancing up and down the number of tools I have at my disposal, wondering what would be best to fix this situation.

But there's nothing here that can help us. Nothing that I've run my fingers over that would give me or it any more comfort and I decide in that moment to give us a chance.

"We can do this," I whisper to myself. "We can be happy this way and I'll never need anything or anyone else, because I have everything I've ever wanted now."

With a happy sigh, I walk back to the table my pet is on and undo the straps.

"I have to teach you to walk again," I say sitting it up. "Then after that—the possibilities are endless."

ABOUT THE AUTHOR

Yolanda Olson is an award winning and international bestselling author. Born and raised in Bridgeport, CT where she currently resides, she usually spends her time watching her favorite channel, Investigation Discovery. Occasionally, she takes a break to write books and test the limits of her mind. Also an avid horror movie fan, she likes to incorporate dark elements into the majority of her books.

You can keep in touch with her on Facebook, Twitter, and Instagram.

Printed in Great Britain
by Amazon

84663384R00147